THE NEWBURY HOUSE TOEFL® PREPARATION KIT

Preparing for the TOEFL®

Daniel B. Kennedy
The Catholic University of America

Dorry Mann Kenyon
George Mason University

Steven J. Matthiesen
Prince George's County Public Schools, Maryland

Newbury House Publishers, New York

A division of Harper & Row, Publishers, Inc.
Philadelphia, San Francisco, Washington, D.C.
London, Mexico City, São Paulo, Singapore, Sydney

Director: Laurie E. Likoff
Text Design: Valerie Greco/Cover to Cover
Cover Design: Delgado Design, Inc.
Cover Illustration/Photo: ACCURATE ART, Inc.: Ronald Houghton
Production Coordinator: Cynthia Funkhouser
Compositor: Waldman Graphics, Inc.
Printer and Binder: Malloy Lithographing, Inc.

NEWBURY HOUSE PUBLISHERS
A division of Harper & Row, Publishers, Inc.

Language Science
Language Teaching
Language Learning

TOEFL test directions are reprinted by permission of Educational Testing Service, the copyright owner of the directions. However, test questions other than the sample questions provided with the directions, and other testing information are provided in their entirety by Newbury House Publishers. No endorsement of this publication by Educational Testing Service should be inferred.

The Newbury House TOEFL Preparation Kit: Preparing for the TOEFL

Copyright © 1989 by Newbury House Publishers, a division of Harper & Row Publishers, Inc. All rights reserved. Printed in the United States of America. No part of this book may be used or reproduced in any manner whatsoever without written permission, except in the case of brief quotations embodied in critical articles and reviews. For information address Harper & Row, Publishers, Inc., 10 East 53d Street, New York, NY 10022.

Library of Congress Cataloging in Publication Data

Kennedy, Daniel B.
    The Newbury House TOEFL preparation kit : preparing for the TOEFL
    Daniel B. Kennedy, Dorry Mann Kenyon, Steven J. Matthiesen.
       p.   cm.
    ISBN 0-06-632611-7
    1. English language—Textbooks for foreign speakers. 2. English language—Examinations, questions, etc. I. Kenyon, Dorry Mann. II. Matthiesen, Steven J. III. Title. IV. Title: TOEFL preparation kit.
PE1128.K426 1989
428'.0076—dc19   89-2888
                                   CIP

92 91 90 89 9 8 7 6 5 4 3 2 1

An Introduction to This Book

The *Newbury House TOEFL Preparation Kit* is the product of lengthy research on the nature of the TOEFL. This research focused on gaining a complete understanding of the TOEFL and the TOEFL program. To do this, the authors carefully reviewed official TOEFL publications written for college admissions officers. These publications include the *TOEFL Test and Score Manual* and several TOEFL Research Reports, distributed by Educational Testing Service, the makers of the TOEFL. The authors also analyzed thousands of actual TOEFL test questions from many forms of the TOEFL. After doing this, the authors classified the questions into groups that have similar characteristics. Then, the authors described the characteristics of each group in writing. Following this, the authors wrote questions with the same characteristics. They then evaluated and revised the questions, if necessary.

Finally, they developed three practice tests using the test questions. These practice tests reflect all the question types tested on the TOEFL. The authors then administered the three practice tests to foreign students studying at universities in the United States and abroad. After they analyzed statistically the responses to each item, they made further changes whenever necessary. In this manner, they obtained questions that not only look like TOEFL questions, but also function like TOEFL questions.

The final version of the three practice tests was administered, with a real TOEFL, to students at several universities in the United States, and scores on the practice tests and the TOEFL were mathematically correlated. The authors then used the mathematical correlations to develop a score conversion table. This scientific process provides the closest thing possible to a real TOEFL score. The *Newbury House TOEFL Preparation Kit* is the only TOEFL preparation program to be developed in this way.

A DESCRIPTION OF THE PROGRAM

The *Newbury House TOEFL Preparation Kit* consists of three parts: this TOEFL preparation book, titled *Preparing for the TOEFL;* which includes three practice tests with answer sheets; a test tape for practicing the Listening Comprehension section of the TOEFL; a *Tapescript and Answer Key;* and a book to prepare you for the Test of Written

English, titled *Preparing for the Test of Written English*. *Preparing for the TOEFL* begins with a basic description of the TOEFL examination, including sample questions. The book then provides detailed answers to over forty questions commonly asked about the TOEFL program and its policies. Each of the next chapters contains a description of the seven major types of questions found on the TOEFL. This description is based on our thorough analysis of TOEFL tests and items. Next, Chapter 10 reviews thirty-one points of English grammar that are frequently tested on the TOEFL. It includes basic rules of grammar and practice questions. These questions show you how each point of grammar is tested on the TOEFL.

At the end of the book, you will find two important appendices. **Appendix A** is a list of the TOEFL scores required by the colleges and universities in the United States with the largest number of foreign students. **Appendix B** provides you with instructions for scoring the practice tests and changing your number of correct answers into TOEFL scores. Appendix B also includes score conversion tables for *A Practice TOEFL, Form 1, Form 2,* and *Form 3*. These are the three practice tests that are included in the *Newbury House TOEFL Preparation Kit*.

Follow the Program to Success

To use these materials, first read Chapter 1, "A Brief Introduction to the TOEFL." This chapter will give you a basic understanding of the test. Then, read Chapter 2, "Some Commonly Asked Questions about the TOEFL." Chapter 2 explains how you can apply to take the TOEFL, what choices you will have as you register for and participate in the TOEFL program, what you can expect at the test center, how universities use and interpret scores, typical university TOEFL score requirements, and important information that you will not find in the *Bulletin of Information for TOEFL*. Chapter 2 will explain TOEFL procedures and policies to you in detail.

You can take *A Practice TOEFL, Form 1* after reading Chapter 1. Or, you may read both Chapter 1 and Chapter 2 before taking this practice test. Use the test booklet, the test tape, and one of the multiple-choice answer sheets included in this kit. Follow the TOEFL time limits for each section. After completing *A Practice TOEFL, Form 1,* score it using the answer key provided in the booklet containing the tapescript and answer key. Then, determine your estimated TOEFL score from your number of correct answers, following the instructions in Appendix B. This score will tell you how well you may do on the actual TOEFL examination. If your estimated TOEFL score is above the minimum required by the college or university of your choice (See Appendix A), you can register for the TOEFL now. Then, continue to study this book to make sure you do the best you can on the actual TOEFL. If your estimated TOEFL score is below the minimum (usually 550) required by the college or university of your choice, then you should wait before you register for the TOEFL. Study Chapters 3 through 9 of this volume, instead.

Chapters 3 through 9 describe TOEFL question types in depth, beginning with the one-sentence Statements found in the Part A of Section 1 of the TOEFL, and continuing through a detailed description of the Reading Comprehension passages and questions found in the second part of Section 3. The chapters also give you strategies for preparing for the different types of questions and for answering them on the test. Study these chapters on TOEFL questions carefully. They will permit you to learn how to recognize and respond to the different problems you will find on the TOEFL. Be sure to review carefully the grammatical descriptions and the practice questions for Section 2 of the TOEFL, *Structure and Written Expression.*

When you are able to recognize the different types of questions on the TOEFL, you will be better able to answer each question correctly. You will also feel much more confident that you are ready to take the test. There is a lot of important information in Chapters 3 through 9, so you may need to read each of these chapters more than once. While doing this, you should look again at the questions in *A Practice TOEFL, Form 1*. These are further examples of each question type. Also, make sure to complete the practice grammar exercises in Chapter 10.

After you have studied Chapters 3 through 10, you should take *A Practice TOEFL, Form 2*. If you have studied them as recommended, your score on *Form 2* should be thirty to one hundred points higher than your score on *Form 1*. If your score is still not high enough for admission to the college or university of your choice, you should carefully review Chapters 3 through 10 again and study your mistakes on *Form 2*. Then, take *A Practice TOEFL, Form 3*. If, after taking *A Practice TOEFL, Form 3*, your score is still not high enough, you should enroll in an English-language course, and continue to review Chapters 3 through 10 of this book. This will help you do as well as you possibly can on the TOEFL, given your level of English ability. When you think you are ready, you may take *A Practice TOEFL, Form 3* again.

You may also want to order *Listening to TOEFL: Test Kit 2*, which is published by the TOEFL program. It includes three more TOEFL exams. Once you have reached an acceptable score on any form of *A Practice TOEFL*, or any of the official TOEFLs in *Listening to TOEFL: Test Kit 2*, you will be ready to register for an actual TOEFL. You should score as high or higher on the actual TOEFL as you did on *A Practice TOEFL*, provided you continue to read in English as much as possible, listen to spoken English in a variety of situations, and remain familiar with TOEFL item types as described in Chapters 3 through 9 of this volume.

If you plan to take the *Test of Written English (TWE)*, which is offered as a required fourth section of the TOEFL during the months of September, October, March, and May, you should read and follow carefully the discussion of the TWE contained in *Preparing for the Test of Written English* by Liz Hamp-Lyons. This book is also part of the *Newbury House TOEFL Preparation Kit*. This volume about the TWE, like the materials devoted to the multiple-choice TOEFL, provides the most comprehensive explanation of this test yet available.

Contents

Chapter 1
A Brief Introduction to the TOEFL   1

    SOME GENERAL TOEFL CHARACTERISTICS   1

    SAMPLE TOEFL QUESTIONS   2

        Section 1: Listening Comprehension   2
            Part A: Statements   2
            Part B: Short Dialogs   3
            Part C: Minitalks and Extended Conversations   3

        Section 2: Structure and Written Expression   5
        Section 3: Vocabulary and Reading Comprehension   6
        The Test of Written English   7

Chapter 2
Some Commonly Asked Questions about the TOEFL   9

TOEFL SECTION 1

Chapter 3
Statements   27

    WHAT YOU SHOULD KNOW   27

    THE STATEMENTS   28

    CHOOSING THE ANSWER   30

    RECORDING YOUR ANSWER   33

Chapter 4
Short Dialogs   34

    WHAT YOU SHOULD KNOW   34

    THE QUESTIONS   35

    CHOOSING THE ANSWER   35

    WHAT IS TESTED?   36

       Idioms   37
       Everyday and Specific Vocabulary   37
       Inference   38
       Emphatic Word Use   39

    A FINAL NOTE   40

TOEFL SECTION 2

Chapter 5
Minitalks and Extended Conversations   41

    WHAT YOU SHOULD KNOW   41

    THE QUESTIONS   42

       Inference Questions   42
       Specific Questions   44

    CHOOSING THE ANSWER   46

       Minitalks   46
       Extended Conversations   49

    A FINAL NOTE   53

Chapter 6
Structure   54

    WHAT YOU SHOULD KNOW   54

    WORKING THROUGH SOME EXAMPLES   55

Chapter 7
Written Expression — 60

WHAT YOU SHOULD KNOW — 60

CHOOSING THE ANSWER — 61

Error Type 1: Grammatical Agreement   61
   A. Errors in the Agreement of Number   61
   B. Errors in the Agreement of Subject and Verb   61
   C. Errors in the Agreement of Verb Tenses   62

Error Type 2: Grammatical Forms   62
Error Type 3: Parts of Speech   63
Error Type 4: Word Usage   64
Error Type 5: Word Order   65
Error Type 6: Omissions and Additions   65
Error Type 7: Style   66

TOEFL SECTION 3

Chapter 8
Vocabulary — 68

WHAT YOU SHOULD KNOW — 68

HOW TO IMPROVE YOUR TOEFL VOCABULARY — 69

What Vocabulary to Study   70
What Vocabulary NOT to Study   71

TAKING THE TEST — 72

STRATEGY REVIEW AND PRACTICE — 74

Chapter 9
Reading Comprehension — 78

DEVELOPING READING STRATEGIES: FIRST STEPS IN READING COMPREHENSION — 78

STRATEGY REVIEW — 83

READING COMPREHENSION: PASSAGES AND QUESTIONS — 84

WHAT YOU SHOULD KNOW	84
THE QUESTIONS	85

    1. Main Idea Questions 86
    2. Factual Questions 87
    3. Inference Questions 89
    4. Analogy Questions 91
    5. Organization Questions 92
    6. Viewpoint Questions 93

STRATEGY REVIEW	94
PRACTICE QUESTIONS	94
KEY	96

Chapter 10
Practice Exercises for Section 2 of the TOEFL   98

    1. Agreement of Tenses 99
    2. Subject-Verb Agreement 100
    3. Two-Word and Three-Word Verbs 101
    4. Active and Passive Verbs 102
    5. Common Verb Errors 103
    6. Subjects and Objects 104
    7. Common Noun Errors 105
    8. Common Pronoun Errors 106
    9. Noun Phrases 107
    10. Gerunds and Infinitives 108
    11. Expressions with *It* 109
    12. Expressions with *There* 111
    13. Common Adjective Errors 112
    14. Common Adverb Errors 113
    15. Comparisons (Structure) 114
    16. Comparisons (Written Expression) 116
    17. Prepositions 117
    18. Prepositional Phrases 118
    19. Adjective, Adverb, Gerund, and Infinitive Phrases 119
    20. Adverb Clauses 121
    21. Adjective Clauses 123
    22. Noun Clauses 124
    23. Conjunctions (Structure) 126
    24. Conjunctions (Written Expression) 128
    25. Negative Constructions 129
    26. Word Order (Structure) 131

27. Word Order (Written Expression)   132
28. Parallelism (Structure)   133
29. Parallelism (Written Expression)   134
30. Redundancy   135
31. Omission and Inclusion   136
Key to Practice Exercises   137

Appendix A
TOEFL Requirements by Institution   139

Appendix B
Guidelines for Scoring Practice Tests and Converting Number-Right Scores to Scaled Scores and Percentile Ranks   144

    SCORE CONVERSION TABLES FOR FORMS 1-3   148

A Practice TOEFL: Form 1   155

A Practice TOEFL: Form 2   191

A Practice TOEFL: Form 3   227

Answer Sheets for Forms 1, 2, and 3   263

CHAPTER 1

A Brief Introduction to the TOEFL

The TOEFL examination consists of 150 questions in three sections. The sections are divided into seven parts. For each part and section, the name, number of questions, and length of time are listed below.

Section 1	*Listening Comprehension*	50 questions	35 minutes
Part A	Statements	20 questions	
Part B	Short Dialogs	15 questions	
Part C	Minitalks and Extended Conversations	15 questions	
Section 2	*Structure and Written Expression*	40 questions	25 minutes
	Structure	15 questions	
	Written Expression	25 questions	
Section 3	*Vocabulary and Reading Comprehension*	60 questions	45 minutes
	Vocabulary	30 questions	
	Reading Comprehension	30 questions	

SOME GENERAL TOEFL CHARACTERISTICS

The TOEFL tests a wide variety of characteristics of spoken and written English as used in the United States. However, there are some things that you will not find on the TOEFL. These include discussion of unhappy topics such as divorce, death, war, and murder. Nor will you find topics or situations on the TOEFL that place women in a position inferior to men. Instead, you may see or hear women in positive roles, such as providing information, giving directions, or showing leadership. Similarly, you will find a number of situations or topics describing the contributions of U.S. ethnic minorities, particularly Blacks and Hispanics, to American scientific and cultural history. Therefore, do not be surprised if you see a Hispanic name on the test.

The language used on the TOEFL covers a wide variety of topics from the natural sciences and social sciences, as well as some topics from literature and the humanities. When references are made to individuals or to geographic sites such as cities, rivers, or mountains, 90% of the time the individual will be an American, and the geographic site will be some place in the United States. However, three to five times in each TOEFL, you will find references to Canadian history or geography. You will not find references to people or geographic sites in countries other than the United States and Canada. Thus, the Eiffel Tower in Paris, for example, would never be on a TOEFL. When reference is made to an individual, a geographic site, or even a scientific process, actual knowledge of the reference is NOT required. Therefore, do not worry if you are not familiar with the topic being discussed. You will be tested on your comprehension of the English language, not your general knowledge.

SAMPLE TOEFL QUESTIONS

Below is a brief introduction to the various types of questions on the TOEFL. Chapters 3 through 9 of this book contain more detailed information and practice for each type of question.

Section 1: Listening Comprehension

This section tests your ability to understand spoken American English. The English you will hear is recorded on tape. After you hear each question, you read four possible answers printed in your test booklet. You must mark on your answer sheet the letter of the answer you think is correct. The voices of only three speakers are on the test tape; all are Americans. Each speaks English clearly, with pronunciation that is normal for educated persons throughout the United States, and with a voice similar to the voices you might hear on an American radio station. Section 1 contains three parts.

Part A: Statements. This is the easiest part, and it comes first. It contains single sentences recorded on tape. After you hear each sentence, you read four sentences in your test booklet. Then, you choose the sentence that is closest in meaning to the one you heard. The following example illustrates the process.

You will hear: Anna thought she'd have three times more people at her lecture.

You will read: (A) People attended the lecture three times.
(B) There were fewer people than she expected.
(C) There was a large crowd at the lecture.
(D) She thought three more people would attend.

In the above example, choice (B) most closely gives the same meaning as the sentence on the tape. All of the other sentences have a meaning different from the sentence on the tape. Therefore, they cannot be the correct answer.

Part B: Short Dialogs. This part contains short dialogs between two people. In each dialog, each speaker will talk only once. Then, a third voice will ask a question about what the first two speakers said. After you hear the question, you must read the four possible answers in the test booklet and choose the best (most correct) answer. The following example illustrates the questions in Part B.

You will hear: (MAN A) I'd like five aerograms and this package sent parcel post.
(WOMAN) Here you are. That's five thirty-five altogether.
(MAN B) Where does this conversation probably take place?

You will read: (A) In a department store.
(B) In a bank.
(C) In an airport.
(D) In a post office.

In the conversation, you learn that the man would like to mail a package and buy aerograms. Thus, you can infer that the man is in a post office. Therefore, the correct answer is (D).

Part C: Minitalks and Extended Conversations. This part is composed of two kinds of listening passages: short lectures (called minitalks) and extended conversations. The minitalks are spoken by only one person; the extended conversations involve two people. Minitalks and extended conversations are at least 40 seconds long, and some are over a minute long. After each, there are between four and eight questions. You must choose the correct answer to each question from among the four choices printed in the test booklet. Then, mark it on your answer sheet. Here is an example of a minitalk.

You will hear: (MAN) Paying income taxes has been a fact of life for Americans since 1913. At that time, the Congress of the United States passed a law that gave the government the power to levy and collect taxes on the income of Americans. The rates were very low at first, but they have been increased from time to time. Now the average American family pays between fifteen and twenty percent of its wages in taxes to the United States government. The tax system is progressive. This means that taxpayers who make less money pay less in taxes. Conversely, a high-income family typically pays more, up to thirty-three percent of its income, in taxes.

(WOMAN) What percent of income is paid in taxes by an average family?

You will read: (A) 3 to 13%.
(B) 10 to 15%
(C) 15 to 20%.
(D) 25 to 33%.

In the fourth sentence of the minitalk, we learn that the typical American family pays between fifteen and twenty percent of its income in taxes. Therefore, choice (C) is the best answer. During an actual TOEFL, you would be asked several additional questions about the minitalk.

Here is an example of an extended conversation.

You will hear: (WOMAN) That sign we just passed up the road said "Deerfield." Isn't Deerfield famous for something?
(MAN A) Well, there's the well known boys prep school ...
(WOMAN) I mean historically.
(MAN A) Oh. Yes. Deerfield was one of the earliest English settlements in western Massachusetts. It's very historic.
(WOMAN) I wonder what it's like now.
(MAN A) I visited it once. There's only one street, and it's lined with restored 18th-century houses. You can take guided tours of the houses. There's a beautiful old graveyard, too—that was my favorite part.
(WOMAN) I'd like to see Deerfield someday.
(MAN A) Let's go today. I'll turn around up ahead, and we can go back and spend a couple of hours there.

(MAN B) What is the main topic of this conversation?

You will read: (A) The old school house
(B) An early settlement
(C) A trip to the country
(D) An animal crossing

The second time the man talks, he says that Deerfield was one of the earliest English settlements. Therefore, choice (B) is the correct answer since the whole conversation centers on Deerfield. During an actual TOEFL, you would be asked several more questions about this extended conversation.

Section 2: Structure and Written Expression

This section contains two types of questions. The first type of question tests your ability to recognize correct English word order or structure. There are 15 "structure" questions on the test. Each contains a sentence with one or more words missing. Of the four possible completions to the sentence in your test booklet, you must choose the best completion. The following sentence is an example.

 Benjamin Franklin served as a diplomat in Europe for twenty-five years, he is usually remembered for his stateside political activities.

(A) Although
(B) However
(C) Therefore
(D) That

In the sentence above, only choice (A) makes a correct grammatical structure, a subordinate clause. Any of the other choices makes an ungrammatical sentence. Therefore, you would mark choice (A) on your answer sheet.

Section 2 also contains 25 "written expression" questions that test your ability to recognize errors in English. In each of these questions, you will read a sentence in your test booklet. In each sentence, there are four underlined words or phrases. One of these must be changed in order to make the sentence correct. You must choose which word or phrase must be changed and mark its letter on your answer sheet. The following sentence is an example.

The oral tradition <u>of some</u> American Indian <u>tribes have</u> allowed
                A   B
many stories <u>to be</u> <u>passed down</u> from generation to generation.
            C   D

In the sentence above, the plural verb *have* should be singular (*has*), since the subject of the sentence (*tradition*) is singular. Therefore, you mark (B) on your answer sheet.

Section 3: Vocabulary and Reading Comprehension

This section also contains two kinds of questions. The first part, Vocabulary, tests your knowledge of English vocabulary. There are 30 sentences. In each sentence, one word or a group of words with a single meaning is underlined. Beneath the sentence are four possible replacements for the underlined part of the sentence. You must choose the word or words that are closest in meaning to the underlined part of the original sentence.

The following question is an example.

Ezra Pound was a discerning and energetic entrepreneur of the arts.

(A) expert
(B) vigorous
(C) perceptive
(D) impressive

Among the possible answers, choice (B) is the best, since it is closest in meaning to the word *energetic*.

The second kind of question in this section tests reading comprehension. There are between five and seven passages, which you have to read. Each passage is followed by four to seven questions about the passage. There are 30 questions in all. You must choose the one best answer to each question and mark its letter on your answer sheet. A sample passage and question follows.

Precipitation is one of the three main processes (evaporation, condensation, and precipitation) that constitute the hydrologic cycle, the continual exchange of water between the atmosphere and the surface of the Earth. Water, evaporated from ocean, land, and freshwater surfaces, is carried aloft as vapor by the air currents, condenses to form clouds, and ultimately returns to the Earth's surface as precipitation. The average global stock of water vapor in the atmosphere is equivalent to a layer of water one inch deep covering the whole Earth. Because the Earth's average annual rainfall is about 40 inches, the average time that the water spends in the atmosphere, between its evaporation from the surface and its return as precipitation, is about 1/40 of a year or about nine days.

According to the passage, how much rain typically falls on each portion of the Earth's surface in a year?

(A) One inch
(B) Nine inches
(C) Ten inches
(D) Forty inches

The last sentence of the passage states that the Earth's average annual rainfall is about 40 inches. Therefore, choice (D) is the best answer.

The Test of Written English

The TOEFL sometimes contains a fourth section called the *Test of Written English (TWE)*. The TWE is included on the TOEFL four times per year, during the months of September, October, March, and May. The TWE tests your ability to write as you will have to write in a North American university.

The TWE consists of a thirty-minute essay on a single topic. The topic may be one of two topic types. One type requires you to compare and contrast two different points of view on an issue, and to take a position in favor of one. The other type of topic requires you to describe and discuss a chart or a graph. The following is an example of the first type of topic.

> Some people prefer to spend their vacation at home relaxing with friends. Others prefer to use their vacation to travel to places they have never visited. Consider the advantages and disadvantages of both types of vacation and explain which type you prefer, giving reasons to support your answer.

A topic such as the above requires you to organize an objective comparison of two alternatives or opposing points of view. Then, you must take a position in favor of one point of view and support that position. Such a task is similar to the kind of writing task you may have to do in almost any course you would take at a university, whether it is a course in philosophy, business, psychology, government, chemistry, or engineering.

The second type of TWE topic requires you to describe and discuss a chart or a graph. The following is an example of this type of topic.

ADMINISTRATIVE CHARACTERISTICS

	Experience	Communication Skills	Friendliness
Administrator A	*****	***	*
Administrator B	*	****	*****
Administrator C	***	**	****

Rating Criteria
*****Excellent   ****Very good   ***Good   **Fair   *Poor

There are three applicants for an administrative position. Each has been interviewed and evaluated on the basis of three personal characteristics. Based on the information given in the chart above, which one would you recommend for the job. Why?

A writing task such as this one also represents the type of writing you might be asked to do in a North American college or university. It requires you to understand data presented visually, then describe and discuss them. Although the topic and the data may be different in your field of study, the task is basically the same.

For additional information on the TWE and how to prepare for it, consult the booklet *Preparing for the Test of Written English*, which is included in the *Newbury House TOEFL Preparation Kit*.

CHAPTER 2

Some Commonly Asked Questions about the TOEFL

This chapter contains forty-three questions that are commonly asked about the TOEFL. A detailed answer follows each question. This chapter does not teach you how to answer questions on the TOEFL examination. Instead, it provides you with important information about the TOEFL program, and it explains TOEFL program procedures and policies in depth. Because there are so many procedures, you will sometimes be told to look for the answer to one question in the answer to a different question.

Because the TOEFL program has so many procedures and policies, you may find Chapter 2 difficult to read, unless you are almost ready to take the TOEFL. If you encounter this problem, you may skip Chapter 2 and come back to it later. Or, you may read it from time to time while you study the rest of this book.

1. Why must I take the TOEFL?

Quite simply, you must take the TOEFL because it is required by 2500 colleges and universities in the United States, Canada, and other parts of the world. These colleges and universities can establish their own admission requirements, and they have decided to require the TOEFL. Foreign professionals such as doctors, nurses, pharmacists, and veterinarians are also required to take the TOEFL by their professional certification boards in the United States and Canada. For example, the TOEFL is required by the Education Commission of Foreign Medical Graduates, the Education Commission of Foreign Veterinary Graduates, the Council of Graduates of Foreign Nursing Schools, and many certification boards of individual states within the United States and the boards of provinces within Canada.

The TOEFL was first offered in 1964, and the number of institutions that require it has grown continuously since then. Your TOEFL score allows an institution to judge whether you have enough proficiency in English to function successfully in an English-language academic environment. While the institutions that require the TOEFL do not all require the same TOEFL score, most American and Canadian universities require a score of 550 for admission to an undergraduate or graduate program. Community colleges, which are two-year college-level institutions, typically require a score of 500 on the TOEFL. Appendix A gives you specific TOEFL score requirements at colleges and universities in the United States that have large numbers of nonnative English-speaking students.

2. Who administers the TOEFL?

The TOEFL is administered by a private American company whose name is Educational Testing Service (ETS). The company is located near Princeton, New Jersey, which is about 60 miles south of New York City. ETS develops each new form of the TOEFL that appears every month. It makes all arrangements for registering examinees and for administering and scoring the test in the United States and Canada. In many other countries of the world, ETS makes an agreement with another private company or organization, or with a government agency, to handle certain TOEFL-related activities. Depending on the agreement, the local organization or agency may register examinees, collect registration fees, supervise the administration of the test, or even report your score to you.

3. What are the differences between the International and Special Center TOEFL testing programs?

The International TOEFL is offered on Saturdays. The Special Center TOEFL is offered on Fridays. The International TOEFL costs about 25% less than the Special Center TOEFL. This is because ETS has to rent special test centers for the Friday administrations, whereas Saturday administrations are usually given in schools or other facilities that charge less for use of their space on the weekends. Both the International and Special Center TOEFL programs are offered six times per year. This means that the TOEFL is given on six Fridays and on six Saturdays each year. It also means that the TOEFL is given twelve times a year, or once a month, on either Friday or Saturday.

4. What is the Institutional TOEFL program?

The Institutional TOEFL program allows colleges and universities to administer the TOEFL on any day the institution wants to. When an institution wants to make use of this program, it contacts ETS and states the date it plans to give the test and the number of examinees it plans to test. The form of the TOEFL that is administered is one that has already been used once in either the International or Special Center program at an earlier date. Because this test form has been used previously, ETS does not guarantee its security. Therefore, under the Institutional program, ETS does not send out official score reports for individual examinees. Instead, ETS sends a list of examinee scores to the institution that administers the test. The institution may use those scores for whatever purpose it wishes. Sometimes, the institution uses them for placement within an English-as-a-Second-Language program. Other times, it may use the scores to admit an applicant to the institution.

Sometimes, an institution will give you a letter or other document stating your scores on the Institutional TOEFL it administered. You are free to present this document to another institution to which you are applying for admission. Often, however, an institution will not accept an Institutional TOEFL score for purposes of admission, unless the test was given at that same institution. This is because each institution that uses the Institutional TOEFL program provides its own test supervisors. Supervisors for the International and Special Center programs are provided by ETS. One common difference between the two types of supervisors is that Institutional TOEFL supervisors are often English-language teachers who are administering the Institutional TOEFL to their own students. Supervisors for the International and Special Center TOEFL are usually professional test administrators and their employees or trainees. Normally, they do not know the examinees.

Institutions pay ETS about US$13 for each examinee tested under the Institutional TOEFL program. The institution then charges examinees whatever price for the test that it wishes to charge. Sometimes the price is only US$13; sometimes the price is US$30 or more.

5. Should I take an Institutional TOEFL?

In general, you should take the International or Special Center TOEFL. Scores from these programs are accepted by all colleges and universities that require the TOEFL. In addition, ETS saves scores earned in these programs and will send official TOEFL score reports to the institutions you designate for a period of two years. Although the International and Special Center programs may cost more than the Institutional program, the services they offer are well worth the difference in price.

You should take the Institutional TOEFL only if you are required to by the English-language program you are enrolled in. If you are thinking about taking an Institutional TOEFL for practice, take one of the forms of *A Practice TOEFL* included in the *Newbury House TOEFL Preparation Kit* instead. Or, take one of the TOEFLs in the TOEFL test kits published by ETS. Both permit you to score your test immediately and to inspect the test. For information on how to order the ETS test kits, see the official *TOEFL Bulletin*. (See question 9.)

6. How will I know that I am not taking an Institutional TOEFL?

If you fill out the registration form in the *TOEFL Bulletin*, you will be taking the International or Special Center TOEFL. The registration form requires you to choose one of these two TOEFL testing programs.

7. Does the TOEFL cost the same in each country?

Yes. The TOEFL costs the same amount in almost every country. However, in some countries, the TOEFL costs more. These countries are Japan, Korea, Taiwan, and the countries of Europe. The TOEFL costs the most in Japan.

8. Do I have to pay for the TOEFL in U.S. dollars?

In depends on the country where you will take the test. If you take the TOEFL in the United States or Canada, you must pay in U.S. dollars. If you take it somewhere else, you *may* not have to. If you have to send your registration form to a location other than ETS, you probably will be allowed to pay for the TOEFL in local currency. Still, in some foreign countries you have to pay for the TOEFL in U.S. dollars. See the *TOEFL Bulletin* that applies to your area of the world for information on the form of payment required in your country. For information on which *Bulletin* applies to your country, see question 9 below.

9. How can I register for the TOEFL?

You can register for the TOEFL by obtaining a copy of the current *Bulletin of Information for TOEFL and TSE*, which we refer to as the *TOEFL Bulletin*. You can get this free publication by writing to:

TOEFL Services
CN 6151
Princeton, NJ 08541-6151, USA

The *TOEFL Bulletin* contains a TOEFL registration form that you must complete, forms for other special services, some practice questions, and information about the procedures that ETS follows in administering the TOEFL.

You can register to take the TOEFL in one of the countries listed below by obtaining a special *TOEFL Bulletin* from the agency that handles TOEFL affairs in that country.

COUNTRY	AGENCY
Algeria, Bahrain, Iraq, Kuwait, Oman, Qatar, Saudi Arabia, Sudan	AMIDEAST Suite 300 1100 17th Street, NW UNITED ARAB EMIRATES Washington, DC 20036-4601

COUNTRY	AGENCY
Brazil	Instituto Brasil-Estados Unidos Av. Nossa Senhora de Copacabana 690-6 Andar 22050 Copacabana Rio de Janeiro, Brazil
Canada	TOEFL Distribution Center P.O. Box 162, Station S Toronto, ON M5M 4L7 Canada
Egypt	AMIDEAST 9 Gamal El-Din Aboul Mahasen Street Apartment 7, Third Floor Garden City, Cairo, Egypt
Europe (all countries, including Cyprus, Great Britain, Iceland, and Turkey)	CITO-TOEFL P.O. Box 1203 6801 BE Arnhem Netherlands
Hong Kong	Hong Kong Examinations Authority San Po Kong Sub-office 17 Tseuk Luk Street San Po Kong Kowloon, Hong Kong or Institute of International Education Hong Kong Arts Centre 12th Floor 2 Harbour Road, Wanchai G.P.O. Box 10010 Hong Kong
India	Institute of Psychological and Educational Measurement 25-A Mahatma Gandhi Marg Allahabad, U.P. 211 001 India

COUNTRY	AGENCY
Indonesia	Institute of International Education P.O. Box 18 KBYCO Jakarta Selatan 12951 Indonesia
Japan	Council on International Educational Exchange Sanno Grand Building Room 216 14-2 Nagata-cho 2-chome Chiyoda-ku, Tokyo 100 Japan
Jordan	AMIDEAST P.O. Box 1249 Amman, Jordan
Korea	Korean-American Educational Commission K.P.O. Box 643 Seoul 110, Korea
Lebanon	AMIDEAST P.O. Box 135-155 Beirut, Lebanon
Malaysia	MACEE TOEFL Services 355, Jalan Ampang 50450 Kuala Lumpur, Malaysia
Mexico	Institute of International Education Londres 16, 2nd Floor Apartado Postal 61-115 Mexico 06600 D.F., Mexico
Morocco	AMIDEAST 25 bis, Patrice Lumumba Apt. No. 8 Rabat, Morocco
Nigeria	African-American Institute Attn: TOEFL P.O. Box 2382 Lagos, Nigeria

COUNTRY	AGENCY
People's Republic of China	China International Examinations Coordination Bureau #35 Da Mu Cang Hu Tong Xi Dan, Beijing People's Republic of China
Singapore	MACEE TOEFL Services 355, Jalan Ampang 50450 Kuala Lumpur Malaysia
Syria	AMIDEAST P.O. Box 2313 Damascus, Syria
Taiwan	The Language Training & Testing Center P.O. Box 23-41 Taipei, Taiwan
Thailand	Institute of International Education Room 219 A.U.A. Language Center 179 Rajadamri Road G.P.O. Box 2050 Bangkok 10501, Thailand
Tunisia	AMIDEAST BP 1134 Tunis, Tunisia
Yemen Arab Republic	AMIDEAST c/o Yemen-American Language Institute P.O. Box 1088 Sana'a Yemen Arab Republic

If you live outside the United States and Canada in a country not listed above, you should request a copy of the current *TOEFL Bulletin, Overseas Edition* at the address below.

TOEFL Publications
CN 6154
Princeton, NJ 08541-6154

10. After I send in my TOEFL registration form, what happens?

After sending in your registration form, you should receive an admission ticket to the test center about two weeks before the test date. If you register two or three months before the test date, you should receive your admission ticket about one month before the test date. The admission ticket will show your registration number, name, and address, as well as the test center, time, and date of the test. This ticket is very important. No one is admitted to the test center without an admission ticket.

11. Can I change the date of my registration?

No. Once you have received an admission ticket, space is reserved for you on a specific date and at a specific test center. However, if you do not take the test, you can get a certificate of $10 (U.S. currency) credit toward the cost of registering for another TOEFL, or you can apply the credit to the purchase of a TOEFL test kit. After the test, you have 60 days to take advantage of this $10 credit. If you want to apply the credit toward the registration fee for another TOEFL, but you do not have time to wait for the credit certificate, send your old admission ticket, a new registration form, and the rest of the test fee to:

TOEFL Services
CN 6161
Princeton, NJ 08541-6161, USA

12. Can I take the TOEFL without registering beforehand?

No. You must register and receive your test center admission ticket in order to take the TOEFL.

13. What if it is not convenient for me to take the TOEFL at the test center on my admission ticket?

Request a change of test center. To do this, complete the Request Form for Change in TOEFL Test Center that is printed in the *TOEFL Bulletin*. There is a $5 charge for this service. Your request form must arrive at ETS before the closing date for registration for the test, which is usually about six weeks before the test date. Thus, unless you register about three months before the test date, you probably won't be able to change your test center.

Note: ETS allows the test center supervisor to admit examinees to a different test center than appears on the admission ticket if space and test booklets are available. You may try this if you wish, but there is no guarantee that there will be space for you.

14. What if I do not go to take the TOEFL?

If you do not go, you may lose your registration money entirely. To avoid this, request a $10 (U.S. currency) credit certificate within sixty days after the test date. You can use the $10 toward the registration fee for a later TOEFL administration for up to two years. (See the description of how to do this in question 11 above.)

15. Is the TOEFL always the same length?

No. Some TOEFLs contain 150 questions, and some contain 200 questions. The TOEFL always contains 150 questions when it is administered outside the United States or Canada. Within those two countries, the TOEFL contains 150 questions five times per year. This is during the Disclosed Administrations discussed in the answer to question 28 below. You should take the TOEFL at one of the Disclosed Administrations if possible. Since the test is shorter, you will not become as tired as you might with the longer form. Therefore, it will be easier to give the test all your attention. You can find out if the short or the long form of the test is given in a certain month by looking in the *TOEFL Bulletin*. Look for the heading "TOEFL Test Forms Given at Specific Administrations." The Disclosed Administrations are usually in September, October, February, March, and May. However, ETS sometimes changes these dates, so be sure to check the *Bulletin* before signing up to take the test during a specific month.

At the other seven administrations each year, the TOEFL you will take in the United States and Canada contains 200 questions. The 50 extra questions are not counted in your score. The extra questions are included so that ETS can develop statistics on the questions' difficulty and quality. The questions will appear on a later TOEFL, and ETS will use the statistics to adjust the scores for differences in the difficulty of different forms of the TOEFL.

Note: You will not know which questions will not be counted when you take the TOEFL. Therefore, if you take a TOEFL with 200 questions, you must do your best on every question.

16. Are all TOEFLs equally difficult?

More or less, but not exactly. The TOEFL tests a wide variety of English, and each TOEFL is only a sample of the English that can be tested. Therefore, the average number of questions answered correctly by examinees may change from one test form to another. However, these differences in test difficulty are eliminated by use of a statistical procedure called *test equating*. Because of test equating, the same TOEFL score from different TOEFL administrations indicates the same level of English proficiency, even if one form is more difficult than another.

17. How long does the TOEFL take?

About three hours. This includes the time necessary for the supervisor to check your identification documents, and for you to fill out your answer sheet and complete the test. If you take the longer, 200-question version of the test in the United States or Canada, the total time required may be almost four hours.

18. Will I have enough time to finish?

Probably, but you must work quickly. Pay attention to the time so that you can complete the test. You should have enough time for Section 1. If time is almost over for Section 2 or 3, and you have not finished, answer the rest of the questions with the same answer—either (B) or (C) only—so you will get some of the questions correct by chance. Remember, your score is not lowered for guessing on the TOEFL. Your score depends only on the number of questions you answer correctly.

19. If I finish a section early, can I go on to the next section?

No. This is cheating. If the test supervisor catches you working on a section other than the one that you should be working on, he or she may collect your test booklet. If this happens, you will not receive a score on the test. Or, the supervisor may report to ETS that you were working on the wrong section. If this happens, ETS may decide to cancel your score, especially if it is a high score. If ETS cancels your score, you have the right to take the TOEFL again without charge.

20. Should I guess if I am not sure about an answer?

Yes, definitely. Guessing is to your advantage on the TOEFL. Incorrect answers do not count against you.

21. If I need to guess, what strategy should I use?

First, decide which choices you do NOT believe are right, and then make your best guess from the remaining choices. If you are not sure any choices are definitely wrong, choose choice (B) or (C), as the correct answer will be one of these 55 to 60% of the time. We have found that choice (A) is the least-used choice on the test. The correct answer is found there only about 19% of the time. This is because test writers think the correct answer will be easier to find if it follows the question immediately. Therefore, they try to "hide" it in the middle of the choices (position B or C). However, they do not always put the correct answer in the middle. They know that if they did, you would soon realize this. Still, choices (B) and (C) are the most frequently used. You should remember this if you have no idea as to the correct answer. For example, if you think that choice (A) is the correct answer, mark (A) on your answer sheet. On the other hand, if you think choices (B) and (D) are wrong, but you cannot decide between choices (A) and (C), then you should mark choice (C).

22. What should I do if I cannot understand the tape recording?

During the beginning of the tape recording, each of the three speakers on the tape makes a statement. If you cannot hear these statements clearly, raise your hand so that the test center supervisor can make adjustments before the test begins.

23. What should I do if I want to change an answer?

If you want to change an answer, you must completely erase your first answer. Then, fill in your new one. It is very important that you completely erase the answer you want to change. If two answers are filled in, the question will be counted as incorrect even if one of the two answers is correct.

24. What should I do if I mark my answers in the wrong places?

This can be a serious problem. You must always be sure to put your answer in the correct space on the answer sheet. If you mark your answers in the wrong places, and you notice it before the end of the section, carefully change them by erasing the incorrect answers completely and filling in the correct answers. If you notice that you have marked your answers in the wrong places after time is over for the section, you may NOT go back and change your answers. Tell the supervisor what you did, and ask him or her to report it to ETS. You should also write ETS about this yourself and request that your test be hand scored. (See question 36 for this procedure.) Remember, *you* are responsible for marking your answer sheet correctly.

25. Is it possible to cheat on the TOEFL?

No. Because there is a possibility that examinees may cheat, ETS does many things to prevent it. Between eight and sixteen versions of the same test form are printed and distributed at each test center. Therefore, each question appears in a different order in different test booklets at the same test center. In addition, different versions of the TOEFL answer sheet are used at the same test center. Therefore, if you copy the answer from the person sitting next to you, you will be copying the answer to a different question. Do not try to cheat on the TOEFL. If you do not know the answer to a question, make a guess and go quickly to the next question. You will do much better on the test this way. Copying answers from other examinees will only hurt your score.

26. What happens if I am caught cheating?

Your TOEFL scores will not be reported, or if reported already, they will be canceled. As indicated above, efforts to cheat on the TOEFL are foolish. Besides copying, other things that are considered cheating are bringing notes on English grammar or vocabulary to the test center, making notes in your test booklet, working on a different section than the one you should be working on, continuing to work on the test after time is over, communicating with another examinee, taking a test booklet out of the test room, or removing a page from the test booklet.

27. Is it possible to get someone to take the TOEFL in my name?

Sometimes examinees try, but it is considered cheating and it may also be illegal. In the past, some examinees have paid someone to take the TOEFL for them. These paid examinees bring false identification documents to the test center. Because of this, the TOEFL now uses the following policy.

You must bring a recent picture of yourself to the test center. This picture must be attached to the Photo File Record (sent with your admission ticket) and presented to the test center supervisor. This picture is kept by ETS, which sends a copy of it to each institution that receives your TOEFL scores. If the person on the score report is not the person who enrolls in the institution, the institution will probably cancel the admission. In the United States, if you pay someone to take the TOEFL for you and then use the TOEFL score to get a visa to study in the United States, you can be sent home by the U.S. government. In addition, the person you paid can be arrested. Therefore, do not try to have someone take the TOEFL for you.

28. Can I keep my TOEFL test booklet after the test?

Maybe. The answer depends on when and where you take the test.

The TOEFL program allows examinees to keep or obtain the test at the five Disclosed Administrations each year. These are usually the September, October, February, March, and May administrations. (See question 15.) If you take the TOEFL at one of these administrations in the United States, Canada, or Puerto Rico, you may keep the test booklet at the end of the test. If you take one of the Disclosed Administrations elsewhere, on the day of the test you must give the test center supervisor an envelope with a stamp and your address on it. The supervisor will then mail the test booklet to you a few days after the test.

For $18 you can get a copy of the cassette tape for the *Listening Comprehension* section of the disclosed TOEFL, a copy of your answer sheet, and a list containing the correct answer to each question on the test. To obtain this material, you must complete the TOEFL Test Materials Order Form in the *TOEFL Bulletin* within four months after taking the test. Then, send it with your check to the address listed in the answer to question 11 above.

We encourage you to take the TOEFL on one of the Disclosed Administration dates and to order a copy of the test materials. It will allow you to inspect the test and to determine where you made mistakes. If you plan to take the TOEFL again, you may use the test for additional practice. Also, if there is an error in the test, it will allow you to discover the problem and write to ETS about it.

29. How can I complain about a test administration?

If you have a complaint about the test administration at your testing center, about either the testing facilities or the supervisor, describe your complaint in a letter and send it within three days after the test date to:

TOEFL Program Office
CN 6155
Princeton, NJ 08541-6155, USA

Be sure to describe your complaint clearly and include the date of the test and the location (city and country) of the test center in which you took the TOEFL. If there was a lot of noise in the test room, or if you could not understand the voices on the tape because the sound equipment was of poor quality, or if there were other problems at the test center, write ETS a letter describing the problem. ETS may allow you to take the test again for free.

30. Can I complain about a question on the TOEFL?

Yes. You may complain about it at the TOEFL test center to the test center supervisor. If the supervisor agrees with you, he or she should tell ETS about your complaint. In addition, on the five Disclosed Administrations each year, when you are allowed to either keep your test or get a copy of the test afterwards, you can check the test and cite the question exactly. If you think that the question has more than one correct answer, or if you think that there is no correct answer, or if you think that ETS has marked the wrong choice as the correct answer, or if you find something else wrong with the question, you may write a letter of complaint to the address below.

SHEP Test Development
Educational Testing Service
CN 6656
Princeton, NJ 08541-6656, USA

In your letter, identify the question and the test form (or test date), and send ETS a photocopy of the page that contains the question.

Describe clearly why you think the question is a bad one. ETS will answer you in writing in about one month. If it agrees with you, it will score your answer sheet again, as well as the answer sheets of all examinees who took the test on that date. If your score has already been sent to a college or university by the time ETS replies, ETS will send corrected scores to all institutions that received your scores, as well as corrected scores for examinees tested on that date. If you receive a copy of your test, go over it carefully. While ETS is good, it is not perfect.

31. How can I get my TOEFL scores sent to a college or university?

You can get your TOEFL scores sent to a college or university in one of two ways. First, on the day of the test you can request that official score reports be sent to as many as three institutions. To do this, mark the code numbers of those institutions on your TOEFL answer sheet. There is no additional charge if you use this method. Second, you can request TOEFL scores by mail by using the official Score Report Request Form, available in the *TOEFL Bulletin*. There is an additional charge of $5 for each score sent through this service. Scores are sent about two weeks after ETS receives the request. For an additional $15, you can have your scores sent within two days of the date ETS receives the request.

32. Can I cancel my TOEFL score?

Yes. There are several ways to do this. The easiest way is to complete the Score Cancellation Section of your TOEFL answer sheet after taking the test. You may also cancel your score by calling ETS at 609-882-6601. Or, you can send a telegram to

EDUCTESTSVC
Princeton, NJ 08541, USA

within seven days of the test date. After seven days, you cannot cancel your TOEFL scores. If you call or send a telegram, you must also immediately send a letter with your signature to:

TOEFL Score Cancellations
CN 6151
Princeton, NJ 08541-6151, USA

33. When will I receive my TOEFL score report?

According to ETS, you will receive your TOEFL score report about one month after the test date. Actually, that is the minimum amount of time you will have to wait. If you live outside the United States, you will probably have to wait six weeks or longer. If you do not receive your TOEFL score report in six weeks, you should write or call ETS between 8:30 A.M. and 4:30 P.M. Eastern standard time at the address and phone number below.

TOEFL Services
CN 6151
Princeton, NJ 08541-6151, USA
Phone: 609-882-6601

34. Can I myself send a score report to an institution?

Yes. Many institutions will accept a score report from an applicant. They will most likely accept one of the two original documents you will receive from ETS. However, many will also accept a photocopy of that document, which is called the *Examinee's Score Record*. If you send a photocopy, be sure to tell the institution that they can check your score by calling ETS at 800-257-9547. This is a free long-distance phone number that ETS provides to institutions for that purpose. By sending score reports in this way, you may be able to save yourself the charges for ordering more than three score reports or for ordering score reports after you take the test.

35. How does ETS get my total TOEFL score?

TOEFL total scores range from below 300 to a high of 677. Although possible, TOEFL scores are rarely below 300, because examinees can answer one-fourth of the answers correctly by guessing. Actually, if you guessed the answer to every question, you would earn about a 330 on the TOEFL. Thus, scores lower than 330 are earned by people who do not even bother to guess, and by people who are unlucky when guessing.

The scores for the three sections of the TOEFL have a similar range. However, they are reported on a scale that is only $\frac{1}{10}$ as large as the scale for total scores. Thus, section scores range from below 30 to a high of 68. Your total score is equal to the total of your section scores, multiplied by $\frac{10}{3}$. For example, if your three section scores are 50, 54, and 52, your total score is figured in the following way.

$$50 + 54 + 52 = 156$$
$$156 \times \tfrac{10}{3} = 520$$

Thus, the total score reported to you is 520. You then compare this score with the score required by the college or university you wish to attend.

If you wish, you may also compare your score on the TOEFL to the score of other TOEFL examinees. To do this, refer to the tables of percentile ranks and the instructions for using them that appear in Appendix B.

36. What can I do if I disagree with my score report?

Ask ETS to score your answer sheet by hand. If you believe that your score is not accurate, you can request that your answer sheet be scored by two individuals. The results of this rescoring will be reported to you about three weeks after ETS receives your request. If there is a change in your score, your new score will be reported to all institutions that received the incorrect score report. In order to use this service, you must fill out the TOEFL Hand Scoring Request Form in your *TOEFL Bulletin* and send it to ETS along with $15.

37. Why might my score report be wrong?

Errors in calculating your score are rarely the mistake of ETS. Most often, errors in TOEFL scores are caused by an examinee. You might mark the answers in the wrong places. Or, you might not erase a mark completely after changing an answer. In either case, the computer at ETS will not notice the error, but ETS employees will notice it when they score your test by hand. ETS may then decide to change your score. If your score does change, ETS will report the new score to you and all other institutions that received your original score.

38. How long does ETS keep my TOEFL scores?

ETS will keep your TOEFL scores for two years. If it has been more than two years since you took the TOEFL, you will have to take it again in order to have ETS send a score report. If you have taken the TOEFL within the last two years and need to have a score report sent to an institution, call or write TOEFL Services. (See question 33 above for the address and phone number.) Be sure to send $5 for each score report you request and write your name (family name, given name, middle name as you wrote it on your answer sheet), your date of birth, registration number, and test date.

39. Can I take the TOEFL again?

Yes. You may take the TOEFL as many times as you wish. Research has shown that most examinees improve their scores each time they take the TOEFL. About 20% of the people who take the TOEFL each year have taken it before. Some take it more than ten times. However, you can save money by taking the practice tests in the *Newbury House TOEFL Preparation Kit*. If you wish to have more practice, you should take the TOEFLs contained in the TOEFL test kits published by ETS. Information on ordering these is available in the *TOEFL Bulletin*. These are real TOEFLs, but they contain little information on the test. TOEFL practice tests published by other publishers are not written by ETS. We have found many questions in them that are unlike the questions that appear on the TOEFL. The TOEFLs and practice exercises in the *Newbury House TOEFL Preparation Kit* are more like a real TOEFL than those in any other books.

ETS will keep your TOEFL scores for only two years. Therefore, if you need official TOEFL scores, and you took the TOEFL more than two years ago, you must take the TOEFL again.

40. If I take the TOEFL more than once, are all my scores reported?

No. Only the most recent score is reported. Because your English proficiency may get better or worse between test dates, ETS sends only the most recent score.

41. What should I do the night before the test?

Get some exercise, eat a healthful meal, and get a good night's sleep. These are the most helpful things you can do the night before the TOEFL. Otherwise, the next day you may feel sick or tired. Many examinees make the mistake of studying late the night before the test. This does not help. And, if it makes you tired during the test, it may even hurt your ability to concentrate or think clearly.

Some people worry too much about tests. If you are such a person, do something else instead. Actually, worrying may make you do worse on the test. It can make you nervous, and this will prevent you from concentrating during the test. If you are very worried about the TOEFL, it is important to get plenty of exercise the day before the test. By getting exercise, you can clear your mind of this worry. Exercise will also make you physically tired, and this will help you go to sleep quickly the night before the test. If you worry, but you do not enjoy physical activity, then do whatever relaxes you. You might read a book, see a movie, sew, cook, or visit with friends.

42. Should I purchase any other TOEFL preparation materials?

You will not need any other TOEFL preparation materials than those contained in the *Newbury House TOEFL Preparation Kit*. If you know the information contained in this kit, and you still do not achieve the score you desire on the TOEFL, then your problem is a lack of English proficiency. No TOEFL preparation kit will correct this problem. In order to correct it, you should enroll in a good English-language study program and make use of every opportunity to read, write, and hear English. If you wish to take additional practice tests, you should order the TOEFL test kits: *Understanding TOEFL, Listening to TOEFL,* and *Reading for TOEFL*. These contain official TOEFL tests published by ETS. Information on ordering them may be found in the *TOEFL Bulletin*.

The authors of this text have found other TOEFL preparation kits containing many questions that are quite different from those found on the TOEFL. Practicing with such tests may be bad for you because they may give you a false idea of the kind of questions you can expect on the TOEFL.

43. Are there any general test-taking strategies I should use?

Yes. Here are five general test-taking strategies you should practice and use.

A. Work as rapidly as you can. Do not spend a lot of time trying to answer a question that you do not know. Instead, make a guess, mark your answer sheet, and then place a light mark in your test book next to the number of the question you are unsure of. In this way, if you have time at the end of the section, you can come back to this question and try it again. Sometimes, especially in Section 2, the answer will seem clearer the second time you look at the question.

B. Do not spend time reading the directions for each section. You will know them thoroughly after using this book. In this way, you will have time to answer two or three questions while other examinees are still reading the directions. This will also help you finish the section on time.

C. Answer every question. If you do not finish a section, rapidly fill in your answer sheet with choice (B) or (C) before the time is over. This takes only a few seconds, and you have a twenty-five percent chance of getting such answers correct.

D. Concentrate as hard as you can on the test questions. Do not daydream or let anything else enter your mind. Do not worry about how you are doing. That will only stop your concentration and hurt your score. Remember, standardized tests like the TOEFL are designed to be fairly hard. The average person will only get slightly more than sixty percent of the answers right. If you get more than this amount of the answers right, you will do better than average.

E. Do not rest. After you answer each question, go immediately to the next question. You can rest between sections or, better yet, rest after the test is over.

Now, if you haven't already done so, take *A Practice TOEFL, Form 1*. Then, score it and go on to Chapter 3.

CHAPTER 3

Statements

Chapters 3, 4, and 5 provide in-depth analysis and training in the three parts of Section 1, *Listening Comprehension*. This is the section of the TOEFL that is given through the use of audio tape. To do well on this section, you must be able to comprehend American English easily. Chapter 3 covers the first part of Section 1. These questions are called *statements*.

WHAT YOU SHOULD KNOW

In this part of Section 1 of the TOEFL, you will hear 20 single statements. The statements are played on tape and are spoken only once by a man or a woman. The purpose of this part is to test your ability to understand accurately single statements made by American men and women. In order to perform well, you will have to understand English sounds, grammar, and vocabulary. Most statements contain between 5 and 18 words.

Listen carefully to each statement and try to understand the main point. You cannot take notes. While you are listening to the statements on the tape, do not look at the test booklet. Instead, look up (or close your eyes), listen, and concentrate on the meaning of each spoken statement. After each statement, there is a 12-second period of silence. During this time, you must make your choice from the four choices in your test booklet. Your choice should be the correct paraphrase or restatement of the statement you heard. After selecting the choice you believe is the correct answer, use a Number 2 pencil to fill in the appropriate oval on your answer sheet until the letter is completely covered. *If you are not sure which of the four choices is the correct answer, you should make a guess. Try to answer every question—don't leave any unanswered.* If you have extra time after you have marked your answer, you may want to look at the vocabulary used in the choices (options) for the next question, just to get an idea of the setting for the statement that will be spoken next. Then, direct your full attention to the next statement on the tape.

THE STATEMENTS

The 20 statements on the tape are complete sentences. Most are declarative sentences, but some are interrogative. There are usually some imperative sentences as well. Statements can be affirmative or negative, and any verb tense can appear. Numbers are often used in the statements and are frequently important for choosing a correct option. Pay attention to and try to remember quantities, street numbers, ages, and other numerical data. Generally, the statements provide a single piece of information to the listener. *You should concentrate on understanding the main point of each statement, since that is what you must identify on this part of the TOEFL.*

To do well on this section of the TOEFL, you need a good understanding of English grammar, but you must also be familiar with spoken American English. The language in the statements is informal and conversational—the kind of language that is used in everyday communication in the United States. The speakers will say each word clearly, but the statements will be spoken at conversational speed, and you will hear many contractions. Each statement is part of a conversation such as you might hear at an American bank, store, school, or any other common meeting place. Some statements might even be heard in telephone conversations.

SAMPLE STATEMENT

You will hear: (MAN) Let's not sign this until we have a lawyer look at it.

Notice the conversational nature of the statement and the use of the contraction *let's*. The use of contractions is common in this part of the TOEFL. The man is apparently talking about a document of some kind; his statement is part of a larger conversation you could hear in many places: in a bank or office, on a bus or elevator, or in an American home.

Also, *because the statements are made in everyday situations, you can expect to hear many common American idioms on this part of the TOEFL.* On some versions of the TOEFL, idioms are used in fifty percent of the statements.

SAMPLE STATEMENT

You will hear: (WOMAN) I'm afraid I won't be able to make it to your party tonight.

Notice the use of the polite conversational expression *I'm afraid* to express regret, as well as the idiomatic phrase *to make it to*, meaning "to attend" or "to come to." This is a statement that might be heard anywhere, either in a face-to-face conversation or on the phone. This sentence, like the previous example, contains contractions.

Many two-word and three-word verbs appear in this part of the TOEFL. These are verb phrases composed of a verb combined with one or two other words, usually prepositions. For example, when the verb *to check* is combined with the preposition *out*, the resulting two-word verb is *to check out*. When used with an object, *to check out* means "to investigate" or "to borrow."

SAMPLE STATEMENT

You will hear: (WOMAN) I doubt that that book has been checked out.

The presence of the words *book* and *checked out* indicates that this is part of a conversation that would most likely be heard in a library. Comprehension of the statement depends on your understanding of the two-word verb *checked out*. In this statement, its meaning is "borrowed from a library." This statement is typical of many in this part of the TOEFL, since it deals with a situation that can occur on a university campus.

Although many of the statements take place in academic settings, they are conversational in tone and rarely use formal academic language. They are most frequently associated with practical matters of university life. Such statements would most likely be heard in dormitories, dining halls, libraries, and other campus areas where students and teachers meet.

SAMPLE STATEMENT

You will hear: (MAN) Returning students can renew their parking permits in Room 412.

The use of the words *students* and *parking permits* tells us that this statement would most likely be heard at a college or university. The word *returning* suggests that it is the beginning of the school year. The language used does not relate to academic subjects, but it is the type of language you could expect to hear in an administrative office at a school. The statement could be an answer to a student's question.

You can expect to hear common American first names, such as *Margaret* or *William*, on this part of the test. Also, because of the informal nature of most of the statements, nicknames (informal, friendly variations of formal names) are likely to appear. Some examples of nicknames are *Peggy*, instead of *Margaret*, or *Billy*, instead of *William*). Often, one or two of the statements will use formal terms of address. Some examples are *Mister Henson* and *Professor Adler*.

SAMPLE STATEMENT

You will hear: (MAN) Jenny thinks everyone will be leaving her apartment at ten.

Notice the use of *Jenny,* a nickname for *Jennifer,* and the phrase *at ten,* a short expression for *at ten o'clock.*

CHOOSING THE ANSWER

After you listen to each statement on tape, you have 12 seconds to consider the four choices in your test booklet and choose an answer. They are listed as (A), (B), (C), or (D). *The correct answer is the one that paraphrases the original statement most closely—the one that gives the listener the same information as the original, but uses different words to do so.*

SAMPLE QUESTION

You will hear: (MAN) Let's not sign this until we have a lawyer look at it.

After hearing this sentence on tape, you read the following choices in your test booklet:

(A) A lawyer should sign this.
(B) We should get legal advice.
(C) We have seen a lawyer.
(D) Let's wait for a lucky sign.

After considering each choice, you see that choice (B), the correct answer, states the important information in the statement but uses different words and grammatical structures to do so. Notice that only one word, *we,* occurs in both the original and the correct answer. *In this part of the TOEFL, the correct answer usually contains very few of the words that are heard in the original statement. Conversely, the choices that contain words or sounds similar to those in the spoken statement are seldom correct.*

Look at the remaining choices. (A) is incorrect because there is no suggestion in the statement that the lawyer needs to sign anything. This choice might attract you if you did not understand the grammar of the original statement. Choice (C) uses the verbs *have* and *look* in the statement to construct a choice using the present perfect form *have seen.* The speaker has not seen a lawyer but clearly intends to. Although (C) is incorrect, the examinee who does not have a complete understanding of the grammar of the sentence might choose it. Choice (D) takes advantage of a possible pronunciation confusion between the words *look* in the statement and *lucky* in the choice, plus a misunderstanding of the verb and noun forms of *sign*. Notice that (D) is also the only one of the four choices that repeats the word *let's,* but (D) does not correspond to the meaning of the spoken statement. As you continue to read the sample statements, notice how the correct answer maintains the meaning of the original statement without using the same words.

SAMPLE QUESTION

You will hear: (WOMAN) I'm afraid I won't be able to make it to your party tonight.

You will read:
(A) I can't make any food for the party.
(B) I'm afraid to accept your party invitations.
(C) I fear I won't be on time for the party.
(D) I can't come to the party this evening.

Here, the correct answer, (D), restates the essential information in the statement, although in a different way. The polite *I'm afraid I won't be able to* is changed to *I can't*. The phrase *make it to your party* is changed to the nonidiomatic phrase *come to the party,* and *tonight* becomes *this evening.* Of the other choices, (A) focuses on the phrase *make it* in the statement, but uses *make* in a different sense. In this choice, the meaning of *make* is "prepare," while in the statement, *make it* means "come." For this reason, and because the word *food* appears in the option but is never mentioned in the statement, choice (A) is incorrect. Choice (B) repeats the word *afraid* heard on the tape but uses it in its more common sense, meaning "fearful." This clearly is not the sense of the polite usage of *afraid* in the original statement. Choice (C) also plays with the meanings of the word *afraid.* However, it states that the speaker might not be on time when, in fact, the original statement tells us that the speaker will not attend the party at all.

Pronunciation also plays a very important role on this part of the TOEFL. Often, at least one of the three incorrect choices presented for each question is wrong because it is based on a misunderstanding of the statement owing to a confusion over pronunciation. Similarly, *when many of the same words or similar-sounding words appear in both the statement and an option, that option is likely to be an incorrect answer.*

SAMPLE QUESTION

You will hear: (WOMAN) I doubt that that book has been checked out.

You will read:
(A) The book is probably available.
(B) Someone has borrowed that book.
(C) I think the book has a checked cover.
(D) I don't think you can borrow that book.

Of the four choices, the correct choice is (A). The vocabulary in the statement (*book* and *checked out*) suggest that the woman is in a library; the speaker says that she doubts that the book has been checked out, which means that it is probably available in the library. Choice (B) is wrong because it states the opposite of what the speaker means. Choice (C) might seem attractive if you are unfamiliar with the two-word verb *check out*. In that case, you might hear only *checked* and think it is an adjective. Finally, in choice (D), *I don't think* paraphrases *I doubt* in the original but concludes that the book cannot be borrowed; actually, the original statement tells us that the book is not checked out and therefore probably can be borrowed.

SAMPLE QUESTION

You will hear: (MAN) Returning students can renew their parking permits in Room 412.

You will read:
(A) Twelve students can return to the room.
(B) New students are permitted to park there.
(C) Old students should go to 412 for permits.
(D) There's enough room for twelve students.

Notice how three of the choices focus on the number *412* in the statement. Here, choice (C) most clearly restates the information in the original. *Old* is substituted for *returning*, and *room* is deleted in the option, but otherwise (C) is a direct paraphrase of the original statement. Choice (A) repeats the number *twelve*, but uses it to specify a number of students. The verb *can return* twists the meanings of *permits* and *returning* in the original. (B) changes the noun *permits* into a verb form *permitted* and makes the verb *renew* into the adjective *new*, but there is no mention of new students in the statement. Finally, (D) takes advantage of a possible confusion over the sounds of *Room 412* (pronounced "room four-twelve") and *room for twelve students*. Notice how choice (D) illustrates the point we made earlier, that *when many similar-sounding words appear in both the statement and an option, that option is likely to be incorrect.*

SAMPLE QUESTION

You will hear: (MAN) Jenny thinks everyone will be leaving her apartment at ten.

You will read:
(A) Everyone is living with Jenny in Apartment 10.
(B) The people will leave Jenny's in ten minutes.
(C) The people are probably going to go at ten.
(D) Jenny will give her thanks to everyone at ten.

The closest paraphrase to the original statement is found in choice (C). The singular *everyone* becomes *the people,* and *will be leaving* changes to *are going to go.* The word *probably* replaces *Jenny thinks* to keep the sense of probability in the original statement. Choice (A) uses a misunderstanding of the pronunciation of *leaving,* making it *living.* (B) confuses the meaning of the phrase *at ten,* making it *in ten minutes;* except for those three words, this choice could be a correct answer. Choice (D) exploits a possible sound confusion between *thinks* and *thanks,* making it an inappropriate choice.

RECORDING YOUR ANSWER

After the statement is played on the tape, you will have about 12 seconds to consider the four choices in your test booklet. When you have decided which option is the correct answer, fill in the appropriate lettered oval on your test paper until the letter is covered completely. *Remember, if you do not know which of the four choices is the correct answer, you should guess. Try to answer every question—don't leave any unanswered.* After you have answered, you may want to look briefly at the vocabulary used in the choices for the next question, just to get an idea of the setting for the next statement that will be spoken by the voice on the tape.

CHAPTER 4

Short Dialogs

WHAT YOU SHOULD KNOW

In Part B of the *Listening Comprehension* section of the TOEFL, you will hear 15 short dialogs between two men or between a woman and a man. These dialogs contain English that is more informal than the English you will usually hear in the classroom or read in a book. In fact, their purpose is to test your ability to understand social or everyday topics of conversation. Thus, they seldom deal with academic subjects.

Since the English is less formal, you can expect to hear many contractions, but the English you will hear is spoken clearly and distinctly. At the end of each dialog, a third voice will ask a question requiring your response. You will hear each dialog only one time, so listen carefully. Pay special attention to the second speaker. *The correct answer can often be determined from information contained in the second statement.*

While you are listening to the dialogs on the tape in this part of the TOEFL, try NOT to look at the test booklet. Instead, look up (or close your eyes), listen, and concentrate on the meaning of each spoken statement. After hearing the short dialog, you will need to select your response to the question. There are four options to choose from for each question. All of the choices are grammatically correct and may seem logical, but only one is the best one. You will have approximately 12 seconds to select your response.

After selecting the option you believe is the correct answer, use a Number 2 pencil to fill in the appropriate oval on your answer sheet until the letter is completely covered. *If you are not sure which of the four choices is the correct answer, you should make a guess. Answer every question—don't leave any unanswered.* If you have time after you have responded, you may want to look briefly at the vocabulary used in the choices for the next question, just to get an idea of the setting for the next short dialog that will be spoken. However, once the dialog begins, direct all your attention to it. *Do not read the choices while the dialog is being spoken.*

SAMPLE DIALOG

You will hear: (MAN A) What's the matter, Jane?
(WOMAN) It's my purse . . . I'm sure I left it right here.

(MAN B) What does the woman mean?

Notice that contractions are used throughout the conversation. Most exchanges use the first-person singular (*I*) and the second-person singular (*you*), and common American names are used in many conversations.

THE QUESTIONS

The question that you will respond to usually begins with a question word (*what, why, who, how, when, where, which*) and is usually spoken in the third-person singular (*he, she,* or *it*). *Usually, you will be asked about the meaning of the second speaker's response. What does the man mean?* and *What does the woman mean?* are the most common questions found in this part of the test.

In addition to the above questions, you will sometimes be asked, *Where does this conversation probably take place?* Other questions will ask you the reason or the cause of a condition described in the dialog. These questions usually begin with *Why*. You will sometimes hear such questions as, *Why is the man happy?* or *Why is the woman so upset?* You may also be asked to make a prediction or draw a conclusion from the conversation. For example, you may hear such questions as, *What does the woman imply?* or *What will the man do next?*

It is very important for you to understand the question. Even if you remember all the information in the dialog, it will not help you if you misunderstand the question. Therefore, as you read through this chapter, pay special attention to the sample questions. You may want to read them aloud, in order to help yourself recognize them when you hear them on the tape. Learning the format of the most commonly asked questions is a useful strategy for preparing for this part of the test.

CHOOSING THE ANSWER

Remember, the second speaker's statement usually contains the information you will need to answer the question correctly. However, sometimes an understanding of the entire conversation is necessary to choose the correct response, since the first speaker's statement can set the context for understanding the meaning of the second speaker's statement.

The correction option may simply state the final line of the conversation in a different way or summarize it, as in Part A.

Also as in Part A, *an option that contains the same words heard in the dialog is usually NOT the correct answer.* Similarly, options that contain words or combinations of words that *sound like* those heard in the conversation are seldom correct.

SAMPLE DIALOG

You will hear: (WOMAN) It looks like it's going to be cloudy and cool.
(MAN A) Well, so much for the picnic we planned.

(MAN B) What will the man and woman probably do?

You will read: (A) Go on a picnic.
(B) Wear coats that look alike.
(C) Postpone the picnic.
(D) Sew a lot.

As is often the case, the information needed for the selection of the correct answer is in the second statement. Choice (C) is correct. Choices (B) and (D) contain words and sounds found in the dialog. Choice (B) contains the expression *look alike,* which sounds similar to *looks like* in the conversation. In the same way, choice (D), *Sew a lot,* contains the same sound found in the expression *so much.* Both of these choices may be attractive if you misinterpret the sounds or contexts of the statements. You can usually eliminate such answers, since they sound similar to the words in the dialog. Choice (A) tests your understanding of the second statement. If you recognize *so much for* as an expression that indicates that an activity will not or did not happen as planned, you will eliminate (A) and mark (C), the best response, on your answer sheet.

WHAT IS TESTED?

Since short dialog questions focus on informal, conversational English, your understanding of idiomatic expressions is tested often. You will also be asked to draw conclusions from the conversations you hear. Sometimes, your knowledge of specific word meanings and everyday vocabulary will be tested. Below, you will find some examples of these types of test questions.

Idioms

This type of question will test your understanding of idiomatic language. It is the most common type of question in this part of the TOEFL. The correct answer will require you to understand the idiom used in the dialog.

SAMPLE DIALOG

You will hear: (MAN A) Why don't you go to the game with me?
(MAN B) I can't stand watching a game I know nothing about.

(WOMAN) What will the man probably do?

You will read: (A) Watch the game sitting.
(B) Learn about the sport.
(C) Stay home.
(D) Play in the game.

This question tests knowledge of the idiom *can't stand*, meaning "cannot tolerate." Choice (C), *Stay home*, answers the question. Options that give you the literal meaning of the words in the idiom, as in (A), *Watch the game sitting*, are almost never correct. The other options may seem possible, but none has the meaning implied in the expression.

Everyday and Specific Vocabulary

These types of test questions are similar. They both test the meanings of key vocabulary words presented in short dialogs.

In "everyday vocabulary" test questions, your knowledge of the vocabulary of daily activities will be tested. Short dialogs of this type will deal with common problems and situations associated with daily living in the United States.

SAMPLE DIALOG

You will hear: (WOMAN) Good afternoon. May I help you?
(MAN B) I'd like <u>to cash this check</u> and <u>make a deposit</u> in my <u>checking account</u>.

(MAN A) Where does this conversation probably take place?

You will read: (A) In a hotel.
(B) At a bank.
(C) In a travel agency.
(D) At a post office.

Short Dialogs

Again, your knowledge of the underlined vocabulary is being tested. All of the words are commonly used in a bank. Therefore, response (B), *At a bank,* is correct. Notice that this type of item does not make use of words in each incorrect option that repeat or sound like those used in the dialog. Instead, all the options are places in which money transactions take place, but only in a bank can a person make a deposit in a checking account.

Specific vocabulary test questions usually present a group of vocabulary words in a conversation about a less common or unspecified everyday subject. The words used are often those closely associated with the specific situation being tested. In these types of questions, you will usually be asked where the conversation takes place or to identify the topic of the conversation.

SAMPLE DIALOG

You will hear: (MAN A) This seam is ripped and I've got to have the waist taken in an inch.
(MAN B) No problem. I'll have them for you next week.

(WOMAN) What are the men talking about?

You will read: (A) Trash.
(B) Rulers.
(C) Pants.
(D) Shirts.

The underlined words relate to (C), *Pants,* which is the correct answer. The example above is less typical of TOEFL items in two ways. First, notice that the key words are in the first statement. In most TOEFL items, they are found in the second speaker's statement. Second, one-word options are not common. Although they are infrequent, you will sometimes find items like this one on this part of the test.

Inference

This type of question requires you to draw a conclusion based on the information you hear in the short dialog. Often, you will be asked, *What will the man/woman probably do next?* Or, you may be asked to indicate what the speaker's response means within the context of the dialog.

SAMPLE DIALOG

You will hear: (MAN A) Our English composition is due soon. How about helping me tomorrow?
(WOMAN) I'm sorry. <u>I've got one of my own to do this week</u>.

(MAN B) What does the woman's response mean?

You will read: (A) She's too busy to help him.
(B) She would not like to help him.
(C) She owns one, too.
(D) She helped him once this week.

You must draw a conclusion about the short dialog. This means that you must understand the message even if it is not directly stated in the conversation. The correct response is (A), *She's too busy to help him*. From her statement, we can conclude that she is too busy to help him because she has a project to do, too.

Responses (C) and (D) are simply combinations of words or sounds heard in the conversation. Such responses can usually be eliminated. The woman apologizes to him, suggesting that she would like to help, but cannot. Therefore, (B) is not a likely choice.

Emphatic Word Use

In this type of question, your ability to hear the stress and the tone of the speaker's voice is important. Differences in stress and the tone of a voice can change the entire meaning of a word or a statement. Consider, for example, the difference between *dessert* as a verb (meaning "to leave") and *desert* as a noun (meaning "the last dish at a meal"). You must listen carefully to the stress to determine the meaning of the pronounced word. Pay special attention to the sample item below.

SAMPLE DIALOG

You will hear: (MAN A) My car is in the shop. Will you lend me yours for the evening?
(MAN B) <u>MY CAR</u>! That's a good one!

(WOMAN) What does the man mean?

You will read: (A) He won't let his friend borrow the car.
(B) He will shop for a car.
(C) He has a good car.
(D) He will lend his car to his friend.

Certain conversations include the use of pronunciation to convey meaning. In the example above, *MY CAR* is heavily stressed. When the words *MY CAR* are pronounced with stress, they convey the idea that the speaker does not agree with the first speaker's request. In this case, he doesn't want to lend the car to his friend. In this part of the TOEFL, it is important to be aware of the speaker's tone of voice and use of stress. Response (A) is correct because it accurately reflects the meaning in the tone of the speaker's voice and his use of stress.

A FINAL NOTE

Do not be surprised to hear men and women playing similar roles throughout this part of the test. You may hear men or women speaking in circumstances that seem unusual to you. For example, men may be found shopping in a supermarket, and woman may be found supervising men on the job. Such conversations are not uncommon in the United States and therefore are included in the test.

If you have considered all of the responses and cannot decide on an appropriate one, GUESS. There is no substitute for a good, educated guess based on your understanding of the conversation you hear. Listen carefully to the conversations, consider what you have learned about the test questions in this part of TOEFL, and make the best choice you can.

CHAPTER 5

Minitalks and Extended Conversations

WHAT YOU SHOULD KNOW

In Part C of the *Listening Comprehension* section of the TOEFL, you will hear two types of longer listening selections: minitalks and extended conversations. A minitalk has only one speaker, a man or a woman. An extended conversation is a long dialog between a man and a woman. There are 15 test questions in this part. Sometimes the questions are based on only two spoken selections, but usually they are based on three. There is always at least one minitalk and one extended conversation. When there are three selections, the type of passage is alternated. Each passage is followed by between four and six questions. However, when there are only two passages, each passage is followed by seven or eight questions.

Both types of listening passages are usually about 130 to 230 words in length, or about 40 to 70 seconds long. They usually contain English speech related to a university setting and involve more formal language than is found in Parts A and B of the *Listening Comprehension* section of the TOEFL. Although the vocabulary may be informal and conversational at times, more often it is specific and academic. The selections usually have to do with topics related to university life, American history and geography, or general science. Be sure to listen for dates, amounts, statistics, and other numerical information.

You will hear each minitalk and extended conversation only one time, and you will NOT be allowed to take notes on what you hear. Therefore, you must concentrate intensely as you listen.

When you hear the man or woman make an announcement such as, *Questions 36 to 42 refer to the following conversation*, get ready to concentrate on the new passage. Do not think about the last passage any more. Give all your attention to the new passage, because you will hear it only one time. Do not think about any previous questions once the conversation or lecture begins. Listen carefully for all important details in the passages.

After you hear each minitalk or extended conversation, you will be asked four to six questions. You will hear each question on tape only ONE time. Then, you will have 12 seconds to read the options in the test booklet and choose the correct answer. Work quickly so that you will be able to concentrate on the next question when it comes.

After you answer each question, look at the next four options. They may provide you with clues about the nature of the next question. However, *do not read the options while you are listening to the question.*

THE QUESTIONS

Your comprehension of spoken English is tested in this part by two types of questions: inference questions and specific questions.

Inference Questions

The first questions following a passage are usually the inference type. Inference questions ask you for information not directly stated in the selection, but implied. You will have to draw your own conclusion from the information that you hear. These questions will test your understanding of the larger context in which the selection takes place. To answer these questions, you should try to become familiar with the kinds of settings students in North America may find themselves in.

There are usually one to three inference questions following a minitalk or extended conversation. Here are some common inference questions you can prepare yourself for, followed by a detailed discussion of some of them.

MINITALK

What is the main topic of the talk?
Who is the speaker?
What is the speaker's profession?
Where does the talk take place?
Whom is the speaker talking to?

EXTENDED CONVERSATION

What is the main topic of the conversation?
Who are the speakers?
Where does the conversation probably take place?
What will the man (woman) probably do next?

The most common general inference question you may hear at the end of a passage comes in two forms: *What is the main topic of the talk?* or *What is the main topic of the conversation?* Either form tests your general comprehension of the selection. In answering this question, be careful not to choose just any topic or detail you heard in the passage. Instead, think about the larger purpose of the talk or conversation. The correct response will reflect the answer to the question, *Why did the speaker give this talk?* or *Why did this conversation take place?*

The next most common inference question has to do with the identity of the speaker in a minitalk or the speakers in an extended conversation. The question is usually, *Who is the speaker?* or *Who are the speakers?* The answer to this question is usually two or three words, such as *a doctor* or *two college students*. Thus, if you see four options in your test booklet that list different professions, the question will probably be about the speaker's job. For example, examine the following options for question 36, the first question in this part of the *Listening Comprehension* section of the TOEFL.

36. (A) An engineer.
    (B) An architect.
    (C) A professor.
    (D) A journalist.

Another common inference question deals with the location of the conversation. This question frequently is, *Where does this talk (or conversation) take place?* Again, the answer to this is only two or three words giving a location, such as *in school* or *on a bus*. Thus, when you read in your test booklet four options that refer to different places, you can guess, even before you hear the passage or question, that the question will be about the location of the talk or conversation. Suppose you read the following options for question 37 in your test booklet:

37. (A) In a classroom.
    (B) In a hospital.
    (C) On a boat.
    (D) On a plane.

If you guess that the question will be, *Where does this talk take place?* you will probably be right.

A less common inference question asks about the audience of a minitalk. Two forms of this question are, *Whom is the speaker talking to?* or *For whom is this talk intended?* The answer to this type of question is usually a group of people, such as *students* or *librarians*. If you read four options that describe a group of people in your test booklet, the question may be about the audience. For example, for question 38, you read:

38. (A) The hospital staff.
    (B) The faculty.
    (C) A group of students.
    (D) A group of nurses.

In this case, you would probably be right if you guessed that the question was, *Whom is the speaker talking to?*

A final inference question that may follow an extended conversation asks about what may happen after the conversation. This question is usually, *What will the man (woman) probably do next?* This question often occurs as the last question about a passage. The answer to this question is generally an action phrase such as the following for question 39 in your test booklet:

    39. (A) Return it.
           (B) Call the librarian.
           (C) Give it to a friend.
           (D) Read it this afternoon.

Specific Questions

The remaining three to five questions on each selection are factual and ask for specific information about details heard in the selection: *who, what, where, when, why,* and *how.* Often, these questions refer to the speaker directly, such as, *What does the speaker say people should do when they . . . ?; What does the speaker suggest is the cause of . . . ?;* or *What does the speaker think about . . . ?* Another type of specific question begins with the words *According to.* An example is, *According to the speaker, what should people do when they . . . ?* In an extended conversation, the word *man* or *woman* is used instead of the word *speaker,* since extended conversations involve two speakers, a man and a woman.

Because these questions are factual and ask for specific information, you must pay close attention to details such as names, places, times, dates, and numbers, as well as to larger pieces of information such as definitions, descriptions, and explanations heard in the selection. Because you cannot take notes, you will need to keep these details in your memory in order to answer the questions.

As with the inference questions above, you may be able to prepare yourself for these factual questions before you hear the passage or the questions. You can gain insight about details of the passage and the questions by looking at the options in the test booklet as soon as you finish Part B. In fact, while the directions and examples for Part C are played on the tape, you have about three minutes to become familiar with the vocabulary of the passages. You can also anticipate the questions by reading the options. Therefore, *do not listen to the directions and examples.* The directions for Part C are always the same, and you will be very familiar with them after using this book.

Let's look at some examples. While the tape is giving the instructions and examples for Part C, you read the options in the test booklet and see:

39. (A) Right away.
    (B) Tomorrow.
    (C) Next week.
    (D) In two weeks.

Before you hear the passage, ask yourself what type of information will you need to answer this question? You can probably guess that the question will begin with *When*. Also, because all of these time expressions relate to the future, you can guess that the question will probably be, *When will (something happen)?* If you know this information before you listen to the passage, you will have an advantage, because you can listen very carefully for the mention of something that will happen at one of the times that appear in the options.

Suppose you read the following options for question 40.

40. (A) By answering all the questions correctly.
    (B) By turning it in on time.
    (C) By leaving a margin on the right.
    (D) By writing it clearly.

What type of question will be asked for these options? Clearly, the question will begin with *How*. What else do the options tell you? They describe how something should be done. With this information, you can guess what the question will be. It probably will be a question like, *How can one get a good grade on the assignment?* When you hear the passage, you will know to listen specifically for information that answers that question.

Now read the options following question 41:

41. (A) One.
    (B) Two.
    (C) Six.
    (D) Ten.

What kind of question does this information answer? If you guess that the question will begin with *How many*, you will probably be right. If you read this before listening to the passage, you will know that one of the questions will ask you for an exact amount and that you need to listen for that amount in the passage. Note that, in the options, the numbers are given in increasing order. Dates and times are also listed this way on the TOEFL. If you know this, you can find a specific option more easily.

Practice these test-taking skills when you take the practice TOEFLs accompanying this book. In Part C, prepare for the inference questions and the specific factual questions by reading the options during the three minutes that the directions and examples are being given.

This will give you a big advantage. However, be careful not to miss the minitalk or extended conversation because you are reading and thinking about the options. Remember, when you hear, *Questions 36 to . . . refer to the following . . .* , get ready to listen carefully.

CHOOSING THE ANSWER

After you hear each question, read the options in the test booklet and select the correct answer. There are four options. Each one is grammatically correct. However, only one of them is the best option. You will have twelve seconds to select your answer.

Although most of the questions are concerned with the details of the passage, the correct answer will almost never contain the same words that are used in the selection. For example, in the selection, you hear the statement, *The entire process takes but a minute and a half.* After the passage, you hear the question, *How long does the process take?* Your choices may be:

(A) One-and-a-half seconds.
(B) Ten-and-a-half seconds.
(C) Thirty seconds.
(D) Ninety seconds.

The correct answer is (D), since one-and-a-half minutes equals ninety seconds. Notice that choice (A) uses many of the same words that are used in the passage, but it is not correct. As in Part B, *options that contain words or combinations of words that sound like those heard in the selection are seldom correct.*

Minitalks

A minitalk has only one speaker. The most common type of minitalk simulates an academic lecture or a situation in a university setting. For example, you may hear a professor describing a course to students on the first day of class. Or, you may hear a speaker give a short introduction to a presentation. Sometimes, it is a short lecture containing a lot of specific information. Usually, the first sentence of the minitalk gives you the context of an academic lecture, while the second or third sentence introduces the topic.

At times, you may hear a minitalk in which the speaker is talking about himself or herself. In this case, the content is usually personal, and the language is not very formal or academic.

Here is an example of a minitalk.

SAMPLE MINITALK

You will hear: (MAN) Questions 36 to 41 refer to the following talk.

(When you hear these words, stop whatever you're doing and get ready to concentrate on understanding what you hear next.)

(WOMAN) Good morning, class. I'm sure you're going to find today's lecture very interesting. We're going to talk about two tribes of American Indians in Virginia. As you know, most Indians in the United States live on reservations in the Western states, but there are a number of reservations in the East as well. Two of these have been set aside for the Pamunkey and Mattaponi Indians in the state of Virginia. The Pamunkey and Mattaponi tribes were first encountered by the English explorer Captain John Smith in 1607, when he was establishing the colony of Virginia. After repeated hostilities with the expanding colony, the Pamunkey and Mattaponi Indians were each given a reservation in 1677 near Richmond, the present-day capital of the state of Virginia. Today, 300 years later, the two tribes still hold their reservations, which are about six miles apart. There are only about 60 Pamunkey and 70 Mattaponi living on the tribal lands, but others who leave the reservations for work often return when they retire. Both tribes maintain small museums to explain their parallel histories to visitors. The Pamunkey and Mattaponi reservations are vivid proof that not all Indian people today are found west of the Mississippi River.

You will hear: (MAN) Question 36. Who is the speaker talking to?

(12-second pause)

You will read: 36. (A) Tourists.
(B) Students.
(C) Indians.
(D) Historians.

Minitalks and Extended Conversations

The correct answer is (B). This is an inference question. In the talk, the speaker greets her students and talks about "today's lecture" in lines 1 and 2.

You will hear: (MAN) Question 37.

(Whenever you hear the question number given, immediately answer the last question if you haven't already done so, and concentrate on the next question.)

Where did Captain John Smith come from?

(12-second pause)

You will read: 37. (A) Virginia.
       (B) North Carolina.
       (C) England.
       (D) New York.

The correct answer is (C). You were told in line 10 that he was an English explorer. Notice that the information needed to answer the question (*English*) was given only once, and it appeared in a different grammatical form from that used in the option.

You will hear: (MAN) Question 38. How could the relations between the Indians and the early colonists be described?

(12-second pause)

You will read: 38. (A) Tolerant.
       (B) Surprisingly cordial.
       (C) Frequently unfriendly.
       (D) Interdependent.

The correct answer is (C). Again, the necessary information is heard only once using different words. (See line 13.)

You will hear: (MAN) Question 39. In what year were the reservations established?

(12-second pause)

You will read: 39. (A) 1607.
       (B) 1677.
       (C) 1760.
       (D) 1767.

The correct answer, (B), can be found in line 15. This is a numerical detail that you have to keep in your memory until you hear the question. Remember, you cannot take notes. Notice that the dates are given in increasing order—all numerical options are listed this way in your test booklet. Also, notice that if you read these options before listening to the minitalk, you will know that a date will be important in answering the question. Therefore, you can pay special attention to dates in the passage.

You will hear: (MAN) Question 40. How does the lecturer characterize the histories of the two tribes?

(12-second pause)

You will read: 40. (A) Lively.
(B) Uninteresting.
(C) Forgotten.
(D) Similar.

The correct answer, (D), can be found in line 23. Notice that the answer used *similar*, which is a synonym for *parallel*, the word heard in the lecture.

You will hear: (MAN) Question 41. What is the Indians' probable attitude toward the reservations?

(12-second pause)

You will read: 41. (A) They are embarrassed by them.
(B) They feel at home on them.
(C) They want to sell them.
(D) They wish the reservations were in the West.

The correct answer, (B), can be found in line 21. This is an inference question. Since you know that Indians who leave the reservation for work often return there when they retire (rather than staying at the place where they worked), you can conclude that they feel at home on the reservation. There was no information given that suggested that any of the other choices were possible.

Extended Conversations

An extended conversation is a dialog between two speakers, a man and a woman. Extended conversations can have two types of content: social or academic. Conversations with social content may take place in stores, at school, in a library, or in any other place where people gather. Generally, the language in such a conversation is informal. It may not contain much academic information. In such a conversation, you may be asked inference questions about the dialog, such as:

Where did this conversation take place?
What are the speakers talking about?
Why are they speaking to each other?
When did the conversation take place?
What is the relationship of the speakers?
Who are the speakers?
What will the man (or woman) probably do next?

Extended conversations with academic content are more common on the TOEFL than conversations with social content. In conversations with academic content, information, such as how an American city got its name or why prices are increasing, may be given. The language of these conversations is more formal, and it is specific to the topic being discussed. The questions following a conversation with academic content deal more with factual details than with inference. An example of an extended conversation with academic content follows.

(*Note:* The numbers in parentheses refer to the question numbers and are not part of the dialog.)

SAMPLE EXTENDED CONVERSATION

You will hear: (MAN) Questions 42 to 46 refer to the following conversation. (Get ready!)

(MAN) Are you enjoying this tour? (43)

(WOMAN) Yes. It's my first time to visit New York. (43)

(MAN) Mine, too. New York is such a big and fascinating place. (43)

(WOMAN) Do you know how New York came to be the largest city in the United States? (42)

(MAN) Well, I suppose because it is one of the country's oldest cities. Besides that, it has a good harbor.

(WOMAN) That's true, but there are other old port cities in the U.S. like Boston, Philadelphia, and Baltimore. In fact, in our early history, the first two played a much larger role than New York. What made New York so different?

(MAN) The big difference is that New York had a water route to travel to the interior of the U.S. that the other cities lacked.

(WOMAN) Do you mean a river?

(MAN) Not a natural one. It was a canal. (44) The Erie Canal, which was completed in 1823, connected New York's port to the Great Lakes in the Midwest. (46)

(WOMAN) So even before the railroad was invented, goods and supplies could travel via a water route from New York to the West.

(MAN) Yes, and corn and wheat from that area could travel to New York for sale elsewhere. (45)

(WOMAN) So New York began to grow faster than the other cities. (42)

(MAN) Yes. In fact, within fifteen years after the canal opened, New York doubled in size. It became the trading capital of the U.S., attracting business, banking, and industry, and providing work for thousands of new immigrants.

(MAN) Question 42. What is the main topic of the conversation?

(12-second pause)

You will read: 42. (A) New York's harbor.
    (B) The Erie Canal.
    (C) New York's growth.
    (D) Early American cities.

The correct answer is (C). This is a general inference question. Notice that the subject of this conversation is introduced in the second question at the beginning of the dialog, and the rest of the conversation discusses that question. Although the other choices are mentioned in the dialog, they are not the main subject.

You will hear: (MAN) Question 43. Who are the speakers?

(12-second pause)

You will read: 43. (A) A tourist and a tour guide.
    (B) A tourist and a bus driver.
    (C) Two tour guides.
    (D) Two tourists.

The correct answer is (D). This is an inference question. The man gives information about New York to the woman, but we learn in the first few sentences that this is the first time both have been to New York.

You will hear: (MAN) Question 44. What gave New York an advantage over other cities?

(12-second pause)

You will read: 44. (A) A harbor.
(B) A railroad.
(C) A canal.
(D) A river.

The correct answer is (C). This is a simple factual question.

You will hear: (MAN) Question 45. What kinds of products traveled to New York from the Midwest?

(12-second pause)

You will read: 45. (A) Farm produce.
(B) Agricultural equipment.
(C) Good livestock.
(D) Interior goods.

The correct answer to this factual question is (A). Corn and wheat, heard in the dialog, are types of farm produce. Notice that, as usual, the printed answer uses words different from those used in the spoken dialog.

You will hear: (MAN) Question 46. About how long ago did New York's rapid growth begin?

(12-second pause)

You will read: 46. (A) Over 100 years ago.
(B) Over 150 years ago.
(C) Over 200 years ago.
(D) Over 250 years ago.

The correct answer is (B). You must remember the date when the Erie Canal opened (1823) to get the answer right. You also must know some basic arithmetic.

One or more questions requiring a knowledge of basic arithmetic usually appear on each TOEFL. When you read options like these before listening to the passage, you know that a date or period of time in the past is going to be important. Since the options do not mention exact dates, you might even imagine that the question will require you to do some basic arithmetic. You will have to do this arithmetic without writing in your test booklet. Questions involving basic arithmetic usually are based on dates, ages, times, sums of money, etc., so you should pay special attention to information involving numbers on the TOEFL. Notice again that the numbers in this set of options are listed in ascending order, as always on the TOEFL.

A FINAL NOTE

You have now completed training on all three parts of Section 1 of the TOEFL. Do you understand all the information that has been covered? Have you learned the test-taking strategies we describe? Probably not, if you are like most TOEFL test-takers. Therefore, go back and reread Chapters 3, 4, and 5. The second time you read them, the information will be easier to understand and remember. Then apply them to the *Listening Comprehension* section of *A Practice TOEFL, Form 1*, which you took before beginning to read Chapter 3. Continue to reread Chapters 3, 4, and 5, until you can apply these strategies to the practice tests in the *Newbury House TOEFL Preparation Kit*.

CHAPTER 6

Structure

Section 2 of the TOEFL, *Structure and Written Expression,* tests your knowledge of the structure of formal written English as it is used in an academic environment. There are two parts to this section. Both present you with problems in sentence structure, but the two parts require different strategies for selecting the correct option. In the first part of this section, you must recognize *correct sentence structure,* while in the second part you must recognize *errors in structure or usage.* The first part consists of 15 sentences; each has one or more missing words. You must choose one of four options offered as the missing word or words. The second part of Section 2 consists of 25 complete sentences. Each sentence contains a grammatical error that you must identify. Altogether, there are 40 questions in Section 2, and you will have 25 minutes to answer them.

WHAT YOU SHOULD KNOW

The "structure" part of the TOEFL tests you on grammar only. You do not have to correct errors in spelling or punctuation, although in some sentences the punctuation might help you to determine the correct option. The language used in this section of the test is academic, the kind you might see in an American college textbook. The sentences will deal with subject matter in the physical and social sciences, and in the arts and humanities. Often, the statements will contain names of famous Americans or American places and landmarks, and occasionally the statements contain references to Canada. You can recognize these proper names by their capital letters. You may not be familiar with the proper names, but that is not important, since you are being tested on grammar only. Other sentences might contain the names of animals, plants, and geographical features found in North America. Again, you will not need to know anything about these people, places, animals, plants, or geographic features in order to choose the correct completion to the sentence.

You will see simple sentences on this part of the test, as well as sentences that are compound and complex. Usually, one or two sentences will be in question form, and negative sentences might also appear. Most of the sentences contain between 9 and 15 words, but a few might be shorter, while others might contain as many as 20 words. The options are much shorter, usually consisting of one to five words, with longer ones appearing occasionally.

When you work on this part of the test, read each sentence carefully. Before reading the options, try to guess what word or words could logically fit into the blank. Then read the options. You may not see the exact word or words that you are thinking of, but you may see a word or words very similar to what you have in mind. The option may be the same part of speech as what you have guessed, or it may be the same type of phrase or clause as you have in mind. Of course, sometimes you will not be able to guess any answer, and after reading the choices, you may think that they are all equally appropriate. When that happens, be sure to choose an answer, even though you are not sure it is correct; don't leave any question unanswered on your answer sheet.

WORKING THROUGH SOME EXAMPLES

SAMPLE SIMPLE SENTENCES

Here is a typical statement that might appear in this part of Section 2:

1. There isn't ------- ink at all in this pen.

Before you read the options, you can see that something in front of the word *ink* is missing. You can see the expletive *there* with the verb *isn't* and noun *ink* as the predicate noun. You might guess that the missing part of the sentence is an adjective. Now look at the complete question, with the sentence and options together, as it would appear on the TOEFL.

1. There isn't ------- ink at all in this pen.
   (A) some
   (B) the
   (C) any
   (D) no

The correct answer is (C). This question tests your understanding of a negative construction in a simple sentence and focuses on the adjective. Notice the four options each consist of one word only; often, the options will be equal in length, though not always.

2. Candles ------- important since ancient times as sources of light.

This sentence has no verb, so you can guess that the options will be verb forms. The presence of the word *since* means that the tense of the verb will be a present or past perfect form.

(A) which have been
(B) have been
(C) have been being
(D) having been

Looking at the options, we see that they all contain present perfect forms of the verb *to be*, but only option (B) makes sense.

Other sentences on the TOEFL similar to this one might focus on the subject of the sentence or on the object of a preposition or an adjective.

SAMPLE COMPOUND SENTENCE

3. Appendicitis can occur at any age, ------- it occurs most commonly in young adults.

Looking at the sentence, we can see that it has two clauses. You might guess that the missing part is some kind of connector or conjunction and is probably only one word.

(A) which
(B) since
(C) or
(D) but

Looking at the list of options, you can see that option (D) is the only choice that makes sense in the statement.

SAMPLE COMPLEX SENTENCES

4. The colonists ------- Jamestown in 1607 were energetic, curious, and versatile.

After reading the sentence, you might guess that the missing part is either a preposition or a relative clause.

(A) settled
(B) who settled
(C) they settled
(D) who they settled

Looking at the options, you can see that the question focuses on a clause. The correct answer is (B). It provides the relative pronoun subject and the verb for the clause.

Notice that this sentence contains the proper noun *Jamestown*. You may not know exactly what it refers to, although the second syllable, *-town*, should tell you that this is the name of a place. However, it is not necessary for you to know this to analyze the grammar of the sentence.

   5. ------- of Roanoke disappeared has never been resolved.

You might find it hard to imagine the answer to this question until you read the options.
   (A) The colony
   (B) Did the colony
   (C) Why the colony
   (D) Why did the colony

Such a question is designed to test your ability to recognize a noun clause as the subject of a sentence. The correct choice is (C). The clause *Why the colony of Roanoke disappeared* is the subject of the sentence.

Again, a proper name, *Roanoke,* is used, but you should not let it stop you from understanding the grammatical structure of the sentence.

Often, when all the options contain two or more words, the words will be similar, as is the case in this example. Notice that the words *the colony* appear in each of the options; the only difference between (C) and (D) is the word *did.* Though you should work quickly, be sure to read the options very carefully. This example shows that only one word can sometimes make the difference between a right and a wrong answer.

SAMPLE COMPARISON

   6. More research has been done on the communication of birds ------- of any other animal.

Looking at the sentence, the word *more* might lead you to expect a comparison of some kind.
   (A) more than
   (B) than more
   (C) than that
   (D) that than

The options are phrases containing comparative words, but the correct choice is (C). The word *that* is needed after the word *than,* to avoid repetition of the words *the communication,* which is what is being compared in this sentence.

SAMPLE PHRASES

   7. Because of ------- wide range, the Canada goose is found in a variety of habitats.

Structure   **57**

After reading the sentence, you might expect the answer to be either an article or some kind of adjective.

(A) their
(B) whose
(C) its
(D) theirs

Looking over the options, you can see that the focus is on the possessive adjective in an adverbial phrase. The correct choice is (C); the word *its* agrees with the word *goose*, a singular noun.

Notice the mention of Canada. Usually at least one of the fifteen "structure" questions will refer to something Canadian.

8. Of all the world's important cultivated foods, tomatoes are the newest, ------- widely used only within the last hundred years.

This is another question whose answer might be difficult to guess before you look at the options.

(A) they became
(B) having become
(C) they have become
(D) have become

The options focus on a verb form. (B) and (C) are both attractive, but the presence of the comma in the sentence makes (B), a verb phrase, the only possible answer. Although you are not being tested for punctuation in the options, the punctuation in the sentence is the key to your selection of the correct option here. If a semicolon (;) were in the sentence instead of a comma, then option (C) would be the right answer.

9. Because there is ------- single melting point for glass, its behavior is often discussed in terms of viscosity.

Here you might guess an article or adjective to be the missing part.

(A) not
(B) without a
(C) except a
(D) no

Looking at the options, you see that the question is designed to test your understanding of a negative construction. The correct answer is (D); the absence of an article makes the adjective *no* the only possible option. The prepositional phrases, (B) and (C), can be eliminated, since they do not make sense in the sentence.

10. The noted explorer and fur trader, Simon Fraser, was born
------- Bennington, Vermont.

When you read this sentence, you might guess that the missing word is a preposition, perhaps *in*.

(A) in what is now
(B) what is now in
(C) now in what is
(D) what is in now

After reading the options listed, you see that the question tests your knowledge of correct English word order. Notice that the same four words appear in each option, but in only one option are the words in proper order. The correct option is (A); the preposition *in* directly follows the word *born*. The clause *what is now Bennington, Vermont*, is the object of the preposition.

SAMPLE PARALLEL STRUCTURE

11. American mathematical physicist Josiah Gibbs founded the science of chemical thermodynamics, ------- to the field of vector analysis, and developed new ideas in statistical mechanics.

This sentence has a subject, two verbs, and a blank. Both the verbs have objects, and there is a prepositional phrase after the blank. The two verbs are in the active voice and the simple past tense. You might guess that the missing part is a verb.

(A) contributing
(B) has contributed
(C) contributed
(D) was contributed

Reading down the list of options, you see four forms of the verb *contribute*. One option, (C), is in active voice and simple past tense. Option (C), the correct choice, parallels (is in the same tense as) the other verbs in the sentence.

Other similar sentences might test your recognition of parallelism with nouns, adjectives, prepositions, or other parts of speech.

The "structure" questions above exemplify and describe the main types of problems that you will find on the first part of Section 2 of the TOEFL. For a greater variety of examples and a summary of important grammar points, see the grammar section of this manual (Chapter 10).

CHAPTER 7

Written Expression

WHAT YOU SHOULD KNOW

The purpose of this part of Section 2 of the TOEFL, *Structure and Written Expression*, is to test your sensitivity to correct formal English grammar and expression. You will see 25 sentences (questions 16 to 40 of Section 2). In each sentence, four words or phrases are underlined and labeled as options (A), (B), (C), and (D). One of the underlined words or phrases makes the sentence incorrect. Each option will be between one and three words long; however, one underlined word is the most common type of option. You must identify which of the four options must be changed or eliminated in order for the sentence to be correct. In other words, you have to choose the part of the sentence that contains an *error* in grammar, expression, or style.

The sentences are written in formal academic English on subjects familiar to college students, such as the natural sciences, humanities, and social sciences. Most sentences are affirmative or negative statements, but at least one sentence in question form appears on each test. Some sentences are very short (as few as seven or eight words), and others are very long (as many as 26 or 27 words). Although the shorter sentences are not easier, you may find you can do the shorter sentences more quickly.

Time is very important in this part of the TOEFL. Remember that this part is not designed to test your reading comprehension. It tests your knowledge of English grammar. Therefore, in addition to reading the sentence, your first task is to check the underlined options to be sure they are grammatically correct. While you may see some unfamiliar words in this part, you can still find the part of the sentence that contains the grammatical error, even if you do not understand the meaning of all the words.

SAMPLE QUESTION

New York is one of the largest city in the world.
        A B   C D

In this example, the correct choice is (C). The statement tells us that the city of New York is one of a group, the group being composed of cities. This is the part of the sentence in which the error occurs.

Option (C), *city*, should be *cities* for the sentence to be correct. On your answer sheet, you would darken the oval marked (C) to indicate that the word marked (C) in the item is incorrect.

CHOOSING THE ANSWER

There are seven different categories of errors that occur in this part of the TOEFL. Below are sample questions to help you identify these seven categories of errors.

Error Type 1: Grammatical Agreement

In this type of error, the problem involves agreement in the sentence between number (singular/plural) in nouns, pronouns, adjectives, subjects and verbs, and in verb tenses. This type of error occurs most frequently on the TOEFL. It is easy to recognize if you have a good understanding of the rules of grammatical agreement in English.

A. Errors in the Agreement of Number. These are errors that occur when a word refers to another word but does not agree with it in number.

SAMPLE QUESTIONS

1. Bears and bobcats are the <u>only</u> <u>remaining</u> <u>predator</u> <u>found</u> in the
                                             A   B   C   D
state of Vermont.

Problem: *Predator*, option (C), is the complement of the sentence, and it refers to *bears and bobcats*, which is plural. Therefore, *predator* must be changed to *predators* for the sentence to be grammatically correct.

2. The <u>earliest</u> American writings were concerned <u>directly</u> with
          A   B
the dream of a new world and the first attempts at <u>their</u>
                                                                  C
<u>realization</u>.
   D

Problem: *Dream* is a singular noun, and so *their*, a possessive adjective that refers to *dream*, should be singular also. *Their* must be changed to *its* to correct the sentence.

B. Errors in the Agreement of Subject and Verb. These errors occur when a singular subject is followed by a plural verb, or when a plural subject is followed by a singular verb.

SAMPLE QUESTION

3. The distinction <u>between</u> wages and salaries <u>are</u> based primarily
                     A   B

<u>on</u> the method of <u>computing</u> payment.
 C   D

Problem: The subject, *distinction*, is singular, but the verb, *are*, is plural. *Are*, option (B), should be *is*. Notice that the singular subject, *distinction*, is separated from its verb by a prepositional phrase containing two plural nouns. This separation of subject and verb occurs frequently in this part of the test.

C. Errors in Agreement of Verb Tenses. These are errors that occur when a sentence contains two verbs that refer to the same point in time but are in different tenses.

SAMPLE QUESTION

4. Although previously <u>thinly</u> populated, the American Southwest
                                  A

was strategically important <u>because of</u> several major transpor-
                                       B

tation routes that <u>cross</u> <u>it</u>.
                        C D

Problem: The first verb, *was*, is in the past tense, and the second verb, *cross*, option (C), is in the present tense. *Cross* must be changed to *crossed*.

Error Type 2: Grammatical Forms

Errors of grammatical form are also commmon on the TOEFL. In this type of error, a word is in an incorrect grammatical form or in a form that does not exist in English. The word can be any part of speech. Grammatical topics such as verb tenses, forms of the comparative, and the use of the articles *a*, *an*, and *the* are tested by this type of question.

SAMPLE QUESTIONS

5. The viper is a <u>poisonous</u> snake with long fangs <u>who</u> <u>fold</u> against
                   A   B C

the roof <u>of</u> its mouth when its jaws are closed.
         D

Problem: The relative pronoun *who*, option (B), which refers to a person, should be *which* or *that*, because the word it refers to (*fangs*) is not a person.

6. Wasps, <u>although</u> <u>similar to</u> bees, are usually <u>more thinner</u> and
          A   B   C
   have less <u>hair</u>.
               D

Problem: This sentence contains two comparative forms. *More thinner*, option (C), should be simply *thinner*. Using the comparative *more* with another comparative, *thinner*, is incorrect.

7. <u>The</u> modern American dictionary is <u>typically</u> a single compact
    A   B
   volume <u>publishing</u> <u>at</u> a modest price.
               C   D

Problem: *Publishing*, option (C), should be *published*, the past participle. It is used here in an adjective phrase that describes the word *volume*.

Error Type 3: Parts of Speech

A word may have different forms depending on its part of speech. For example, the word *correct* may take the following forms: *correction* (noun), *corrected* (verb), *correct* (adjective), *correctly* (adverb), *correcting* (gerund), *to correct* (infinitive). Error type 3 usually involves the use of an incorrect part of speech (noun, verb, adjective, adverb, preposition, gerund, or infinitive) for a word. To make the sentence correct, the meaning of the word in the option will not change but the form of the word will.

SAMPLE QUESTIONS

8. In 1954, the first <u>successfully</u> kidney transplant <u>was</u> performed
                             A   B
   <u>when</u> surgeons replaced a man's kidney with one from <u>his</u> iden-
     C   D
   tical twin brother.

Problem: Option (A) must be an adjective, since it modifies the noun compound *kidney transplant*. However, the word that precedes kidney transplant is *successfully*, an adverb. It should be changed to the adjective *successful*.

9. The <u>direct</u> sources <u>of</u> fresh water in lakes <u>are</u> rain and melted
         A   B   C
   <u>snowy</u> and ice.
     D

Problem: The statement names three sources of lake water, which should all be nouns. However, the second source is *snowy*, an adjective.

The word should be changed to the noun *snow*.

10. A <u>given</u> force may <u>generation</u> high or low pressure
        A   B
    <u>depending</u> on the area <u>to</u> which it is applied.
        C   D

Problem: In option (B), a verb must follow the word *may*. Therefore, the word in option (B) should be the verb *generate*, not the noun *generation*.

11. <u>Is it</u> actually possible <u>separating</u> the contributions of heredity
       A   B
    <u>and</u> environment <u>to the</u> characteristics of plants?
     C   D

Problem: After an impersonal expression such as *it is possible*, a verb must be in the infinitive form. Therefore, *separating*, a present participle, should be replaced by *to separate*, an infinitive.

Error Type 4: Word Usage

Unlike type 3 errors, which involve incorrect parts of speech, this type of error involves an incorrect word. Although the part of speech is correct, the word is incorrect for the context. The incorrect word can be a noun, verb, adjective, adverb, preposition, or conjunction.

SAMPLE QUESTIONS

12. The flavor, color, and <u>composition</u> of honey varies according
                            A
    <u>from</u> the type of floral nectar from <u>which</u> it is <u>derived</u>.
     B   C   D

Problem: The word *from* in option (B) is a preposition, but the word preceding it, *according*, is not used with that preposition. The phrase should read *according to*. Therefore, option (B) is the correct choice.

13. The Curtis-Lee Mansion, <u>both</u> known <u>as</u> Arlington House, is
                         A   B
    <u>one</u> of the <u>finest</u> Greek Revival houses in America.
     C   D

Problem: The word in option (A) should be the adverb, *also*. In correct written English, *both* is used to refer to two antecedents (words that appeared earlier in the statement), but there is only one antecedent in this statement, *the Curtis-Lee Mansion*.

14. <u>During</u> the last hundred years, population growth in Canada
       A

    has been stimulated by rapid <u>economical</u> development,
                                              B

    <u>moderately</u> high fertility, and massive <u>immigration</u>.
        C   D

Problem: In option (B), the wrong form of the adjective is used. *Economical* is an adjective meaning "cost-saving," but the meaning desired here is "pertaining to the economy." The correct adjective for this meaning is *economic*.

Error Type 5: Word Order

In this type of error, there is a mistake in the order of the words in one part of the sentence. English has rules regarding word order. Two word order rules that are often tested relate to the use of frequency adverbs and the use of *enough*.

SAMPLE QUESTIONS

15. Georgetown and Alexandria <u>retain still</u> <u>some</u> of the atmos-
                                                           A   B

    phere and <u>much</u> of the scale and texture of <u>colonial</u> river port
                 C   D

    towns.

Problem: In a simple sentence, a frequency adverb comes before all verbs except the verb *to be*. Therefore, the word *still* in option (A) should come before the verb *retain*. The correct word order is *still retain*.

16. The modern tugboat is a floating <u>power</u> plant, just
                                                A

    <u>enough large</u> <u>to accommodate</u> engines, crew, and <u>supplies</u>.
        B   C   D

Problem: The word *enough* may be used before a noun or after an adjective or verb. Since *large* is an adjective, *enough* should follow *large* in option (B). Thus, option (B) is the correct choice. The correct word order is *large enough*.

Error Type 6: Omissions and Additions

In this type of error, a necessary word is missing, or an unnecessary word has been added. Although this error type is rare on the TOEFL, you should check for missing words if you cannot find any other error among the options.

SAMPLE QUESTIONS

17. New York's status as a national business center $\underline{\text{stems its}}$ his-
    A
    toric appeal $\underline{\text{to firms}}$ that require a central location
    B
    $\underline{\text{to carry out}}$ their $\underline{\text{functions effectively}}$.
    C$$D

Problem: In option (A), the missing preposition *from* should follow the verb *stems*. Because the preposition is missing, option (A) should be marked on your answer sheet. The correct phrase is *stems from its*.

18. $\underline{\text{As}}$ the wife of the first president, Martha Washington per-
    A
    formed $\underline{\text{her social duties}}$ $\underline{\text{with}}$ $\underline{\text{the generous hospitality}}$, dig-
    B$$CD
    nity, and reserve.

Problem: In English, abstract nouns are usually not preceded by articles unless they are followed by a phrase or clause. The three abstract nouns listed above—*hospitality, dignity*, and *reserve*—are not followed by a phrase or clause. Therefore, in option (D), *the* is an unnecessary and incorrect addition. Option (D) should simply be *generous hospitality*.

Error Type 7: Style

In some of the items in this part of the TOEFL, the error is more a matter of good English style than of grammar. There are two important conventions of style in English you need to understand. The first is *parallelism*, and the second is *avoidance of redundancy*.

In English, when items are in a series or list, they should all be parallel (written in the same part of speech and having the same word form). This means that the series should be all nouns, all verbs, all adjectives, or all adverbs. Errors of parallelism are rare on the TOEFL, but whenever you see a series, check to see if the underlined options following the series contain this type of error.

SAMPLE QUESTIONS

19. Some critics suggest $\underline{\text{that historians}}$ $\underline{\text{have underrated}}$ the con-
    AB
    tributions of $\underline{\text{New York's}}$ modernist architects, musicians,
    C
    painters, and $\underline{\text{photography}}$ during the 1930's.
    D

Problem: The sentence contains a series of professionals. Therefore, the word *photography*, which is a profession, should be *photographers* to make it consistent with the other words in the series.

In errors of redundancy, the sentence contains an extra, unnecessary word. Even if the word does not make the sentence wrong, it should be taken out because it is repetitious. There are few such errors on the TOEFL. However, whenever you see two underlined words together that have the same meaning, you may find this type of error.

20. Wherever pottery has been developed <u>to any extent</u>, the group
                                                                          A
   <u>responsible</u> <u>has been</u> an <u>agricultural, farming</u> community.
       B   C   D

Problem: Here, the word *farming* in option (D) is unnecessary because it has the same meaning as *agricultural*. Therefore, option (D) is an error and should be marked as your choice on your answer sheet. *Notice in such cases that both words are underlined. This is the way errors of redundancy are always displayed on the TOEFL.*

Another example of a redundancy error involves the use of an unnecessary subject pronoun following a subject, as in the phrase *the scientist he*.

You can practice further what you have learned here in the grammar exercises section of this book (Chapter 10). It contains 217 practice questions for Section 2 of the TOEFL.

CHAPTER 8

Vocabulary

WHAT YOU SHOULD KNOW

Section 3 of the TOEFL is called *Reading Comprehension and Vocabulary*. It contains 60 questions and is divided into two parts. The 30 questions in the first part test vocabulary, and the 30 questions in the second part test reading comprehension. You will have 45 minutes to complete all 60 questions. It is necessary to complete the vocabulary questions as quickly as possible, since the 30 reading comprehension questions are much longer and take more time to answer. Many examinees do not finish Section 3 because of the reading comprehension questions.

Each vocabulary question consists of one sentence followed by four choices: (A), (B), (C), and (D). The sentences are written in academic, formal English. Subjects used in the sentences are those a typical first-year college student in North America may study: natural sciences (biology, chemistry), social sciences (psychology, economics, geography), business, and the liberal arts (history, art, music). Some of the sentences refer to American cities, states, and rivers. Some other sentences refer to American history and include important individuals and dates. Some sentences are very short (six or seven words), while others are quite long (26 or 27 words).

In each sentence, a word or phrase is underlined. You must choose from the four choices the one that is the closest synonym (has most nearly the same meaning) to the underlined word or phrase. When the choice replaces the underlined word or phrase in the sentence, the sentence should still have its original meaning.

SAMPLE QUESTION

1. In American folklore, Paul Bunyan was always accompanied by his *huge* blue ox named Babe.

    (A) friendly
    (B) old
    (C) large
    (D) wonderful

The correct answer is (C). *Large* is a good synonym for *huge*. When *large* is placed in the sentence, the sentence keeps its original meaning.

HOW TO IMPROVE YOUR TOEFL VOCABULARY

One way to improve your vocabulary is to read. You should read the kind of material that a college student would read: newspapers, magazines, books, and encyclopedia articles about a variety of subjects. (Scientific subjects as well as American history and geography may be most helpful.) This is the kind of material TOEFL tests.

Another good way to learn vocabulary is to make lists of new words that you learn. However, do not write out the definition of the word, and do not write the equivalent of the word in your native language. Instead, write the word in one column of your list and then write a synonym in another column. As you study the word, cover the synonym and try to remember it.

Another way to learn more TOEFL vocabulary is to use a set of small cards. Write the new word on one side of the card and its synonym on the other side. You should review your words and synonyms at least once a week.

In order to improve your TOEFL vocabulary, you will need two books: a good thesaurus (a dictionary of synonyms) and a monolingual English dictionary (a dictionary written only in English for native speakers of English). When you find a word you don't know, first use the thesaurus. It will give you synonyms for the word. If the word is not in a good thesaurus, it will not be tested on the TOEFL, since the TOEFL uses synonyms to test vocabulary. If you find synonyms but you don't know the meaning of the word, look up the word in the English dictionary. The dictionary will give you the meaning of the word, as well as other words that are related to it. Being able to use an English language dictionary is important if you wish to learn TOEFL vocabulary.

Another good technique is to learn prefixes. The words TOEFL tests often contain prefixes. To answer the question correctly, you must recognize the meaning of the prefix. A prefix can make a difference in the meaning of a word. For example, *content* means "happy," but *malcontent* means "unhappy." Make a list of prefixes as you find them. Then look them up in the dictionary. Here are a few common prefixes and words that contain them.

Prefix	Meaning	Example
a-	"without"	*amorphous*
bi-	"two"	*biweekly*
circum-	"around"	*circumference*
dis-	"negative"	*disbelief*
en-	"to make"	*endanger*
in-	"not"	*inaccessible*
mis-	"bad"	*misbehave*
non-	"not"	*nonpartisan*
ob-	"inverse"	*obscene*
per-	"through"	*pervade*
re-	"again"	*realign*
super-	"great"	*superlative*
trans-	"beyond"	*transcend*
ultra-	"very"	*ultramodern*

Of course, these are not all the prefixes in English. Most prefixes can have more than one meaning and many have more than one form. For instance, the prefix *ab-* is simply another form of the prefix *a-*. As you learn a prefix, learn different words that contain the prefix and its different forms. This way, you will learn its different meanings and its different forms.

It is also helpful to learn English suffixes. They can give part of the meaning of the word. However, they are not tested on this part of the TOEFL. Suffixes usually show grammatical meaning and part of speech (example: *comfort* vs. *comfortable*). This is tested in Section 2 of the TOEFL.

What Vocabulary to Study

There is no specific vocabulary list you can study for this section. However, here are guidelines about the kind of vocabulary that may appear in this section and the kind of vocabulary that will not appear. This information is based on an analysis of words tested on past TOEFL exams. It will help you improve your own selection of words to study for the vocabulary part of the TOEFL. It will also prevent you from studying words that will not appear on the TOEFL.

1. *Learn the words the TOEFL has already tested*. The underlined words tested in this part of the TOEFL are not tested again. However, they may be used again in the choices as synonyms for other words that are tested. Since these are good words to know for all kinds of reading, make a list of these vocabulary words and learn them. You can make this list from words that have been tested on any previous TOEFLs you

have, or from the words in the TOEFL test kits available from ETS. You can also include in your list the underlined words included in the practice TOEFLs included in the *Newbury House TOEFL Preparation Kit*. In addition, write down the words used in the choices in all of the above tests. These words are on the test because they are possible synonyms for other words. And words that can be synonyms for other words are the words you need to know to score high on the TOEFL.

2. *Learn words that are in general use*, current, and likely to appear in the kinds of material a college or university student in North America would read in newspapers, magazines, encyclopedias, or books. These words are used in many contexts and types of reading material. Students who read widely will meet these words again and again.

3. *Learn words of Latin origin.* About half of the words that appear in this part of the test are of Latin origin. Therefore, if you do not speak or read a language that comes from Latin, learn as many Latin words as you can. Focus on the meaning of the root of the word and notice how the root is used in other related words. During the test, focus on the root of the word also. If you do speak or read a language of Latin origin, examine the root of the word for clues to its meaning when taking the test. Do the same for the choices.

4. *Learn adjectives and verbs*. Most English words are nouns. Yet, adjectives and verbs are tested as often as nouns on the TOEFL. Adjectives can easily be made into adverbs (usually by adding the suffix-*ly*), and adverbs are also tested on the TOEFL.

What Vocabulary NOT to Study

In order to know what vocabulary not to study, you will need a monolingual English dictionary. Each dictionary has a "Guide" in the front, before the definitions of words beginning with the letter *A*. Notice that the guide lists the *labels* that are used in the dictionary. The authors of the dictionary use these labels to identify words, or specific meanings of words, that are unusual or special in some way. These unusual or special words are not a part of the *general* vocabulary; therefore, they are not tested on the TOEFL. The labels that identify unusual or special words are *Nonstandard, Informal, Slang, Vulgar, Archaic, Rare, Poetic, Regional* (plus labels indicating a specific region of the United States), *British*, and foreign language labels such as *French*. If you have a dictionary printed in Great Britain, it will include the label *American*. Again, any word that carries such labels will not be tested on the TOEFL.

The dictionary also contains subject labels. These are labels that identify technical words or words that have specific meanings within a subject or occupation. Such words are not found in a variety of settings, but only in specific and/or technical contexts. Some examples and the field each represents are: *mitochondrion* (biology), *lumen* (physics), *duodenum* (anatomy), *enzyme* (chemistry), and *eocene* (geology). Whenever you see such subject labels in the dictionary, you do NOT have to learn these words for the TOEFL.

The dictionary also contains *idioms*. An idiom is a common expression in which a group of words has a different meaning from what its individual words mean. Idioms are used commonly in everyday speech and make the language colorful. Idioms are usually identified in a dictionary by very heavy or dark print and then defined. Although they often appear in Parts A and B of Section 1 of the TOEFL, they are *never* tested in the vocabulary section. Some examples of idioms follow.

Idiom	Meaning
feel blue	"feel depressed"
be a chicken	"be a coward"
talk turkey	"talk seriously"
jump the gun	"begin before one is supposed to"

The dictionary also contains *phrases*. Phrases are groups of words conveying one meaning, such as *in general, on the whole,* and *little by little*. Phrases are also identified in the dictionary by very heavy or dark print, followed by a definition. They are usually listed under the main word in the phrase. For example, *on the whole* is included in the definition of *whole*. Phrases rarely appear on this part of TOEFL. The vast majority of vocabulary questions are *single* vocabulary words. However, two-word and three-word verbs (phrasal verbs such as *blow up, pay homage to, carry out,* and *hand in*) do occasionally appear on the vocabulary part of the test.

Names of types of animals, birds, clouds, fish, foods, minerals, plants, rocks, etc., require a definition rather than a synonym, and thus *could NOT be tested* here. Some examples and their definition are: *owl* (a kind of bird), *porcupine* (a kind of animal), *starfish* (a kind of fish), *potatoes* (a kind of food), *tulip* (a kind of plant), and *granite* (a kind of rock). In a dictionary, such words contain a subject label.

Don't forget! The TOEFL does not test every word in the English language. The words likely to appear on TOEFL are words that can be found in a variety of contexts in university-level reading and can easily be given a synonym. These words can be nouns, verbs, adjectives, and, less frequently, adverbs.

TAKING THE TEST

The 30 vocabulary questions in this section of the test are designed to test your knowledge of vocabulary, NOT your reading comprehension. Therefore, it is usually not necessary to read the sentence that each word appears in. Instead, you should look only at the underlined word and choose its synonym from among the four choices.

This strategy is the most successful one because it will save you much time and help you avoid confusion. Time is very important in Section 3 of the TOEFL. Many students find that the reading selections take a long time to read. Therefore, you must save time on the vocabulary questions. The sentences in the vocabulary questions will often contain unfamiliar vocabulary and most likely an unfamiliar context that may take you a long time to understand. But, more importantly, *the sentences are not written to help you understand the meaning of the word*. If you don't know the meaning of the word, all four choices can fit into the sentence equally well.

Note: If two (or more) of the choices can be synonyms for the underlined word, you must read the sentence to determine which meaning is correct. However, this occurs very rarely on the test.

Here are some examples to help you look at the underlined word only. Try to choose the correct answer for each.

1. *** *** *** *** *** *** *** *** *** *** *** *** *** *intelligent*.
   - (A) hopeful
   - (B) trustworthy
   - (C) smart
   - (D) careful

2. *** *** *** *demonstrated* *** *** *** *** *** *** *** *** *** ***.
   - (A) associated
   - (B) proved
   - (C) excluded
   - (D) profited

3. *** *** *education*, *** *** *** *** *** *** *** ***.
   - (A) work
   - (B) service
   - (C) assignment
   - (D) schooling

In each case, if you know the meaning of the word, you can find the answer without reading the sentence. The answers are: 1. (C), 2. (B), and 3. (D).

The following two examples will show you that if you don't know the underlined word, any of the four choices will be possible in the sentence.

Vocabulary

1. The *Scarlet Letter* is Nathaniel Hawthorne's ******** novel.
    (A) longest
    (B) best
    (C) most popular
    (D) most quoted

2. The two towers of the World Trade Center are ******* New York landmark.
    (A) a notable
    (B) a much-photographed
    (C) a well-known
    (D) an enormous

The above examples show you the importance of studying the underlined word first. The above examples also show that reading the sentence is not necessary in order to find the correct option. Reading each sentence may only waste your time. You should read the sentence *only if* you feel it will help you when you are undecided between two or more choices, or if you have no idea about the correct choice. Then, the sentence may remind you of the meaning if you have ever learned the word before.

STRATEGY REVIEW AND PRACTICE

Remember, there are three basic strategies you should use in the vocabulary part of Section 3:

1. Work as fast as you can so you will have enough time for the Reading Comprehension questions that follow.
2. Read the underlined word first and try to find the correct answer. Do *NOT* read the sentence unless you don't know the meaning of the underlined word.
3. Examine the root of the word for clues to its meaning, if you speak or read a language derived from Latin.

Below are 20 sample vocabulary questions. You should practice the above strategies with these questions. Answer them as quickly as you can and do not read the sentences unless you absolutely must. You should complete the exercise within 10 minutes.

1. Few executives realize how critically important their *appearance* may be to an employer.
    (A) work
    (B) looks
    (C) health
    (D) attitudes

2. Thomas Jefferson, third president of the United States, was known as a remarkably *gifted* and versatile man.

   (A) wise
   (B) talented
   (C) courageous
   (D) loyal

3. Birds *exhibit* unusual adaptations to their environment.

   (A) require
   (B) develop
   (C) attempt
   (D) display

4. The cooperation of *amateurs* has made the scientific study of birds possible.

   (A) biologists
   (B) volunteers
   (C) agencies
   (D) nonprofessionals

5. San Francisco has become the *financial* center of the western United States.

   (A) literary
   (B) monetary
   (C) industrial
   (D) cultural

6. Weather forecasters must know as much as possible about the *state* of the atmosphere.

   (A) location
   (B) condition
   (C) organization
   (D) composition

7. Chemical changes during the curing of tobacco alter its *aroma*.

   (A) smell
   (B) flavor
   (C) shape
   (D) weight

8. Many reptiles are often classified as *beneficial* to humans.

   (A) harmful
   (B) relevant
   (C) useful
   (D) undesirable

9. In ancient times, *exchanges* of goods occurred through barter.
   (A) demand
   (B) increase
   (C) production
   (D) trade

10. Fish have lived on the earth longer than any other backboned animal and show great *diversity* in their way of life.
    (A) variation
    (B) adaptation
    (C) evolution
    (D) satisfaction

11. Tidal pools are *a singular* place to study shore life.
    (A) an accessible
    (B) a popular
    (C) an impressive
    (D) a unique

12. Gems are the most *prized* and famous of all minerals.
    (A) costly
    (B) beautiful
    (C) valued
    (D) unusual

13. Learning how to *execute* any skill should be kept enjoyable.
    (A) teach
    (B) perform
    (C) practice
    (D) evaluate

14. Amphibians are *curious* reminders of animal life of long ago.
    (A) extraordinary
    (B) explicit
    (C) specific
    (D) significant

15. Observers unacquainted with an individual can glean clues about that person from his or her *conduct*.
    (A) voice
    (B) height
    (C) behavior
    (D) image

16. Members of any *coalition* find themselves in an important relationship to one another.
    (A) alliance
    (B) corporation
    (C) fraternity
    (D) syndicate

17. Some desert reptiles, being cold-blooded, become *dormant* in midsummer.
    (A) inactive
    (B) aggressive
    (C) sensitive
    (D) feverish

18. The atmosphere moderates daytime temperature and *retards* night heat loss.
    (A) aids
    (B) slows
    (C) prevents
    (D) increases

19. Parents may become frustrated by the *incessant* demands of their children.
    (A) complicated
    (B) unnecessary
    (C) endless
    (D) tiring

20. Personal experience is often *an inadequate* basis on which to form generalizations.
    (A) a precarious
    (B) a compelling
    (C) a deficient
    (D) a trivial

CHAPTER 9

Reading Comprehension

This chapter contains two parts. The first part describes strategies that can help you improve your reading comprehension. Although a sample TOEFL text will be used to discuss these strategies, the strategies can be used when reading any text. The second part of this chapter describes in detail the kinds of questions you will find in the reading comprehension part of Section 3.

DEVELOPING READING STRATEGIES: FIRST STEPS IN READING COMPREHENSION

The best way to prepare for the reading comprehension part of the TOEFL is to become an *active* reader and to practice good reading habits. Unfortunately, many students are "passive" readers, both in their native language and in English. They concentrate only on the meaning of the words. They just try to read each word, word by word. They don't think about the ideas they are reading. Active readers, on the other hand, have the following habits.

1. *Active readers read with a purpose.* They think about the *ideas* they are reading, not the words. Active readers are always "talking" with the author while they read. They are always asking themselves questions about the text. These are the same questions the TOEFL will ask you. Examples of such questions are:

What is the main idea the author is trying to tell me?
What reasons does the author give to support his or her ideas?
What is the author going to tell me next?
What is the author's attitude toward his or her topic?

When active readers read, they are always asking and answering these kinds of questions to themselves. You can practice this skill when you read on your own, both in your native language and in English.

2. *Active readers make a connection between the ideas they read and their lives.* For example, good readers may say to themselves:

The information in this reading is similar to . . .
What the author says about this topic I can also use in . . .

On the TOEFL, there are two types of reading comprehension questions that ask you to apply what you read to other situations.

3. *Active readers form opinions or draw conclusions* about the ideas they read. For example, they may say to themselves:

I think I have to agree with this author because . . .
I don't think the author really supports his or her ideas well because . . .
I really disagree with what the author says because . . .

Thus, you see that good readers not only read words, they think about the ideas they are reading. TOEFL reading comprehension questions are designed to test whether or not you have this skill, because this skill is so necessary for success at a college or university.

4. Perhaps most importantly, *active readers concentrate on what they read*. Can you do many things while you're having an important discussion with a friend? Probably not. Your mind and attention are on the topic you are discussing. You may ask and answer different questions in the discussion to get more information. However, you cannot talk about many different topics at the same time. Good readers have the same experience when they read. They concentrate on what the author is saying, the questions they are asking themselves, and the answers they are finding. They become involved with what they are reading; they do not think about other things. You will find that concentration is especially important while taking the reading comprehension part of the TOEFL. Practice concentration whenever you read.

You can become a better reader by practicing active reading on your own in both your native language and in English. Below is a short passage like the ones you will find on the TOEFL. The complete passage is at the end of this section. First, we are going to go through the passage step by step to see what active readers do while they read.

Before you even begin to read, the first question you should ask yourself immediately is, *What subject is the author going to write about*? When you have an answer to this question, you can prepare to think about the ideas. You can prepare your mind to use all the information you already know about the topic to help you understand the ideas in the passage better. In most cases, the very first sentence gives you the information you need to answer that question. In our TOEFL passage, the first sentence is:

> Photosynthesis, which means "putting together with light," is the process by which green plants and certain other organisms transform light energy into chemical energy.

What is the author going to talk about? Is the topic animals? American history? Computers? Probably not. What you expect after reading the sentence, and what you prepare yourself for, is a scientific passage about the process of photosynthesis. Do you know anything about photosynthesis already? You have probably read or learned something about how plants make food sometime in your life. Think about what you already know and you will be prepared to understand the passage. And as you read, think about what information the author is adding to what you already know about photosynthesis.
Let's read the rest of the first paragraph.

> During photosynthesis in green plants, light energy is captured and used to convert water, carbon dioxide, and minerals into oxygen and energy-rich organic compounds.

What is the purpose of this sentence? Why did the author write it to follow the first sentence? Does it tell you his or her point of view? Does it tell you what the author is going to say about photosynthesis? Actually, it does not do either of these things. It just gives us more information about what photosynthesis is. The author wants to be sure you understand the process he or she is going to talk about.
Let's read the next sentence, which begins a new paragraph.

> It would be impossible to overestimate the importance of photosynthesis in the maintenance of life on Earth.

Does this sentence just give us information, or does it give us an idea the author has about photosynthesis? The meaning of this sentence is that, according to the author, the ongoing process of photosynthesis is extremely important for life to continue on our planet. Do you agree? What do you expect the author to say next? If you are an active reader, you know that he or she must now support this idea. The author needs to support it because it is more than just common information. He or she has a certain idea about the topic. Remember that an author writes with a purpose, not just to put words on paper. An author is trying to say something to the readers.

Let's read the rest of this paragraph.

> If photosynthesis ceased, there would soon be little food or other organic matter on Earth. Most organisms would disappear, and in time the Earth's atmosphere would become nearly devoid of gaseous oxygen. The only organisms able to exist under such conditions would be the chemosynthetic bacteria, which can utilize the chemical energy of certain inorganic compounds and thus are not dependent on the conversion of light energy.

What did the author intend in writing these sentences? The sentences support the author's statement that photosynthesis is necessary for life on Earth. What support does the author give? Without photosynthesis, there would be no food; most organisms (including humans) would die, and only tiny bacteria would be able to survive. Do these reasons make you agree that photosynthesis is important?

Now think about the ways active readers think about the ideas they are reading. Examples of active readers' questions and reactions that were mentioned at the beginning of this chapter appear again below. Do they help you learn more about this short passage?

1. *What is the main idea the author is trying to tell me?*
2. *What reasons does the author give to support his or her ideas?*
3. *What is the author going to tell me next?*
4. *What is the author's attitude toward the topic?*
5. *The information in this reading is similar to . . .*
6. *What the author says about this topic I can also use in . . .*
7. *I really disagree with what the author said because . . .*
8. *I don't think the author really supports his or her ideas well because . . .*
9. *I think I have to agree with this author because . . .*

Here are some ideas for answering these questions and ways of "talking" with the author of this short sample TOEFL text on photosynthesis.

1. The main idea the author is trying to tell the reader is that photosynthesis is extremely necessary to life on Earth.
2. The author supports this idea by pointing out that, without photosynthesis, there would be no oxygen, and, therefore, most life on Earth would die except for a certain type of bacteria.
3. After these two paragraphs, the author may go in several directions. Perhaps he or she will talk about a possible threat to the continuation of photosynthesis on Earth. Perhaps the author will

talk about ways to make sure that this important process continues.
4. The author's attitude is that this topic is very important. The author shows this attitude by the choice of vocabulary in the second paragraph: *It is impossible to overestimate the importance of photosynthesis . . .*
5. This passage is similar to other passages about processes that must continue in order to maintain life on Earth, such as the need to have clean air for breathing, clean water for health, and so on.
6. What the author says about this topic can also be used in thinking about all processes necessary to maintain life on earth. Photosynthesis is only one of those processes.

7–9. It is hard to disagree with the author on the main idea. Photosynthesis is an important process we often fail to notice. There are other ways the author could have strengthened the main idea, such as by stating that human life would end without photosynthesis.

The above example shows how good readers think about the ideas they are reading. Of course, this thinking process occurs very quickly and naturally in active readers. Because they have developed good reading habits, active readers follow this process automatically. You should practice this kind of active reading whenever you read in your native language or in English. Below are the two paragraphs from the passage we just read together, with a third paragraph that follows. Reread the entire passage and practice reading the third paragraph actively before you continue in this section.

> Photosynthesis, which means "putting together with light," is the process by which green plants and certain other organisms transform light energy into chemical energy. During photosynthesis in green plants, light energy is captured and used to convert water, carbon dioxide, and minerals into oxygen and energy-rich organic compounds.
>
> It would be impossible to overestimate the importance of photosynthesis in the maintenance of life on Earth. If photosynthesis ceased, there would soon be little food or other organic matter on Earth. Most organisms would disappear, and in time the Earth's atmosphere would become nearly devoid of gaseous oxygen. The only organisms able to exist under such conditions would be the chemosynthetic bacteria, which can utilize the chemical energy of certain inorganic compounds and thus are not dependent on the conversion of light energy.
>
> Requirements for food, materials, and energy in a world where human population is rapidly growing have created a need to increase both the amount of photosynthesis

and the efficiency of converting photosynthetic output into products useful to people. One response to these needs—the so-called "Green Revolution"—has achieved enormous improvements in agricultural yield through the use of chemical fertilizers, pest and plant disease control, plant breeding, and mechanized tilling, harvesting, and crop processing. This effect has limited severe famines to a few areas of the world despite rapid population growth, but it has not eliminated widespread malnutrition.

The next part of this chapter will provide you with more details on the specific types of reading comprehension questions you will be asked on the TOEFL. Remember that the goal of the TOEFL questions is to discover whether you are an active reader or not. Therefore, don't forget to practice active reading in preparation for the TOEFL and for advanced academic work.

To prepare yourself for the reading comprehension part of TOEFL, the best thing to do is to read. Choose appropriate material that will acquaint you with the style of American academic writing. You can find examples of this style in textbooks used in American high schools and colleges. Another excellent place to find examples is encyclopedias; the style of writing found there is very close to the style that the TOEFL uses in Section 3. Pick some scientific subjects in the encyclopedia, such as "Geology" or "Astronomy," or some American historical topics such as "Mark Twain" or "Gettysburg," and read them for practice. Start with topics you are interested in and that you already know something about. Do this to become familiar with the writing style. The American academic writing style is different from the writing style used in newspapers or literature, for example. By reading textbooks and encyclopedias, you will get used to the characteristics of this style—its punctuation, vocabulary, order of ideas, paragraph structure, and organization.

STRATEGY REVIEW

What is the best strategy for you to use when taking the reading comprehension part of the TOEFL? It is the same strategy that active readers always use. The only difference between reading on the TOEFL and the academic reading of good readers is that the TOEFL asks you the questions that good readers ask themselves anyway. Thus, the TOEFL makes your job a little easier because you don't have to make up your own questions. Therefore, you should read the questions about a passage before you read the complete passage. In this way, you will know what to look for while you read. In addition, some students find it helpful to read the first sentence of the passage (and perhaps the last) before reading the questions. The first sentence usually introduces the topic, and sometimes the last sentence summarizes it. This will help you understand the questions in the context of the topic. When you finish reading this chapter, use this strategy on the practice questions and as you review *A Practice TOEFL, Form 1*. Then use this strategy and as you take *A Practice TOEFL, Form 2* and *Form 3*, and when you take the TOEFL at an official administration.

READING COMPREHENSION: PASSAGES AND QUESTIONS

WHAT YOU SHOULD KNOW

This part of the TOEFL consists of five or six reading passages followed by four to seven questions each. The passages are usually written in an academic style and mostly have to do with academic topics. They are similar to passages you can find in a typical American college textbook. The style of writing is appropriate for a first-year college student, although the vocabulary used, especially in scientific passages, might be technical.

This part of the TOEFL usually includes at least one passage about the physical sciences, especially biology, chemistry, and physics. These are the typical science courses American students study in college. Passages about events in American history are common too. Sometimes, these are in the form of biography, for example, the life of an American writer, politician, or athlete. Other subjects you might find in this part of TOEFL include economics, social sciences, and the arts. You will not find literary prose, poetry, or other "artistic" types of writing in this part. The emphasis will be on academic information, using a writing style that a first-year American college student can understand.

Although some of the vocabulary words will be technical, you will usually be able to understand their meaning from the passage. Sometimes, a technical word is defined for you in the passage; other times, you must try to understand the meaning of the word from the context of the passage. In fact, some questions ask you the meaning of a word or a phrase in the context of the passage. With most technical words, you don't have to understand the exact meaning at all. However, you do have to understand the relationship of the ideas in the passage that involve that word.

THE QUESTIONS

There are six types of questions that appear in this part of the test. Each of the question types has a clear purpose. Learning how to identify the purpose of the question will help you to make the correct choice for your answer.

Each of the four choices for a question will seem possible and will be grammatically correct. Therefore, you must read the passage carefully before you mark your answer. In the explanation below, words that are typical of each type of question are underlined. Identification of these words can help you determine the type of question you find.

SAMPLE PASSAGE

A sample passage is presented below to give you an opportunity to read a typical TOEFL passage and choose answers to the six types of reading comprehension questions on the TOEFL. Remember, understanding the purpose of the questions will usually help you to choose the correct answer or to know which choices cannot be correct. To work through the explanations below, read the passage first, then read the introduction to each question type. After each introduction, there is a sample question, based on the passage. Answer each sample question, using the information in the passage. After you choose the answer, read the explanation of the choices. Alternate versions of each type of question appear at the end of the discussion of each question type.

A cartoon originally was and still is a drawing: a full-size pattern for execution in painting, tapestry, mosaic, or other form. The cartoon was the final stage in the series of drawn preparations for painting in traditional Renaissance
5   studio practice. In the early 1840's, when that studio practice was rapidly decaying, cartoons rather suddenly acquired a new meaning: that of pictorial parody, almost invariably a multiply reproduced drawing, which by the devices of caricature, analogy, and ludicrous juxtaposition (frequently high-
10   lighted by written dialog or commentary) sharpens the public view of a contemporary event, folkway, or political or social trend. It is normally humorous but may be positively savage. Just as the personal caricature was for an audience that knew the original, so the cartoon was and is based on wide ac-
15   quaintance with the subject. It serves as a capsule version of editorial opinion when it makes political satire, and it is a running commentary on social change, sometimes intended as a corrective to social inertia.

1. Main Idea Questions

This type of reading comprehension question will ask you to identify the main purpose, topic, or idea of the *whole* passage. You can easily identify these questions by finding one of the following phrases in the question:

. . . main point . . .
. . . mainly discuss . . .
. . . main idea . . .
. . . best title . . .
. . . main purpose . . .
. . . mainly concerned . . .

The following "main idea" question is based on the passage.

SAMPLE MAIN IDEA QUESTION

What does the passage mainly discuss?

(A) The development of caricatures
(B) The evolution of the cartoon
(C) The history of political satires
(D) The styles of editorial opinions

This is a typical "main idea" question. The four options seem possible. They all contain words or phrases that appear in the passage.

The answer to this type of question best summarizes the main idea or topic of the *entire passage*. Options that summarize small portions of the text are usually incorrect. There is usually one "main idea" question for each passage.

Careful examination of the passage shows that (A) cannot be the correct choice, since caricatures are mentioned only in reference to the development of the cartoon. Option (C) seems possible, but, since political satire is only one of the forms of cartoons mentioned in the passage, it cannot be correct. Similarly, option (D) cannot be correct. The cartoon may be a statement of editorial opinion, but, according to the passage, it is not the only purpose of cartoons. Option (B) is correct. The passage mainly describes the development and styles of cartoons over the years.

A careful reading of the first and last sentences of the passage will often help you choose the correct answer to this type of question. In many passages, the main topic is introduced in the first sentence and summarized in the last sentence. A "main idea" question usually follows each reading passage.

"Main idea" questions can take different forms. You may be asked to choose the best title for a reading passage. If asked this type of "main idea" question, look for the title that summarizes best the content and purpose of the passage. You may also be asked to choose the main purpose of the passage or the main point of the author. Four versions of the "main idea" question are:

What is the <u>best title</u> for the passage?
What is the author's <u>main point</u>?
What is the <u>main purpose</u> of the passage?
What is the <u>main topic</u> of the passage?

Occasionally, "main idea" questions are written so you will have to choose the best clause to complete the sentence. In fact, half of the reading comprehension questions are written this way.

The main topic of the passage is the . . .

Be sure not to choose an answer just because it contains a word or a phrase found in the passage. The correct choice will reflect the main idea but will not necessarily contain any words used in the passage. Remember, good readers work with the ideas in the passage, not just the words.

2. Factual Questions

The majority of reading comprehension questions are factual questions. There are two types of factual questions on the TOEFL. The first asks for specific information found in the passage. The second asks you to identify information NOT found in the passage. The first type asks about details and ideas specifically stated in the text. These details often *support* the author's opinion or the main idea of the passage. You can find most answers to this type of factual question directly in the passage. Factual questions often contain *wh-* question words, such as *who, what, where, which,* or *why*. Often the phrase *According to the author* or *According to the passage* comes before a factual question. The following is an example of this type of question:

SAMPLE FACTUAL QUESTION—TYPE 1

According to the passage, to appreciate modern-day cartoons, one must

(A) know about the subject
(B) understand political matters
(C) enjoy various forms of art
(D) be highly educated

This is a factual question. The question asks what a person must possess to understand and enjoy cartoons. The answer to this question

Reading Comprehension **87**

is located in lines 13 and 14 of the passage. Key phrases, such as *audience that knew the original* and *based on a wide acquaintance with the subject*, lead you to choose the correct answer, (A). Nothing is said in the passage about choices (B), (C), or (D). Therefore, you can eliminate these options, even though they might seem like possible answers if you didn't understand the passage.

Be sure to *answer this type of question within the context of the passage*. Do NOT select an answer based on your experience or knowledge of the subject.

Factual questions usually contain key words or phrases that can be used to find the information necessary to choose the correct answer. Look for these words and phrases in the passage, but remember that the correct answer will probably not contain the exact words from the passage. Look for the same *idea* from the passage said in a different way in the options. Sometimes, you can find the answers in a list or series of facts in the passage. Also, the correct answer to factual questions can sometimes be identified by process of elimination. If you are unable to identify the answer, try to eliminate those options that do not appear in the text. There are usually two or three factual questions on each TOEFL reading passage.

Other examples of this type of factual question appear below.

<u>Which</u> of the following does the author mention as the new meaning of the cartoon?

The passage answers <u>which</u> of the following questions?

According to the passage, <u>what</u> is the current use of the cartoon?

<u>When</u> did the cartoon take on new meaning?

The next example is typical of the second type of factual question on the TOEFL. This type of question asks you to identify details that are NOT included in the passage. These questions will contain the words *NOT* or *EXCEPT*. Other questions of this type contain the words *LEAST* or *MOST*. They ask you to identify an order or rank of details mentioned in the text. Note the following examples:

SAMPLE FACTUAL QUESTION—TYPE 2

Which of the following is NOT mentioned as a function of the cartoon?

(A) To draw public attention to an issue
(B) To provide an impetus for social change
(C) To supply a commentary on current events
(D) To depict historical events objectively

This item is typical of *negative* factual questions. In this type of question, you must identify the information that does NOT appear in the passage. Information with the same meaning as choice (A) appears in lines 10 to 11. Information with the same meaning as choices (B) and (C) appears in lines 17 to 18. The correct choice is (D). There is no information in the passage to support this option. In fact, (D) contains an idea that is contrary to the content of the passage. The cartoons described in the passage are not historical or objective in nature.

Other examples of this type of exclusion or negative question are given below. The key negative words are always capitalized on the TOEFL.

The author mentions all of the following reasons for the popularity of the cartoon EXCEPT...

Which of the following is NOT mentioned as a purpose of cartoons?

According to the author, which is the LEAST savage type of cartoon?

3. Inference Questions

There are two types of inference questions that appear on the TOEFL. The first type of inference question asks you to draw conclusions based on information that is clearly stated in the text. For example, the passage may give you the information you need to solve a problem and ask you to find the solution. Usually, the questions direct you to the information in the passage. Then, they ask you to use that information to form a conclusion. Below are sample test questions for the first type of inference question.

SAMPLE INFERENCE QUESTION—TYPE 1

In which of the following would a cartoon be LEAST likely to appear?
(A) Magazines
(B) Novels
(C) History texts
(D) Newspapers

To solve this question, you must use your understanding of the passage. Based on that understanding, you must choose the *least likely* option. The answer is not directly stated in the passage. This question asks you to order the options to find the most unlikely place where a cartoon would appear. Choices (A) and (D), *magazines* and *newspapers*, both talk about issues that are contemporary and political. As a result, you can assume that both could contain cartoons. Many historical events and important issues are discussed in history texts. Therefore, option (C) is also a place where you may find cartoons. Option (B) is the least likely option. Novels are stories in which cartoons seldom appear. The subject matter of most novels makes them an unlikely place to find a cartoon. Therefore, option (B) is the correct answer, since it is the least likely place a cartoon would appear.

Other examples of this type of question are:

The author <u>implies</u> that cartoons are not suitable for use in which types of publications?

It can be <u>inferred</u> from the passage that cartoons would be most useful to which of the following groups?

Note that the phrase *it can be inferred that* identifies many inference questions for you.

The second type of inference question asks you to apply the understanding you have gained from the passage to relevant situations outside the passage. The information that appears in the question and the choices does not directly appear in the passage. Therefore, the question does not lead you to a specific section of the passage. The questions are relevant to the passage but test your understanding of the ideas in the passage by using those ideas in a different situation.

SAMPLE INFERENCE QUESTION–TYPE 2

Cartoons, as described in the passage, can most likely be found in which one of the following?

(A) Science textbooks
(B) Presidential campaigns
(C) Government publications
(D) Renaissance museums

This example asks you to choose one of four places where you would most probably find the use of cartoons. None of the answers is in the passage itself. You must use your understanding of the information in the passage to choose the correct answer. Choice (B) is the correct answer. While not directly mentioned in the passage, a presidential campaign is a contemporary and political event. You can conclude that cartoons would probably be used during such an event. Choices (A) and (C) do not fit any of the situations in which you would likely find cartoons. Science textbooks and government publications are almost always objective and hardly ever humorous. These options can be eliminated. Option (D), *Renaissance museums*, is directly related to information found in the beginning of the passage. However, the Renaissance studio practice did not produce cartoons as described in the passage. Therefore, such a museum would not contain cartoons. Option (D) can be eliminated.

Similar questions of this type include the following:

Which of the following is most likely to be the subject of a cartoon?

Which of the <u>following statements</u> is true of all cartoons <u>mentioned</u> in the passage?

Another form of this type of inference question follows below. It asks you to identify thoughts that the author may or may not agree with on the basis of the facts in the passage.

The <u>author</u> of the passage would most <u>likely agree</u> with which of the following statements?

As with factual questions, this type of inference question may contain key words or phrases that can be used to find the information necessary to develop the correct conclusion.

The three types of reading comprehension question that you have studied up to now are those found most often (75% to 80% of the time) in the TOEFL. In addition, there are three other types of questions that are found less frequently. They are analogy, organization, and viewpoint questions.

4. Analogy Questions

Analogy questions ask you to find similarities between ideas in the passage and ideas provided in the choices following the question. You need to figure out how *things and activities* in the options are *similar* to those in the passage. You may need to compare possible *situations* with a situation that appears in the passage. Find the phrase *comparable to* or *analogous to* to identify this type of question.

SAMPLE ANALOGY QUESTION

The function of drawing a cartoon makes it most comparable to which of the following activities?

(A) Writing a letter of protest
(B) Watching a T.V. newscast
(C) Writing an article for a newspaper
(D) Reading a political biography

This analogy question asks you to compare the activities in the options to drawing cartoons. The option that is most similar to the function of drawing a cartoon is the correct answer. In this question, (A) is the correct choice. The purpose of writing a letter of protest makes it most similar to drawing a cartoon. The activities are similar because they both require active involvement and personal opinion. They also talk about a problem or situation that may need some action. (See line 18 of the passage.) Options (B) and (D) are passive activities that inform but require no active involvement on the part of the viewer. Option (C) seems possible, but an article in a newspaper is written from an objective viewpoint. Opinions are not usually expressed, and articles are not usually designed to change people's opinions.

Other examples of analogy questions based on the sample passage appear below.

Which of the following is <u>comparable to</u> drawing a cartoon?

Drawing a cartoon would be <u>analogous to</u> which of the following activities?

5. Organization Questions

This type of question asks about how the author uses his or her logic to organize and develop the passage. It does not ask about the meaning of the passage. The question may ask about how or why the author used certain supporting details. It may ask about the meaning of a word in a passage. You may be questioned about antecedents. Antecedents are words, usually nouns, that are replaced by pronouns after their first appearance in the passage. The question may also ask you to identify the topic of the previous or the next paragraph. The "organization" question below asks you to identify an antecedent.

SAMPLE ORGANIZATION QUESTION

The word *it* in the fourth sentence refers to

(A) the caricature
(B) the reproduced drawing
(C) the studio practice
(D) the pictorial parody

The question directs you to a specific pronoun in the passage and asks you to identify the earlier word that refers to *it*. The choices are usually found in the text. Read only the text that appears before the sentence that contains the pronoun. Usually, the correct choice is a word in that sentence. Choices that contain words two or three sentences from the pronoun are usually wrong. Always read carefully the sentence that contains the pronoun. The meaning of the sentence will help you to choose the correct option. The correct answer above is (D).

Another example of an "organization" question is:

SAMPLE ORGANIZATION QUESTION

In which of the following ways does the author present the discussion of the cartoon?

(A) As a description of contemporary cartoons
(B) As a historical interpretation of cartoons
(C) As a description of the development of cartoons
(D) As a criticism of cartoons to the present time

The question asks you to identify the way the passage is organized and developed. Choice (A) can be eliminated because the passage does not talk only about contemporary cartoons. Choice (B) can also be eliminated because the writer's style is more a description than an interpretation of cartoons. Likewise, choice (D) is wrong; the author does not use a critical style when writing about cartoons. The passage is an objective description of the evolution of the forms and uses of cartoons. Option (C) is correct.

Another form of "organization" question you may find on the TOEFL requires you to think about the topic of a paragraph that follows the passage you have read.

In the next <u>paragraph</u>, the author <u>will</u> most probably <u>discuss</u> . . .

6. Viewpoint Questions

"Viewpoint" questions ask you how the author feels about the topic of the passage, about issues or people mentioned in the passage, about the tone of the passage, or about the author's purpose or attitude when writing the passage. An example of a "viewpoint" question is:

SAMPE VIEWPOINT QUESTION

Which of the following best describes the author's attitude toward cartoons?

(A) Critical
(B) Persuasive
(C) Humorous
(D) Neutral

It has already been said that the passage is an objective presentation of facts about cartoons. Choices (A), (B), and (C) do not accurately describe the tone (feeling) of the passage. Choice (D), the correct answer, best describes the tone of a descriptive, nonjudgmental passage and therefore, the viewpoint of the author.

Another form of this type of question is:

Which of the following describes the author's <u>attitude</u> toward the use of cartoons for political ends?

"Viewpoint" questions appear rarely in the TOEFL. Most short academic passages do not show the author's viewpoint. If you find this type of question, look for judgments or opinions stated by the author and use them to determine how the author feels about the topic. For example, a sentence followed by an exclamation point or a sentence that contains words such as *exciting, surprising,* or *boring* may give you clues to determine the viewpoint of the author.

Practicing active reading habits and understanding the purpose of TOEFL reading comprehension questions will help you do your best on this section of the TOEFL. Be sure to practice active reading habits and use your knowledge about TOEFL questions when you do the exercises below, when you take *A Practice TOEFL, Form 2* and *Form 3*, and when you take the TOEFL at an official administration.

STRATEGY REVIEW

1. Read the first and last sentence of the passage first.
2. Read the questions following the passage.
3. Read the entire passage.
4. Practice active reading.
5. Answer each question.

PRACTICE QUESTIONS

Try to practice the strategies in this chapter as you answer the 10 practice questions below. Try to complete the 10 questions in 10 minutes. After you finish, carefully check your answers with the key on pages 96–97.

Some seventy-five years ago, there was a heated controversy about whether or not any higher forms of life exist on Mars. Percival Lowell, on the one hand, maintained that the surface of Mars was criss-crossed by a network of lines,
5 or canals, and that the geometrical regularity of the network, together with its variations through the Martian year, indicated it to be an artifact constructed by intelligent beings. At the other extreme were the views of E.E. Barnard, views with which the great majority of astronomers now agree. Barnard
10 said Mars gave him the impression of "a globe whose entire surface had been tinted with a slight pink color on which the dark details had been painted with a grayish colored paint supplied with a very poor brush, producing a shredded or streaky and wispy effect in the darker regions." Suggesting,
15 perhaps, that it was unwise to draw over-firm conclusions from such scant visual evidence, he added that "no one could accurately delineate the remarkable complexity of detail of the features which were visible in moments of the greatest steadiness."

1. What is the main topic of this passage?
   (A) The network of canals on Mars
   (B) The extreme views of E.E. Barnard
   (C) An astronomical argument
   (D) An influential astronomer

2. According to the passage, Lowell felt that the apparent geometrical designs on Mars's surface were
   (A) canals that irrigate vegetation on Mars
   (B) constructed by intelligent forms of life
   (C) artistic shapes that were formed artificially
   (D) an indication of the seasons of the Martian year

3. From the passage, it can be inferred that Barnard felt the existence of life on Mars may be
   (A) likely because of the evidence
   (B) probable on the basis of the evidence
   (C) possible although there's no real evidence
   (D) improbable in light of the evidence

4. The way Barnard views Mars is analogous to which of the following?
   (A) Studying a painting in a museum
   (B) Examining a specimen under a microscope
   (C) Watching a movie in a darkened room
   (D) Looking at a distant sign through dirty eyeglasses

5. Lowell's views most probably had the greatest influence on
   (A) other scientists
   (B) the U.S. space program
   (C) science fiction writers
   (D) romantic idealists

When an individual enters the presence of others, they commonly seek to acquire information about him or her or to bring into play information about the person already possessed. They will be interested in his or her general socioeconomic status, conception of self, attitude toward them, competence, trustworthiness, etc. Although some of this information seems to be sought almost as an end in itself, there are usually quite practical reasons for acquiring it. Information about the individual helps to define the situation, enabling others to know in advance what he or she will expect of them and what they may expect of the individual. Informed in these ways, the others will know how best to act in order to call forth a desired response from him or her.

6. According to the passage, what is the most important use of personal information?

   (A) To build friendships
   (B) To establish mutual trust
   (C) To know how to behave toward others
   (D) To provide a topic of conversation

7. The author mentions the need for all of the following personal information EXCEPT

   (A) self-concept
   (B) state of health
   (C) skills and abilities
   (D) social class

8. A typical college student may most vividly experience the situation described in the passage above when

   (A) attending a class for the first time
   (B) conversing with friends in the library
   (C) deciding what courses to take the next semester
   (D) preparing for an important exam in a difficult subject

9. With which of the following maxims would the author be most likely to agree?

   (A) You only live once.
   (B) I think, therefore I am.
   (C) Beauty is in the eyes of the beholder.
   (D) Always make a good first impression.

10. In the second sentence, *his or her* refers to

    (A) the author
    (B) the individual
    (C) the other
    (D) the self

KEY

1. (C) This is a "main idea" question. Although all of the choices are discussed in the passage, (C) best summarizes what the *entire* passage is about. This topic is introduced in the first sentence of the passage. Note that the word *controversy* is used in the passage while *argument* is used in choice (C).
2. (B) This is a factual question, type 1. The answer is found in line 6: *indicated it* (the geometrical designs) *to be an artifact constructed by intelligent beings*. Note how the answer does not contain the exact words from the passage. *Intelligent beings* in the passage is replaced by *intelligent form of life* in the question choices.

3. (C) This is an inference question, type 1. The answer is not clearly stated in the passage. However, from the passage, we know that Barnard's argument with Lowell was not about the existence of life on Mars. His disagreement with Lowell was on concluding that there was life on Mars on the basis of very little clear evidence. Since the passage did not state directly that Barnard believed life on Mars was impossible, (C) is the best answer.
4. (D) This is an analogy question. In the quote in lines 10 to 14 and 16 to 19, Barnard's opinion was that looking at Mars was like looking at something that was not very clear at all. (D) is the most similar activity. In all the other choices, the objects can be seen clearly.
5. (A) This is an inference question, type 2. None of the four choices are mentioned in the passage. However, from the passage, it is clear that in Lowell's opinion of seventy-five years ago, there was strong evidence for intelligent life on Mars. That idea has been widely repeated in science fiction writing since that time.
6. (C) This is a factual question, type 1. In the passage, the author emphasizes that people try to gain information about others in order to make judgments about the relationship between them. This is clearly summarized in the last two sentences of the passage.
7. (B) This is a factual question, type 2. The only way to answer this type of question is to check each choice to see if it is in the passage. The correct answer is the one that is NOT in the passage.
8. (A) This is an analogy question. Since the passage mainly talks about the situation of meeting a person for the first time, (A) is the best choice. When a student attends a class for the first time, he or she probably tries to find out as much as possible about the professor in order to know what to expect from the professor during the semester. Therefore, in situation (A), a student is most likely to have an experience similar to the one described in the passage.
9. (D) This is an inference question, type 2. Again, since the author is mainly concerned with what happens between people at their first meeting, (D) is the best choice.
10. (B) This is an "organization" question that asks about an antecedent. In the first sentence, the individual is introduced and then referred to as *him or her*. *Others* is a plural word. In the second sentence, *others* are referred to as *they*. Thus, *his or her* refers to the individual.

CHAPTER 10

Practice Exercises for Section 2 of TOEFL

In this chapter, we review the points of English grammar that appear most frequently on Section 2 of TOEFL, *Structure and Written Expression*. We describe briefly each point of grammar. Then, we give you an example of how the point may appear in a sentence in Section 2. Following this, there are hints as to what to check for when you see these sentences on the TOEFL. Finally, there are seven example questions that test the grammar point. These sentences are just like those you will find on an official TOEFL. Practice applying the hints to find the correct answer. If you can answer these sentences correctly, you will have no trouble with Section 2 of the TOEFL. If you cannot answer them correctly, you may wish to consult a good book on English grammar for students of English. Below are three books that review rules and provide practice exercises in English grammar.

Cathleen Cake and Holly Deemer Rogerson. *Gaining Ground: Intermediate Grammar*. Cambridge, MA: Newbury House Publishers, 1986.

Polly Davis. *English Structure in Focus*. Cambridge, MA: Newbury House Publishers, 1987.

Blanche Ellsworth. *English Simplified*. Fifth Edition. New York: Harper and Row Publishers, 1985.

Other grammar books, including books you already have, may be helpful to you also. If you do not understand these sentences or the explanations in a good grammar book, you may need to take an intermediate or advanced course in English grammar.

Different aspects of grammar are tested in the two parts of this section. "Structure" questions test your ability to identify correct structure. "Written expression" questions test your ability to identify incorrect structure or inappropriate style. (See Chapters 6 and 7.) Some points of grammar are tested by "structure" questions, while others are tested by "written expression" questions. Some points are tested by both types of questions. The examples below show the type of question, "structure" or "written expression," that is used to test each point.

1. Agreement of Tenses

Check to make sure that verbs in main and subordinate clauses agree with respect to tense. For example, a complex sentence with a past tense verb in the main clause will generally be followed by a subordinate clause with a past tense verb.

    Tense Agreement: Henry Ford **was** a businessman who **possessed** great managerial skills.

Check to be sure that a verb has not been replaced by an incorrect verb form or by another part of speech in the same word family.

1. The novel and the short story are the literary <u>forms</u> <u>most</u> com-
                                                                                                  A   B
   monly called "fiction," but contemporary <u>narrative</u> poetry and
                                                                                  C
   drama <u>were</u> also forms of fiction.
           D

2. The basic <u>principle</u> of fiber optics <u>has</u> been <u>understood</u> since
                A   B   C
   1870, but major developments in this field <u>occur</u> primarily since
                                                               D
   1951.

3. Without <u>careful budgeting</u>, a family <u>can dissipate</u> a good in-
                   A   B
   come so that there <u>was not</u> money for larger expenditures
                           C
   <u>such as</u> furnishings or the care of elderly parents.
     D

4. The fuzzy, overstuffed quality of nineteenth-century prose <u>resulting</u> from <u>using</u> ten words <u>where</u> one would have <u>sufficed</u>.
       A   B   C   D

5. Noah Webster's *Dictionary* <u>is</u> first published in 1828 and has
                                   A
   been <u>extremely</u> influential in American language <u>usage</u> <u>since</u>
            B   C   D
   then.

6. <u>Browsing</u> horses <u>had</u> become very rare <u>by</u> the early Pliocene
       A   B   C
   era and soon <u>become</u> extinct.
                D

7. <u>Although</u> navigation of the Hudson Strait <u>in Canada</u> is difficult,
       A   B
   it <u>was</u> still used <u>frequently</u> by ships even now.
      C   D

Practice Exercises for Section 2 of TOEFL

2. Subject-Verb Agreement

The subject and verb of a sentence must go together. Singular subjects must be matched with verbs in the singular form. Plural subjects must be matched with verbs in the plural form. The subject and its corresponding verb may be separated by a clause or a phrase. Identify the verb of the sentence, then check to be sure that the subject agrees with it.

Singular Subject: The **heart** of the hummingbird **beats** incredibly fast.

Plural Subject: The **Great Smoky Mountains are** located in western North Carolina.

The **use** of pesticides in agriculture **has** been debated for years.

1. The king <u>snakes</u> is a <u>medium-sized</u>, nonpoisonous snake
           A   B
   <u>so named</u> because it feeds <u>mainly</u> on other snakes.
     C   D

2. Washington is at the <u>southern</u> edge of the fall line, which is an
                     A
   area about ten miles wide <u>where</u> the waters from the Piedmont
                            B
   Plateau <u>rumbles</u> to the <u>coastal</u> plain.
          C   D

3. Wampum beads <u>made of</u> clamshell <u>was used</u> by Indian tribes
               A   B
   <u>in the</u> northeastern United States as a <u>kind of</u> money.
     C   D

4. A society that <u>emphasizes</u> religion and social hierarchy
                 A
   <u>tend to</u> depict its leaders as abstract, idealized symbols of per-
    B
   manent values <u>rather than</u> as distinct personages.
               C   D

5. The leaves of the lemon verbena plant <u>is</u> rich in aromatic <u>oil</u>,
                         A   B
   with a clear <u>lemon-like</u> flavor and scent.
    C   D

6. Prisms <u>made of</u> Iceland spar <u>is</u> <u>used as</u> light-polarizing
        A   B C
   <u>devices</u> in microscopes.
    D

7. <u>Most</u> cases of ichthyosis are genetically determined, <u>but</u> each
    A   B
   <u>are</u> inherited <u>differently</u>.
    C   D

3. Two-Word and Three-Word Verbs

A two-word or a three-word verb usually consists of a verb followed by one or two prepositions. These words function as a unit in a sentence and have a single meaning.

Two-word Verbs: Some companies rely so heavily on computers that there are major problems when their computer systems **break down**.

White blood cells called macrophages help to **carry out** the processes of healing a wound.

Three-word Verbs: American college students can typically **look ahead to** four years of undergraduate study before beginning graduate school.

Check to be sure that the correct preposition is used and that the two-word or three-word verb conveys the correct meaning within the context of the sentence. Check to be sure that no prepositions are missing.

1. Early American rock-and-roll lyrics from the 1950s <u>dealt of</u>_A teenage <u>concerns</u>_B like <u>school</u>_C, parents, cars, and, especially, <u>young love</u>_D.

2. The <u>way</u>_A a junior college is organized and financed depends <u>at</u>_B <u>whether</u>_C it is a public or private <u>institution</u>_D.

3. The climate of Kansas is <u>subject</u>_A <u>of</u>_B the wide fluctuations <u>characteristic</u>_C of interior <u>continental</u>_D areas.

4. As a child grows <u>on</u>_A, its physical health <u>is affected</u>_B <u>by</u>_C <u>many elements</u>_D in the air, water, and food.

5. Honeybees are social insects <u>whose</u>_A colonies are made <u>up on</u>_B a queen, several <u>thousand</u>_C workers, and usually <u>a few</u>_D drones.

6. Jimmy Hoffa, the <u>labor leader</u>_A, left school in the 1930s and was caught up <u>to</u>_B the <u>growing</u>_C <u>union movement</u>_D.

7. The <u>tissue</u>_A portion of <u>the</u>_B kidney consists <u>to</u>_C two distinct <u>layers</u>_D.

Practice Exercises for Section 2 of TOEFL

4. Active and Passive Verbs

Verbs are words that indicate a state of being or action in the sentence. Do not confuse active and passive verb forms. Remember, passive forms always require the verb *to be*.

Active: Planes **have transported** mail across the nation since 1918.

Large trees **surround** many colonial plantation houses in the South.

Passive: Mail **has been transported** across the nation by planes since 1918.

Many colonial plantation houses in the South **are surrounded** by large trees.

Choose the option that completes the sentence correctly with respect to form, tense, and subject-verb agreement.

1. The Doppler effect ------- the observed frequency of a wave produced by the motion of the wave's source or receiver.
   (A) change
   (B) changes
   (C) changed
   (D) is changed

2. The light from a firefly is said to be "cold" because the insect's utilization of the energy is so efficient that little of it ------- into heat.
   (A) is conversion
   (B) converting
   (C) to be converted
   (D) is converted

3. A camera with an interchangeable lens mount can ------- other lenses besides the normal lens for that camera.
   (A) accept
   (B) accepts
   (C) accepted
   (D) accepting

4. The initial objects with which scientists ------- are the objects of perceptual experience.

   (A) concerned
   (B) concerning
   (C) are concerned
   (D) to be concerned

5. The international language known as Esperanto ------- to be simple and logical, with a flexible vocabulary and a grammar contained in sixteen basic rules.

   (A) designed
   (B) designing it
   (C) was designed
   (D) it was designed

6. Colorful posters were ------- in San Francisco in the 1960s to publicize rock shows.

   (A) print
   (B) prints
   (C) printed
   (D) printing

7. The southern tip of Florida would be tropical evergreen forest and swamp if it ------- undisturbed.

   (A) left
   (B) were left
   (C) leaves
   (D) is leaving

5. Common Verb Errors

Check to make sure that each verb is in its correct form and has not been replaced by another part of speech in the same word family. Also check the sentence for a missing or an unnecessary verb. Be sure that the meaning of the verb is correct for the context of the sentence.

Computers **will continue** to have an impact on every field of endeavor into the twenty-first century.

1. Before mechanical <u>means of</u> propulsion were invented,
                                      A
   <u>humans dependent</u> upon wind and water currents and
          B
   <u>their own</u> muscles <u>to move</u> boats.
       C   D

2. Most name-brand bakery <u>goods</u> are sold <u>by</u> driver-salespeople
                                         A   B
   who service and <u>delivery</u> to the major <u>retail</u> stores.
                      C   D

3. Grease <u>fires</u> in the kitchen can <u>best</u> be <u>fight</u> with a carbon dioxide fire <u>extinguisher</u>.
             A   B   C
            D

4. <u>Beyond</u> the simple pleasures <u>of</u> flying, kites have been <u>use to</u> lift or <u>tow objects</u>.
      A   B   C
          D

5. <u>Throughout</u> its history, the Johns Hopkins University <u>has noted</u> for <u>providing</u> innovative programs and for <u>its emphasis</u> on graduate study.
     A   B   C
     D

6. The <u>desert</u> in <u>southern</u> Arizona is <u>dominant</u> by cacti and <u>deep-rooted</u> shrubs.
          A   B   C
       D

7. Angles <u>lie</u> <u>outside</u> a polygon <u>are</u> <u>called</u> exterior angles.
           A   B   C   D

6. Subjects and Objects

Nouns, noun clauses, pronouns, gerunds, or infinitives can appear as the subject or object of a sentence. Make sure that the subject and object of a sentence are in the correct form. Be especially careful with pronouns. Remember that a pronoun changes its form depending on whether it is used as a subject or an object.

Though he was born in Kansas, **Calvin Trillin** now lives in New York, where **he** writes.

A parade is usually given for returning **astronauts** to publicly honor **them**.

1. ------- who work for large corporations usually receive more progressive benefits.
   (A) The woman
   (B) Women
   (C) Women those
   (D) Any woman

2. Presented annually since 1945, ------- Lasker award is considered a stepping stone to the Nobel Prize.
   (A) when the
   (B) which
   (C) the
   (D) so that

3. Although oysters are marine mollusks, ------- prefer waters that are slightly brackish.
   (A) but
   (B) that
   (C) they
   (D) to

4. How does an animal or a plant, originating in a single cell, attain ------- ?
   (A) its specific form
   (B) to form it specifically
   (C) the form specific
   (D) as a specific form

5. The Indians in Oklahoma array ------- in colorful costumes for their elaborate dances.
   (A) they
   (B) are
   (C) themselves
   (D) oneself

6. Poison sumac leaves have 7 to 15 leaflets, and ------- margins are never toothed.
   (A) they
   (B) their
   (C) it
   (D) its

7. The importance of Willis Lamb's research in physics was recognized when a Nobel Prize was awarded to ------- in 1955.
   (A) he
   (B) him
   (C) they
   (D) them

7. Common Noun Errors

A noun denotes a person, place, thing, or idea. Make sure that each noun is in its correct form and that it has not been replaced by another part of speech. Check to see that the noun is appropriate in meaning to the sentence.

> Early **observers** of the **phenomenon** known as **phosphorescence** called it "**St. Elmo's Fire.**"

1. Gingham is a kind of <u>cloths</u> <u>woven</u> <u>in many</u> weights, such as
                          A   B   C
   sheer, medium, <u>or heavy</u>.
                D

2. There <u>is no</u> agreement <u>among</u> philosophers on the question
         A   B
   <u>of how</u> their subject stands in <u>relative</u> to the sciences.
     C   D

3. A <u>pendulum swings</u> back and forth in isochronous <u>motion</u>
             A   B
   around a pivot <u>points</u> at the opposite end of a <u>supporting rod</u>.
                   C   D

4. Phonetics is <u>of</u> primary <u>important</u> for <u>any</u> true <u>understanding</u>
                 A   B   C   D
   of the nature of language.

5. Allen Ginsberg's <u>poetry</u> has sometimes <u>been</u> criticized <u>for</u> oc-
                     A   B   C
   casional carelessness of <u>technician</u> and lack of decorum.
                                 D

6. The Bluegrass area <u>of</u> Kentucky developed a <u>distinctly</u> agrarian
                       A   B
   <u>and</u> advanced plantation <u>cultured</u>.
    C   D

7. Because of <u>its</u> value as a landing place <u>for</u> planes, Johnston
                A   B
   Island in the Pacific <u>was</u> proclaimed a naval defense <u>areas</u> in
                         C   D
   1941.

8. Common Pronoun Errors

A pronoun usually takes the place of a noun, gerund, or infinitive. Remember that a pronoun changes form depending on its function in a sentence. Check pronouns for subject, object, and possessive forms. Make sure that each pronoun agrees with its antecedent (the noun it replaces) in number (singular or plural) and gender (masculine, feminine, or neuter).

> **None** of the women who work on a collaborative quilt knows for sure which part of it is **hers**.

Check to see that the pronoun is necessary in the sentence, and make sure that no necessary pronoun has been omitted and that no unnecessary pronoun has been added.

1. The architecture at Harbor Point in Boston was designed with
      A   B   C
   the residents in mind, and they appreciate them.
                                       D

2. Copper plaques were made by Northwest Coast Indians, who
                      A
   used as a medium of exchange and a standard of value.
     B   C   D

3. Most weevils, or snout bettles, are of a somber color, but a few
    A   B   C
   of they are brilliantly colored.
      D

4. Its surprises people when they learn that Jamestown was
    A   B
   established twelve years earlier than the Plymouth colony.
       C   D

5. Most existing American canals are for barges and do not exceed
        A   B
   them twelve feet in depth.
    C   D

6. Gaston Lachaise produced many ornamental sculptures, some
                          A   B
   of that for Rockefeller Center in New York.
     C D

7. The study of land use encompasses the various ways in that
         A   B
   land serves to provide humans with their needs and wants.
       C   D

9. Noun Phrases

A noun phrase is made up of one or more nouns, together with any modifiers, such as adjectives or articles. Check to see that articles have been used correctly, and that all necessary articles have been included. Make sure that adjectives of quantity, such as *many* and *much*, are appropriately used. *Many* is used with countable nouns, such as books, drinks, hours, and dollars. *Much* is used with noncountable nouns such as education, water, time, and money.

Much early controversy over Andy Warhol's paintings centered on his use of **many identical repeated images**.

1. Coal, though the much more abundant energy source
                  A   B
   than either oil or gas, is still a finite resource.
         C   D

2. Several important rivers and much small streams empty into
         A   B   C   D
   the Chesapeake Bay.

3. When Columbus had made up the mind to find a new route to
                    A   B
   the Indies, no one could dissuade him from the idea.
             C   D

4. The major cities of Utah are located on the western slopes
         A   B   C
   of Wasatch Mountains.
        D

5. Much of the fresh vegetables consumed in the United States
    A   B
   are grown by truck farmers.
    C   D

6. True land crabs have a thickly, dense hard shell.
        A   B C D

7. Diplomatic protocol prescribes the arrangement and etiquette
                      A   B
   of the diplomatic conduct and ceremonies.
      C   D

10. Gerunds and Infinitives

Gerunds and infinitives are verb forms that can be used in a sentence as a noun would be. Both can appear as either a subject or an object of a sentence, and a gerund can also appear as the object of a preposition.

Infinitive: **To vote** was the duty of comparatively few in the early United States.

Gerund: Seminole Indian women make beautiful clothing by **sewing** many small scraps of cloth together.

Check to see that the infinitive or gerund is appropriately used and is in its correct form.

1. The carve of the monumental heads of the presidents on Mount
         A   B   C
   Rushmore in South Dakota took fourteen years.
                            D

2. Chemical bond between atoms of oxygen and atoms of gold,
        A   B   C
   silver, and platinum is weak.
                         D

3. In the year 1864, Robert E. Lee concentrated all his attention
      A   B C
   on win the Civil War.
       D

4. Derive mineral resources from sedimentary rocks is a major
     A   B   C   D
   modern industrial activity.

5. Use a stethoscope enables a physician to hear sounds produced
    A   B   C
   in the body, especially heart and lung sounds.
    D

6. It is possible determining that French explorers reached the
      A   B
   juncture of the Kansas and Missouri rivers in the seventeenth
           C   D
   century.

7. Sorghum leaves occasionally contain enough hydrocyanic acid
            A   B
   killing livestock.
     C   D

11. Expressions with *It*

It is used when the true subject comes after the verb.

> **It takes** much less time to cross the Atlantic in the supersonic "Concorde" than in a standard jumbo jet.

> **It is possible** that factories will one day rely almost entirely on robots for routine work.

> **It is necessary** to understand American culture in order to appreciate American literature.

It is also used with common expressions, such as time and weather.

> When **it is five o'clock** in New York, **it is two o'clock** in Los Angeles.

> Many cities in the Southern part of the United States have difficulty keeping traffic flowing when **it snows**.

Do not confuse the use of *it* with *there*.

---

1. For many Americans, ------- Emily Post who remains the final authority on proper etiquette.

   (A) they are
   (B) there is
   (C) she is
   (D) it is

2. Although colonial grievances against British rule were held throughout the colonies, ------- a concentration of people and ideas in cities to give direction to the movement for independence.

   (A) it took
   (B) they took
   (C) had taken
   (D) to take

3. ------- to learn a new language in the latter years of life.

   (A) Although it's easy
   (B) Isn't it easy
   (C) Because it's easy
   (D) It isn't easy

4. ------- sometimes appear that children are crying when they are actually laughing.

   (A) They may
   (B) It may
   (C) He may
   (D) There may

5. ------- difficult to determine the origins of a person's responses to perceived competition.

   (A) There's
   (B) Here's
   (C) It's
   (D) That's

6. The echo-sounding machine, developed in 1911, made ------- take a sounding from a ship at full speed.

   (A) the possibility
   (B) it possible to
   (C) possibility the
   (D) possible to

7. ------- known whether Myles Standish, captain of New Plymouth, ever became a Puritan.
   (A) Is it
   (B) If it is
   (C) Is not
   (D) It is not

12. Expressions with *There*

There is usually used with the verb *to be* and is used mostly to describe a situation or condition.

There have been many Americans who have achieved fame in the arts not only nationally, but internationally as well.

There was much excitement across the nation as Americans prepared to celebrate the bicentennial of the United States in 1976.

Most theatre people agree that **there is** no other city quite like New York for professional opportunities.

Do not confuse the use of *there* with *it*.

1. ------- actually more beneficial insects than pest species.
   (A) It is
   (B) It was
   (C) There is
   (D) There are

2. ------- any comprehensive definition of jazz music?
   (A) Is
   (B) Is it
   (C) Is there
   (D) Are there

3. ------- no sharp scientific distinction between porpoises and dolphins.
   (A) Theirs
   (B) There's
   (C) They're
   (D) There

4. Although no one knows exactly when the earliest printing press was used, ------- is no doubt that it was invented by 1439.

   (A) there
   (B) it
   (C) that
   (D) when

5. ------- no important pieces of American fiction published in America before 1819.

   (A) It was
   (B) There were
   (C) When was
   (D) Why were

6. ------- several botanical names for the soybean plant.

   (A) For are
   (B) To be
   (C) There is
   (D) There are

7. Since the 1960s, ------- has been a revival of the art of mime in the United States.

   (A) there
   (B) what
   (C) how
   (D) it

13. Common Adjective Errors

Adjectives modify, describe, or limit nouns. Make sure that each adjective is in its correct form and has not been replaced by another part of speech in the same word family. Check to make sure that all nouns and pronouns agree with their corresponding possessive adjectives.

Transient adaptation refers to **rapid** fluctuations in the sensitivity of the eye.

Each man or woman on a rowing team must subordinate **his or her** personal goals to the team effort.

Every village of the Pueblo Indians has **its** distinct style of design.

1. The major advantages <u>of</u> the Wankel-type engine are <u>its</u> small
                                   A   B
   space requirement, low <u>weight</u> per horsepower, and <u>smoothly</u>
                                 C   D
   and vibrationless operation.

2. An isotope is one <u>of</u> two or more specimens of the same chem-
                        A
   ical that <u>have</u> <u>difference</u> atomic <u>weights</u>.
             B   C   D

3. The small Pennsylvania <u>town of</u> Jim Thorpe <u>was named</u> for the
                                A   B
   <u>fame</u> Indian football player <u>who is</u> buried there.
     C   D

4. The Navajo Indians <u>have displayed</u> a <u>marked</u> ability to incor-
                             A   B
   porate aspects of other cultures <u>into</u> a changing, <u>flexibility</u> life-
                                C   D
   style.

5. *Thermal agitation* is the name <u>given</u> to the <u>continuously</u> motion
                                  A   B
   of atoms <u>that</u> is present in all <u>kinds</u> of matter.
            C   D

6. Arthur Miller, in *Death of a Salesman*, <u>questions</u> the American
                                          A
   <u>ideal of</u> prosperity <u>because it</u> entails <u>danger</u> moral compro-
      B   C   D
   mises.

7. From 1946 <u>to</u> 1980, the average <u>seasonally</u> number <u>of</u> icebergs
             A   B   C
   below the 48th <u>parallel</u> was 300.
                   D

14. Common Adverb Errors

Adverbs give information about verbs, adjectives, or other adverbs. They can also be used to describe complete sentences. Many adverbs are formed by adding *-ly* to an adjective. Check to make sure that each adverb is in its correct form and has not been replaced by another part of speech in the same word family, especially by an adjective.

Because they **always** worked **hard** and **rarely** left their self-contained communities, the Shakers **eventually** prospered.

---

1. Except <u>in</u> meteorites, iron <u>as</u> a <u>free</u> metal is <u>rare</u> found on earth.
           A   B C   D

2. Plums <u>are</u> the <u>most wide</u> <u>distributed</u> <u>of the</u> stone fruits.
          A   B   C   D

3. The modern problems of <u>environmental</u> pollution are <u>basely</u>
                                  A   B
those of rapid human population <u>growth</u> and <u>expanding</u> technology.
                                      C   D

4. Scientists have <u>noted</u> <u>that</u> chimpanzees sometimes <u>appear</u> to
                      A   B   C
communicate warmly and <u>friendly</u> with each other.
                                  D

5. The Lost Colony in North Carolina <u>mysterious</u> disappeared
                                               A
<u>between</u> 1587 and 1590, when <u>its</u> founder returned from
   B   C
<u>a visit</u> to England.
  D

6. Benjamin Franklin's contribution to <u>heating</u> in 1742 was
                                                   A
<u>actual</u> a <u>cast-iron</u> fireplace, <u>not a</u> stove.
  B   C   D

7. <u>Virtual</u> all animals <u>make</u> interferon, <u>but</u> the protein is <u>highly</u>
   A   B   C   D
species-specific.

15. Comparisons (Structure)

Special forms or words are necessary when using adjectives and adverbs in comparisons.

EQUALITY (*as......as*)

The Matterhorn in Switzerland is not **as high as** Mount Everest.

Very few scientists become **as famous as** Albert Einstein.

COMPARISON OF TWO NOUNS (*more/-er*)

Mount Everest is **higher** than the Matterhorn.

Can you think of a scientist who is **more famous** than Albert Einstein?

COMPARISON OF THREE OR MORE NOUNS (*most/-est*)

Mount Everest is **the highest** mountain in the world.

Albert Einstein is clearly one of **the most famous** scientists who ever lived.

When the sentence is making a comparison, check to make sure the adjective or adverb is in the correct form.

1. Scott Joplin is clearly the world's ------- composer of ragtime music.
   (A) a famous
   (B) famous
   (C) more famous
   (D) most famous

2. The history of wearing jewels is as ------- as the history of humankind.
   (A) old
   (B) older
   (C) oldest
   (D) the oldest

3. Ezra Pound became one of the most ------- authors in the development of twentieth-century English writing.
   (A) influence
   (B) influences
   (C) influential
   (D) influencing

4. Most retail stores in North America look forward to the months before Christmas as their ------- period of the year.
   (A) busy as
   (B) the busiest
   (C) busiest
   (D) the most busy

5. Studies show that students with high self-esteem have ------- ratings from both themselves and their teachers in their speech than students with low self-esteem.
   (A) high
   (B) higher
   (C) highest
   (D) the highest

6. Springs with ------- temperatures than their surroundings are called thermal springs.
   (A) the highest
   (B) higher
   (C) high
   (D) highly

7. Although potatoes are cultivated in every state, Idaho produces ------- crop.
   (A) large
   (B) the large
   (C) the larger
   (D) the largest

16. Comparisons (Written Expression)

Special forms or words are necessary when using adjectives and adverbs in comparisons.

EQUALITY (*as. . . . . .as*)

The Matterhorn in Switzerland is not **as high as** Mount Everest.

Very few scientists become **as famous as** Albert Einstein.

COMPARISON OF TWO NOUNS (*more/-er*)

Mount Everest is **higher** than the Matterhorn.

Can you think of a scientist who is **more famous** than Albert Einstein?

COMPARISON OF THREE OR MORE NOUNS (*most/-est*)

Mount Everest is **the highest** mountain in the world.

Albert Einstein is clearly one of **the most famous** scientists who ever lived.

When the sentence is making a comparison, check to make sure the adjective or adverb is in the correct form.

1. In the diet of most Northern Europeans, the potato is a
   A   B
   usualer source of starch than rice.
   C   D

2. One of the most odd and most primitive of all living mammals
              A   B   C
   is the platypus.
   D

3. Many psychologists believe that the early one is exposed to love
   A   B   C
   and discipline, the more easily one will learn responsibility.
                                    D

116   Chapter 10

4. <u>Of</u> the two <u>hourly</u> rates of pay, workers will <u>be paid</u> the
      A   B   C
   <u>highest</u> for overtime work.
     D

5. The <u>bigger</u> of the three daily meals <u>for</u> most American families
        A   B
   <u>is</u> dinner, <u>served</u> about six o'clock.
    C   D

6. Roughly <u>half of</u> the population of Miami <u>is</u> Hispanic, <u>the high</u>
             A   B   C
   percentage of any <u>major</u> U.S. city.
                         D

7. <u>Perhaps</u> the <u>better known</u> of <u>all the</u> agencies <u>of the</u> Department
       A   B   C   D
   of the Interior is the National Park Service.

17. Prepositions

A preposition is a word or a group of words that shows a relationship between the object of the preposition and another word in the sentence. Choose the preposition or prepositional phrase that is appropriate for the context of the sentence.

In due course, Washington and Baltimore are each destined to grow outward **until** merging **into** one metropolitan area.

1. ------- in the United States, Texas is the leading cattle producer.
   (A) All the states
   (B) Of all the states
   (C) Not all the states
   (D) There are all the states

2. In the electric catfish, the electric organ cloaks most of the body ------- the skin.
   (A) and beneath
   (B) beneath only
   (C) just beneath
   (D) that beneath

3. Jogging burns calories ------- about one hundred per mile.
   (A) of rate
   (B) of the rate
   (C) at the rate
   (D) at the rate of

4. ------- a laser to operate, stimulated emission must predominate over absorption throughout the laser medium.

   (A) Ordering to
   (B) For ordering
   (C) In order for
   (D) The order of

5. ------- of academic leadership, Milton Eisenhower was frequently called to Washington.

   (A) By his years
   (B) His years were
   (C) During his years
   (D) There were his years

6. The Washington Monument on the Mall is a hollow shaft without a break ------- its surface except for the tiny entrance.

   (A) with
   (B) in
   (C) from
   (D) to

7. Large losses may occur from insurance claims made by people ------- legal action.

   (A) since
   (B) through
   (C) to
   (D) until

18. Prepositional Phrases

A preposition and its object form a prepositional phrase. Check to be sure that an appropriate preposition is used in the phrase and that another part of speech is not used in its place.

In proportion to the general population, the number **of fine artists in the United States** who live **on the proceeds of their work** is quite small.

1. Will Rogers's <u>particular</u> brand of satiric humor, heavily loaded
                    A
   with homespun philosophical <u>comment</u>, won <u>him</u> great popu-
                              B   C
   larity <u>of</u> the American people.
        D

2. As <u>by</u> <u>many</u> domestic animals, the <u>origin</u> of the present-day
        A   B   C

   chicken is <u>somewhat</u> obscure.
                   D

3. <u>From</u> its system of parks and forest preserves, Chicago has
    A

   <u>much</u> to offer the <u>seeker</u> of outdoor <u>recreation</u>.
     B   C   D

4. The most important <u>figure in</u> the history of the
                                A

   <u>theory evolution</u>, and <u>one of</u> the most important in the history
         B   C

   of <u>human culture</u>, is Charles Darwin.
          D

5. <u>Past</u> the <u>ages</u>, herbs have been used <u>both</u> to preserve food and
    A   B   C

   to enhance <u>its</u> flavor.
              D

6. <u>To</u> a treaty <u>in</u> 1861, Potawatomi Indians were <u>given</u> individual
    A   B   C

   <u>allotments</u> of land.
      D

7. In spite <u>for</u> its brevity <u>of form</u>, the sonnet is capable <u>of</u> pre-
        A   B   C

   senting deep and universal <u>insights</u>.
                            D

19. Adjective, Adverb, Gerund, and Infinitive Phrases

A phrase adds information to a sentence. It is often used to complete the idea of a sentence. A participle phrase includes a present or past participle and one or more other words. An infinitive phrase includes an infinitive with an object. A gerund phrase consists of a gerund with an object. Note the examples of each type of phrase.

Infinitive:	Thomas Edison liked **to conduct complicated experiments**.
Gerund:	**Spinning cotton** was a tedious task before the invention of the cotton gin.
Present Participle:	**Capitalizing on Russia's need for funds**, the United States purchased Alaska at an excellent price.
Past Participle:	**Given the power of computers**, it is not surprising to find them everywhere in business.

Choose the phrase that is correct in form. Avoid options with unnecessary pronouns.

1. In October, 1776, Benjamin Franklin accepted an appointment as one of three commissioners to France, the others ------- Silas Deane and Arthur Lee.

    (A) being
    (B) being with
    (C) were being
    (D) who were being

2. Streams cause more erosion than all other geological ------- .

    (A) agents combine
    (B) combining agents
    (C) agents combined
    (D) are combined agents

3. Of all the Western world's important cultivated foods, tomatoes are the newest, ------- widely used only within the last hundred years.

    (A) they became
    (B) having become
    (C) they have become
    (D) have become

4. In the last six months of 1818, Sam Houston mastered a course in law usually ------- eighteen months.

    (A) it required
    (B) was requiring
    (C) requiring
    (D) that required

5. In biology, a cell is defined as the smallest unit of life ------- all the components required for independent existence.

    (A) contains
    (B) is contained
    (C) it contains
    (D) containing

6. ------- to many people, the famous cowgirl Calamity Jane wrote a series of touching letters to her daughter.

    (A) Unknowing
    (B) Unknown
    (C) Unknowingly
    (D) Unknowns

7. With the aid of new technology, people can now travel faster than ------- possible even 25 years ago.
   (A) believe
   (B) believes
   (C) believed
   (D) believing

20. Adverb Clauses

Adverb clauses give additional information about the main idea of the sentence. They are introduced by words such as *when, where, because, although, before*, and *if*. Make sure that each introductory word is correct in meaning for its sentence.

The City Beautiful Movement flourished in America **when national optimism was at its peak**.

Although many Chinese live in the United States, only one town, Locke, California, is entirely Chinese in population.

Hispanic villages in New Mexico have evolved a distinctive culture **since Mexican rule came to an end**.

Note that the subject and verb in the clause may sometimes be left out. In this case, the introductory word is followed by a phrase rather than a clause.

Clause: **Although it is fishlike in form**, the dolphin is a mammal.
Phrase: **Although fishlike in form**, the dolphin is a mammal.

1. ------- often happens in American literary lives, Sherwood Anderson came to celebrity after his best work had been done.
   (A) When
   (B) As
   (C) It
   (D) So

2. Sulfur is used so extensively in an industrial economy ------- its rate of usage is cited as an index of industrialization.
   (A) than
   (B) so
   (C) that
   (D) as

3. ------- bluefin tuna is found throughout the world, it is most often caught in the temperate waters of the Atlantic.

   (A) Because
   (B) Although the
   (C) That some
   (D) Whenever any

4. ------- healthy and thoroughly amiable, the foxhound makes a difficult house pet.

   (A) Ever since
   (B) Because
   (C) As if
   (D) Though

5. ------- the WPA posters of the 1930s were intended only for short-term use, most of them have been lost.

   (A) Without
   (B) Because
   (C) Regarding
   (D) Usually

6. ------- in ancient inscriptions, monograms remain difficult to interpret.

   (A) Appear frequently
   (B) They appear frequently
   (C) Although they're appearing frequently
   (D) Although appearing frequently

7. The iris has large, showy flowers that are regular and, ------- their elaborate appearance, relatively simple.

   (A) because
   (B) since
   (C) despite
   (D) whenever

21. Adjective Clauses

Adjective clauses give descriptive information about a noun, pronoun, gerund or infinitive. They are introduced by words such as *that, which, when, where* and *who*.

> The Louisiana environment, **which has dramatic weather and light as well as picturesque cities, swamps, and bayous**, inspires many noted photographers.

> John Dewey, **who was a philosopher as well as an educator**, had a large impact on American education.

> The time **when the sun crosses the equator**, making night and day equal in length, is called the equinox.

Make sure that the words agree with their antecedents: *that* and *which* can refer to persons and things, but *who* can refer only to persons.

Note that the introductory word and the verb *to be* in an adjective clause may sometimes be left out.

> Doubokors, Hutterites, and Sephardim are only a few of the exotic ethnic groups **(that are) found in Washington State**.

1. The types of gas masks ------- to purify the air generally consist of a facepiece and a canister.
   - (A) are used
   - (B) been used
   - (C) that are used
   - (D) which have used

2. In the 1940's, Charles Eames developed a chair ------- a molded plywood seat and back on metal legs.
   - (A) with form
   - (B) that had
   - (C) forming by
   - (D) by that

3. The snapping turtle, ------- many to be an aggressive animal, is actually quite docile.
   - (A) which
   - (B) believing
   - (C) are not
   - (D) believed by

Practice Exercises for Section 2 of TOEFL

4. Between the Rockies and the Pacific lie plateaus and mountains ------- the driest parts of the United States are situated.
   (A) where
   (B) that
   (C) which
   (D) whose

5. The region around Waterloo, Ontario, was settled by Mennonites ------- at the beginning of the nineteenth century.
   (A) arrival
   (B) arrived
   (C) whose arrival
   (D) who arrived

6. Iodine is an element of the halogen family, a group ------- the elements fluorine, chlorine, and bromine.
   (A) include
   (B) that includes
   (C) included
   (D) who includes

7. The Eskimo culture area comprises the longest continuous stretch of terrain ------- any culture group on Earth.
   (A) occupies
   (B) to occupy
   (C) occupying
   (D) occupied by

22. Noun Clauses

Some clauses are used in sentences as nouns would be used. They are called noun clauses. A noun clause can appear as the subject or object of a sentence, or as the object of a preposition. Noun clauses are introduced by words such as *that, who, how, why, when,* and *where*.

Noun Clause as Subject:	**That Columbus discovered America** is disputed by many.
Noun Clause as Object:	No one really knows **why the Mesa Verde Indians abandoned their cliff homes in Colorado.**
Noun Clause as Object of Preposition:	Robert Motherwell has written eloquently about **how the creative process takes place.**

Choose the word or phrase that introduces the noun clause and is correct for the meaning of the sentence.

1. ------- are master craftspeople is evidenced by the quality of their work over the centuries.

    (A) Blue Ridge potters
    (B) Because Blue Ridge potters
    (C) Blue Ridge potters who
    (D) That the Blue Ridge potters

2. It has never been known ------- the Washington Monument was built off its axis.

    (A) to
    (B) than
    (C) why
    (D) there

3. ------- dinosaurs today is the product of a vital interaction between science and art.

    (A) How the perception of
    (B) Perceive
    (C) Its perception
    (D) How we perceive

4. Slashing brushstrokes were fundamental ------- the Abstract Expressionists wanted to achieve in their paintings.

    (A) in that
    (B) to what
    (C) but also
    (D) and for

5. Woodworkers are advised to consider ------- linseed oil darkens with age.

    (A) but
    (B) since
    (C) and
    (D) that

6. Indiana Territory was created in 1800 and included ------- become the states of Indiana, Illinois, and Wisconsin.

    (A) has
    (B) that has
    (C) what has
    (D) that what has

Practice Exercises for Section 2 of TOEFL

7. William James, the nineteenth-century psychologist, believed ------- consciousness functions in a purposeful way to organize thoughts.

   (A) that
   (B) if
   (C) in
   (D) what

23. Conjunctions (Structure)

There are two types of conjunctions used to join clauses.

COORDINATING CONJUNCTIONS

Not all Americans vote in every election, **and** there are some who never vote at all.

Many tourists enjoy their visit to New York, **but** others find the city too overwhelming.

At most universities in the United States, graduate students may live on campus, **or** they may prefer to find quiet quarters off campus.

SUBORDINATING CONJUNCTIONS

Because choosing a college major is a difficult process, most students change their majors at least once during their college career.

Whenever they have the opportunity, many Americans take their vacations away from home.

An increasing number of parents are choosing to send their children to private schools, **although** it may mean economic hardship for the family.

Choose the conjunction that has the correct meaning for the sentence.

1. The poinsettia is commonly used as a holiday houseplant in the North of the United States, ------- in Florida it is a popular outdoor flowering shrub.

   (A) as
   (B) while
   (C) if
   (D) for

2. Polyphony is a synonym of counterpoint, ------- the term *counterpoint* is generally associated with the technique of polyphonic music.
   (A) not unless
   (B) formerly
   (C) though
   (D) additionally

3. ------- the Pony Express was a financial failure, it was a sensational method of providing fast mail service in the wild West.
   (A) Unfortunately
   (B) That
   (C) It was
   (D) Although

4. Public transportation in many parts of North America is inadequate, ------- owning a car is a necessity for many people.
   (A) in addition
   (B) as if
   (C) so that
   (D) nevertheless

5. Edward Bellamy's book *Looking Backward* influenced many Americans, ------- Bellamy clubs were formed to discuss and promote his ideas.
   (A) and
   (B) it was
   (C) but
   (D) that

6. Human behavior is mostly a product of learning, ------- the behavior of an animal depends mainly on instinct.
   (A) whereas
   (B) so
   (C) unless
   (D) that

7. The philosophy of science is as old as science itself, ------- there have always been scientists who reflected on the process of inquiry.
   (A) why
   (B) for
   (C) even
   (D) that

24. Conjunctions (Written Expression)

There are two types of conjunctions used to join clauses.

COORDINATING CONJUNCTIONS

Not all Americans vote in every election, **and** there are some who never vote at all.

Many tourists enjoy their visit to New York, **but** others find the city too overwhelming.

At most universities in the United States, graduate students may live on campus, **or** they may prefer to find quiet quarters off campus.

SUBORDINATING CONJUNCTIONS

Because choosing a college major is a difficult process, most students change their majors at least once during their college career.

Whenever they have the opportunity, many Americans take their vacations away from home.

An increasing number of parents are choosing to send their children to private schools, **although** it may mean economic hardship for the family.

Check to make sure the conjunction has the correct *meaning* for the sentence.

---

1. Much of Edgar Allan Poe's best work <u>is concerned</u> with terror
                                                   A
   and sadness, <u>because</u> in <u>ordinary</u> circumstances he <u>was</u> a pleasant companion.
                B   C   D

2. The relationship <u>of</u> poetry to society <u>has changed</u>; <u>in addition</u>,
                     A   B   C
   it is <u>still</u> vital.
         D

3. <u>Although</u> the handling of goods and the <u>servicing</u> of vessels at
     A   B
   ports <u>require</u> large labor forces, ports are usually associated
         C
   <u>with</u> cities.
     D

4. The design of posters <u>is</u> a challenge to the artist, <u>whereas</u> be-
                                    A   B
   sides <u>their</u> value as commercial objects, many posters are of
          C
   <u>aesthetic</u> interest.
     D

5. <u>Moreover</u> the large amount of time <u>devoted</u> to <u>listening</u> every
       A   B   C
   day, most college students do not listen <u>effectively</u>.
                                                  D

6. The Rocky Mountains <u>have a</u> large volume of low-density rock
                            A
   <u>beneath</u> them, <u>that</u> the core of the Appalachians <u>has almost</u> dis-
     B   C   D
   appeared.

7. Chronolithographs <u>became</u> very popular in the nineteenth cen-
                           A
   tury, partly <u>in fact</u> Currier and Ives <u>published prints</u> on such a
               B   C
   <u>large range</u> of subjects.
     D

25. Negative Constructions

Many negative constructions require a specific word order where the verb precedes the subject.

Not only does the Potomac River flow past Washington, D.C., but the Anacostia flows through the city as well.

Most viewers of the Armory Show of 1913 did not understand the art, and **neither did** the critics.

The earliest ceramics were not made on a wheel, **nor did they have** handles.

Remember that *not* is used with verbs, adjectives and adverbs, and that *no* is used with nouns.

It was **not** until the development of metal cavity implants that tooth care gained some predictability.

There were **no** Catholics in the American colonies until the establishment of Maryland in 1634.

Choose the option with the correct negative form and correct word order.

1. The decline of the mechanical player piano is attributed to the spread ------- piano music, but of all forms of music played by phonograph, radio, and television.

    (A) not
    (B) not to
    (C) not only of
    (D) not only to

2. Virtually ------- improvement in plumbing systems was made from the time of the Romans until the nineteenth century.

    (A) no
    (B) not
    (C) none
    (D) nor

3. ------- the speaker nor the listener can successfully communicate without the other's active participation.

    (A) Both
    (B) Neither
    (C) But
    (D) Not

4. Much of what is called "senility" or "senile psychosis" is ------- more than the reaction of aged people to isolation.

    (A) a thing
    (B) everything
    (C) anything
    (D) nothing

5. Engineers, ------- scientists involved in basic research, work toward the solution of specific practical problems.

    (A) although unlike
    (B) are unlike
    (C) unlike
    (D) who unlike

6. For years, American primitive paintings were not costly; ------- sought by collectors.

    (A) they were nor
    (B) were nor they
    (C) nor they were
    (D) nor were they

130   Chapter 10

7. Washington, D.C., has a problem with air pollution during the summer, although there is ------- industry there.

(A) not no
(B) never
(C) no
(D) none

26. Word Order (Structure)

Certain "structure" questions test for correct word order in the missing part. Be sure that the order of the subject and the verb and the placement of adjectives and adverbs are correct.

Were it not for the Washington Monument and the Capitol, Washington, D.C., would be a **completely horizontal city**.

1. ------- American painter George Inness interested in art, but he showed a strong concern for social issues as well.

   (A) Only was not
   (B) Only not was
   (C) Not only was
   (D) Not was only

2. Some historians believe that John Jay could have played ------- in America's early history as James Madison.

   (A) as an important role
   (B) as important a role
   (C) an important role as
   (D) a role important as

3. Katherine Anne Porter's experiences living abroad as well as ------- in the South are reflected in her stories.

   (A) her childhood those of
   (B) her childhood of those
   (C) those her childhood of
   (D) those of her childhood

4. In most countries, egg and chicken production is by far ------- of the poultry industry.

   (A) the most important aspect
   (B) the most aspect important
   (C) the aspect most important
   (D) the aspect important most

Practice Exercises for Section 2 of TOEFL   131

5. An automobile is often the largest single investment that most ------- .

   (A) will make families ever
   (B) will ever make families
   (C) families will ever make
   (D) families make ever will

6. Nordic skiing consists of ------- with the skier providing propulsion over the terrain.

   (A) country-cross travel
   (B) cross-travel country
   (C) cross-country travel
   (D) travel country-cross

7. During World War II, Hollywood films sought to uplift the spirits of Americans ------- .

   (A) at home both and abroad
   (B) both at home and abroad
   (C) abroad and both at home
   (D) at both home and abroad

27. Word Order (Written Expression)

Certain "written expression" questions test for the correct word order in a short phrase. Especially be sure to check the location of an adverb in relation to a verb or adjective.

Los Angeles and Miami continue to be two of the **fastest growing** cities in the United States.

1. American author Sarah Orne Jewett determined <u>to perpetuate</u>
                                                      A
   in writing the <u>disappearing rapidly</u> traditions <u>of provincial</u> life
                        B   C
   <u>about her</u>.
       D

2. Porcupines <u>are</u> clumsy, <u>methodical</u>, <u>moving slow</u> animals
                 A   B   C
   <u>that show</u> little fear of other animals.
        D

3. <u>Collecting</u> picture postcards <u>was</u> <u>immensely a</u> popular hobby
        A   B   C
   <u>in the first</u> decade of the twentieth century.
        D

Chapter 10

4. Sacajawea, a Shoshone Indian, was <u>only the</u> woman <u>to travel</u>
                                   A   B   C

   with Lewis and Clark <u>on their expedition</u> to the Pacific.
                                 D

5. <u>The purpose</u> of empirical research in the <u>sciences social</u> is to
       A   B

   <u>provide answers</u> to questions <u>about behavior</u> using the scientific method.
        C   D

6. <u>The Earth's</u> atmosphere is simulated for <u>the space</u> traveler by
       A   B

   a <u>support system</u> that provides <u>oxygen necessary</u>.
        C   D

7. <u>Early in</u> his life <u>it</u> was already clear <u>that</u> Henry Ford had an
      A   B   C

   <u>aptitude natural</u> for mechanical things.
       D

28. Parallelism (Structure)

The term *parallelism* refers to the mode of presentation of a series of words that have the same function in a sentence. While more than one option may be grammatically correct, it is style, not necessarily grammar, that is being tested in questions involving parallelism. Check to see that each word in the series has the same grammatical form.

Major causes of power outages are **failed power lines, violent storms,** and **fallen trees.**

Modern political leaders are expected **to lead, to inspire,** and **to provide** moral example to the electorate.

1. Carnegie Hall in Pittsburgh is equipped with one of the world's largest, most powerful, and ------- organs.
   (A) fine
   (B) finer
   (C) finest
   (D) finesse

2. The U.S. Geological Survey distributes maps that are local, regional, and ------- .
   (A) nationalistic
   (B) nation
   (C) nationally
   (D) national

3. The largest groups of American Gypsies are the Romnichels, or English Gypsies, the Roms, or Serbian Gypsies, and the Ludari, or -------.

   (A) the Romanian
   (B) Romanian
   (C) Romanian Gypsies
   (D) are Romanian

4. Extrasensory perception is the awareness of an object, event, or ------- without the aid of the ordinary sensory channels.

   (A) and thinking
   (B) thought
   (C) thoughts
   (D) to think

5. Functionalist architects strip a building of unnecessary elements to define it as a function rather than -------.

   (A) as a symbol
   (B) symbolically
   (C) for a symbol
   (D) to symbolize

6. Folk art is a spontaneous expression of the feelings, attitudes, and ------- the lower classes of a society.

   (A) need
   (B) need of
   (C) needs
   (D) needs of

7. There are four primary taste sensations: sweet, bitter, sour, and -------.

   (A) salt
   (B) salts
   (C) salted
   (D) salty

29. Parallelism (Written Expression)

The terms *parallelism* refers to the mode of presentation of a series of words that have the same function in a sentence. Each word in the series should be of the same grammatical form.

Early American fur traders often adopted Indian clothing: **raccoon skin hat, fringed buckskin shirt and pants, and beaded leather moccasins**.

Many modern architects oppose **applying** ornament in favor of **diffusing, directing**, or otherwise **manipulating** light in bare spaces.

1. In 1921, Isadora Duncan <u>was invited</u> to <u>establish</u> a school of the
                                         A   B
   dance in the Soviet Union, <u>similar to</u> her other two schools, one
                                                  C
   in Germany, <u>the other French</u>.
                          D

2. <u>The</u> introduction of the <u>horse</u> changed <u>the culture of</u> the Plains
    A   B   C
   Indians irrevocably, profoundly, and <u>with great speed</u>.
                                                                    D

3. <u>Air</u> transportation's <u>importance</u> in the United States is
    A   B
   <u>marked by</u> a swelling interest in acquiring property, obtaining
       C
   equipment, and <u>to hire</u> employees.
                          D

4. <u>The</u> leaves <u>of most</u> coniferous trees <u>are long</u>, slender, and
    A   B   C
   <u>needles</u>.
    D

5. The Hudson Bay Company <u>was among</u> the most active <u>agents</u>
                                         A   B
   to explore, chart, and <u>giving descriptions of</u> western Canada.
                                             C   D

6. The <u>speech</u> of Irish, Italian, German, and <u>Eastern Europe</u> im-
       A   B
   migrants <u>produced</u> the <u>Brooklyn accent</u>.
             C   D

7. Flax produces <u>a</u> strong thread <u>used</u> for sewing, netting, weav-
                       A   B
   ing, <u>and</u> <u>towels</u>.
        C   D

30. Redundancy

Redundancy is saying the same thing twice when once is enough. Check for extra words with the same meaning and words that are unnecessary to the meaning of the sentence.

The **last, final** stage of the traditional Hispanic image-carving art in New Mexico is **often frequently** referred to as its golden age.

In the sentence above, there are two redundancies. One of them is the use of *final* and *last* together. One of the words should be eliminated.

The second redundancy is the use of *often* with *frequently*. Again, one of the words should be eliminated.

1. The parents and mothers of preschool children play perhaps
      A   B
   the most important role in the child's eventual emotional
                                               C
   growth and stability.
        D
2. The first public-school kindergarten in the United States it was
       A   B
   opened in St. Louis in 1873 by Susan Blow.
     C   D
3. Invention seems to be a universal, widespread characteristic of
              A   B
   humankind, found at all times and all places of human history.
              C   D
4. The first permanent settlement in North America, Jamestown,
              A
   it was named in honor of King James I of England.
   B   C   D
5. The term *plastics* refers to synthetic materials
                           A
   that are capable of being formed and made into usable prod-
        B   C
   ucts by various processes.
           D
6. The common foxglove grows wild but is often grown as a
                                   A   B
   decorative ornamental flower in gardens.
              C   D
7. Toward the end of his life, Ben Shahn's paintings became more
      A   B   C
   abstract and conceptual.
              D

31. Omission and Inclusion

Check for extra or missing words in the sentence. Be especially aware of omitted articles, prepositions, and adverbs. Check for extra pronouns and unnecessary verbs.

1. Norman Rockwell is well-known painter of magazine covers
                         A   B   C
   and illustrations, principally for the Saturday Evening Post.
                          D
2. The idea of free, universal, tax-supported school system in
              A   B
   every American state began around 1830.
                       C   D

3. The history of the United States has been profoundly
                A   B
   affected the Supreme Court's assertion and exercise of judicial
         C   D
   review.

4. Until the early eighteenth century, when the Cherokee Indians
     A
   began to unite into a tribal state, all political authority rested
             B   C
   it within individual villages.
   D

5. The nine planets of the solar system were formed when were
                                                        A
   condensed out of a great cloud of gas and dust over four billion
       B   C
   years ago.
   D

6. The Indian Arts and Crafts Board was one of greatest successes
                                   A   B
   of the New Deal Indian policy in the 1930s.
                         C   D

7. Most shales contain from 25 to 50 to percent quartz, with a few
     A   B
   varieties containing more than fifty percent.
             C   D

Key to Practice Exercises

PE-1	PE-2	PE-3	PE-4	PE-5	PE-6
1-D	1-A	1-A	1-B	1-B	1-B
2-D	2-C	2-B	2-D	2-C	2-C
3-C	3-B	3-B	3-A	3-C	3-C
4-A	4-B	4-A	4-C	4-C	4-A
5-A	5-A	5-B	5-C	5-B	5-C
6-D	6-B	6-B	6-C	6-C	6-B
7-C	7-C	7-C	7-B	7-A	7-B

PE-7	PE-8	PE-9	PE-10	PE-11	PE-12
1-A	1-D	1-A	1-A	1-D	1-D
2-D	2-B	2-B	2-A	2-A	2-C
3-C	3-D	3-B	3-D	3-D	3-B
4-B	4-A	4-D	4-A	4-B	4-A
5-D	5-C	5-A	5-A	5-C	5-B
6-D	6-C	6-D	6-B	6-B	6-D
7-D	7-B	7-C	7-C	7-D	7-A

PE-13	PE-14	PE-15	PE-16	PE-17	PE-18
1-D	1-D	1-D	1-C	1-B	1-D
2-C	2-B	2-A	2-A	2-C	2-A
3-C	3-B	3-C	3-B	3-D	3-A
4-D	4-D	4-C	4-D	4-C	4-B
5-B	5-A	5-B	5-A	5-C	5-A
6-D	6-B	6-B	6-C	6-B	6-A
7-B	7-A	7-D	7-B	7-B	7-A

PE-19	PE-20	PE-21	PE-22	PE-23	PE-24
1-A	1-B	1-C	1-D	1-B	1-B
2-C	2-C	2-B	2-C	2-C	2-C
3-B	3-B	3-D	3-D	3-D	3-A
4-C	4-D	4-A	4-B	4-C	4-B
5-D	5-B	5-D	5-D	5-A	5-A
6-B	6-D	6-B	6-C	6-A	6-C
7-C	7-C	7-D	7-A	7-B	7-B

PE-25	PE-26	PE-27	PE-28	PE-29	PE-30
1-C	1-C	1-B	1-C	1-D	1-A
2-A	2-B	2-C	2-D	2-D	2-B
3-B	3-D	3-C	3-C	3-D	3-B
4-D	4-A	4-B	4-B	4-D	4-B
5-C	5-C	5-B	5-A	5-C	5-C
6-D	6-C	6-D	6-D	6-B	6-C
7-C	7-B	7-D	7-D	7-D	7-D

PE-31

1-A
2-A
3-C
4-D
5-A
6-B
7-B

APPENDIX A

TOEFL Requirements by Institution

Here is a list of the minimum TOEFL scores at one hundred community colleges, colleges, and universities in the United States with large foreign student enrollments. As you can see, the TOEFL requirements change from one institution to another. Most often, community colleges require a score of 500 on the TOEFL. Colleges and universities most often require a score of 550 for undergraduate or graduate admission. However, a few colleges do not require the TOEFL at all, and a few others require scores of 600 or above.

Some colleges require TOEFL scores, but they do not require a minimum score. These colleges take into account your TOEFL score plus your grades, other test scores, and other information you put on your application. Therefore, if you do poorly on the TOEFL, but you have good grades, you may still be accepted by such colleges.

Some colleges that require the TOEFL, and some of those that do not require the TOEFL, will make you take their English-as-a-Second-Language courses until you can pass their own English-language proficiency examination.

At some universities, particularly those with a large number of Masters and Doctoral programs, the TOEFL score requirement varies by department or field of study. These requirements are set by the professors in each program based on their experience with foreign students entering with different TOEFL scores. The TOEFL score requirements of departments may change frequently, but the requirements of a university do not change often. While minimum score requirements may be set for all graduate school applicants by a university, sometimes individual academic departments within that university set requirements that are 30 or even 50 points higher. Thus, in universities that require a minimum TOEFL score of 550 of all graduate school applicants, some departments may require 580 or 600 of their applicants.

Colleges and universities almost *never* take TOEFL section scores into account when making a decision on an application. Similarly, at present only a few institutions require the TWE, and even fewer require a minimum score on the TWE. Generally, however, admissions officers like to see a score of 4 or above on the TWE.

The following minimum score requirements represent the variety of policies at American universities. If you want to apply to a graduate program, you should write the department you plan to apply to in order to determine the minimum TOEFL score they require, even if your university is listed below.

Institution	MINIMUM SCORE REQUIREMENTS	
	Undergraduate	Graduate
Alabama Agricultural and Mechanical University	500	500
American University	N. Req.	N. Req.
Arizona State University	500	Varies
Boston University	550	550
Brigham Young University	500	550
Brigham Young University, Hawaii Campus	450	NA
Broward Community College	500	NA
California State University, Fresno	500	550
California State University, Long Beach	500	550
California State University, Los Angeles	550	550
Central State University	500	550
City College of Chicago, Loop College	N. Req.	NA
City University of New York, Baruch College	500	550
Colorado State University	500	550
Columbia University	Varies	Varies
Cornell University	550	550
DeKalb Community College	460	NA
Eastern Michigan University	500	500
Florida International University	500	500
Florida State University	550	550
George Mason University	550	Varies
George Washington University	550	550
Georgetown University	550	Varies
Georgia Institute of Technology	550	550
Georgia State University	525	550
Harvard University	600	Varies
Howard University	500	525
Indiana State University	500	550
Indiana University, Bloomington	550	550
Iowa State University	500	500

	MINIMUM SCORE REQUIREMENTS	
Institution	Undergraduate	Graduate
Kansas State University	550	550
Kent State University	525	525
Louisiana State University	500	525
Michigan State University	550	550
Miami-Dade Community College	Req.	NA
New York Institute of Technology	450	N. Req.
New York University	N. Req.	N. Req.
North Carolina State University	500	500
Northern Illinois University	520	550
Northern Texas State University	Req.	Req.
Ohio University	N. Req.	550
Ohio State University	500	500
Oklahoma State University	500	550
Oregon State University	500	500
Pace University	500	550
Pennsylvania State University	550	550
Purdue University	550	Varies
Rockland Community College	N. Req.	NA
San Diego State University	550	550
Southeastern University	500	550
Southeastern Oklahoma State University	500	550
Southern Illinois University	525	550
Stanford University	575	575
State University of New York, Stony Brook	550	550
Syracuse University	500	525
Texas A & M University	550	550
Texas Tech University	550	500
University of Akron	500	550
University of Alabama	500	500
University of Arizona	500	Req.
University of Bridgeport	500	500
University of California, Berkeley	550	550
University of California, Los Angeles	N. Req	550

Institution	MINIMUM SCORE REQUIREMENTS	
	Undergraduate	Graduate
University of Cincinnati	515	515
University of Colorado, Boulder	500	500
University of Denver	500	500
University of the District of Columbia	500	550
University of Florida	550	550
University of Georgia	500	Varies
University of Hawaii at Manoa	450	Varies
University of Houston, Downtown	550	550
University of Houston, University Park	550	550
University of Illinois, Chicago Circle	480	510
University of Illinois, Urbana-Champaign	520	520
University of Iowa	530	530
University of Kansas	N. Req.	570
University of Kentucky	525	550
University of Maryland, College Park	Req.	Req.
University of Miami	550	550
University of Michigan	Req.	Req.
University of Minnesota, Twin Cities	Req.	Req.
University of Missouri, Columbia	500	500
University of Nebraska, Lincoln	500	500
University of New Orleans	500	500
University of Oklahoma	550	550
University of Pennsylvania	Varies	Varies
University of San Francisco	550	550
University of Southern California	Varies	Varies
University of Tennessee, Knoxville	525	525
University of Texas, Arlington	N. Req.	550
University of Texas, Austin	550	550
University of Texas, El Paso	500	550
University of Toledo	500	550
University of Utah	500	500
University of Wisconsin, Madison	525	Req.
University of Wisconsin, Milwaukee	500	550

	MINIMUM SCORE REQUIREMENTS	
Institution	Undergraduate	Graduate
Utah State University	500	500
Virginia Polytechnic Institute and State University	600	600
Wayne State University	500	550
West Virginia University	550	550
Western Michigan University	550	550
Wichita State University	500	525
Yale University	600	Varies

N. Req.: Not required.
Req.: TOEFL is required, but there is no minimum score.
Varies: Minimum score requirement varies by field of study.
NA (Not applicable): There is no graduate program at this institution.

APPENDIX B

Guidelines for Scoring Practice Tests and Converting Number-Right Scores to Scaled Scores and Percentile Ranks

Because of the very careful and scientific way in which the *Newbury House TOEFL Preparation Kit* has been developed, we can give you the following procedures for determining how you would probably perform on an actual TOEFL. If you follow these procedures carefully, you can determine what your TOEFL score would be with a high degree of accuracy.

After you have taken *A Practice TOEFL, Form 1*, score the test and determine how well you did. Do this according to the following procedure.

TO SCORE YOUR TEST

1. Find the key (list of correct answers) that corresponds to the form of *A Practice TOEFL* that you took. Each key is on a separate page in the Tapescript and Answer Key booklet.
2. Score your answer sheet using the key. Place a C next to each correct answer.
3. Count the number of answers you got correct in each section of the test. Write that number in the space called Number Right below.

Section	Number Right	Scaled Score
Section 1	_____	_____
Section 2	_____	_____
Section 3	_____	_____

To Determine Your Scaled Section Scores

1. Find the Score Conversion Table for the form of *A Practice TOEFL* that you took. Each score conversion table is on a separate page at the end of Appendix B, beginning on page 148.
2. Each score conversion table is divided into three sections; these sections correspond to the three sections of the test. Each section consists of a Number Right column and a Scaled Score column. On the score conversion table, find your number-right score (you wrote this on page 194) for each section of the test. To the right of this score is your scaled score for that section. Find your scaled score and write it on page 144 also.

To Determine Your Total Scaled Score

1. Add your three scaled scores together.
2. Multiply the sum by 10.
3. Divide the product by 3.

This is the scaled total score you would earn on the TOEFL, based on your performance on this form of *A Practice TOEFL*.

Example: If your three scaled scores were 49, 50, and 51, you would calculate your scores as follows.

$$
\text{Step 1} \quad \begin{array}{r} 49 \\ 50 \\ \underline{51} \\ 150 \end{array}
$$

$$
\text{Step 2} \quad \begin{array}{r} 150 \\ \underline{\times\ 10} \\ 1500 \end{array}
$$

$$
\text{Step 3} \quad \frac{1500}{3} = 500
$$

To Determine Your Percentile Rank

The above procedures describe how to determine your number-right scores on *A Practice TOEFL* and how to convert this score to an estimate of the equivalent TOEFL scaled scores. To determine the percentile rank that corresponds to your TOEFL scaled scores, see the tables below.

The information in these tables is based on the results of official TOEFL examinees. Use it to interpret your official TOEFL scores *after* you receive them. Your scores on *A Practice TOEFL* can also be looked up in this table. The percentile ranks in the table will tell you how your English skills compare with the English skills of official TOEFL examinees.

TOEFL SECTION SCORE PERCENTILE RANKS

Scaled Score	Section 1 Listening Comprehension	Section 2 Structure and Written Expression	Section 3 Vocabulary and Reading Comprehension
68		99	
66	99	97	99
64	96	95	97
62	92	91	93
60	88	87	89
58	82	80	82
56	75	72	74
54	66	63	64
52	57	53	53
50	45	43	42
48	34	34	33
46	23	25	24
44	15	18	17
42	8	11	12
40	5	7	8
38	2	4	4
36	1	2	2
34		1	1
32		1	1
30			

Source: TOEFL Test and Score Manual, 1987–88 Edition. Princeton, New Jersey: Educational Testing Service, p. 21.

Now, let's learn how to use this table of percentile ranks. In the first column on the left, called Scaled Score, are numbers ranging from 68 to 30. Find your score on each section of the test in this column. The three columns to the right show the percentile rank that corresponds to each section score. The percentile rank is the percent of TOEFL examinees whose score on that section was lower than yours.

For example, consider the person who scored 50 on Section 1, 54 on Section 2, and 52 on Section 3. Now find the scaled score of 50 in the first column. Notice in the next column that the Section 1 percentile rank that corresponds to it is 45. This means that this person scored below average on the Listening Comprehension section, but still scored higher than 45% of the people who took this section.

Now, find the scaled score of 54 in the first column. Notice in the second column to the right that the Section 2 percentile rank that corresponds to 54 is 63. This means that this person scored above average on the *Structure and Written Expression* section, and scored higher than 63% of the people who took this section.

Now find the scaled score of 52 in the first column. Notice in the third column to the right that the Section 3 percentile rank that corresponds to it is 53. This means that this person scored above average on the *Vocabulary and Reading Comprehension* section, and scored higher than 53% of the people who took this section.

Now, let's learn to interpret the TOEFL total score. The table below gives many total scaled scores and the percentile ranks that correspond to them. Find the total scaled score of 520 in the table. The number to the right that corresponds to it is 55. This means that this person scored above average on the TOEFL total score, and scored higher than 55% of the people who took the test.

TOEFL TOTAL SCORE PERCENTILE RANKS

Total Scaled Score	Percentile Rank
660	99
640	97
620	94
600	90
580	84
560	77
540	67
520	55
500	43
480	32
460	22
440	14
420	8
400	5
380	2
360	1
340	
320	
300	

Source: *TOEFL Test and Score Manual, 1987–88 Edition.* Princeton, New Jersey: Educational Testing Service, p. 21.

There are score conversion tables like the two you have just seen for different groups of people, such as graduate school applicants, undergraduate applicants, applicants for professional licenses, men, and women. A table of average scores for each country whose citizens take the TOEFL is also available. You can get these tables by writing ETS for a free copy of the current edition of the *TOEFL Test and Score Manual*. Send your request to TOEFL Services, CN 6151, Princeton, NJ 08541-6151, USA.

Score conversion tables help you to compare yourself with others who took the test. However, it is more important for you to compare your score with the score required by the institution you want to attend. For a list of scores required by the American institutions with the largest number of foreign students, see Appendix A on pages 139–143 of this book.

SCORE CONVERSION TABLE
A Practice TOEFL, Form 1

SECTION I: LISTENING COMPREHENSION		SECTION II: STRUCTURE AND WRITTEN EXPRESSION		SECTION III: VOCABULARY AND READING COMPREHENSION	
Number Right	Scaled Score	Number Right	Scaled Score	Number Right	Scaled Score
50	68	40	68	60	67
49	68	39	66	59	66
48	67	38	65	58	66
47	66	37	64	57	65
46	65	36	63	56	65
45	64	35	62	55	64
44	63	34	60	54	63
43	62	33	59	53	62
42	61	32	58	52	61
41	61	31	57	51	60
40	60	30	56	50	59
39	59	29	55	49	59
38	58	28	54	48	58
37	57	27	52	47	58
36	57	26	51	46	57
35	56	25	50	45	57
34	55	24	49	44	56
33	54	23	48	43	55
32	53	22	47	42	54
31	52	21	46	41	54
30	51	20	45	40	53
29	50	19	44	39	53

SCORE CONVERSION TABLE
A Practice TOEFL, Form 1 (*Cont.*)

SECTION I: LISTENING COMPREHENSION		SECTION II: STRUCTURE AND WRITTEN EXPRESSION		SECTION III: VOCABULARY AND READING COMPREHENSION	
Number Right	Scaled Score	Number Right	Scaled Score	Number Right	Scaled Score
28	49	18	43	38	52
27	48	17	42	37	52
26	47	16	41	36	51
25	47	15	40	35	50
24	46	14	39	34	49
23	46	13	38	33	48
22	45	12	37	32	47
21	44	11	36	31	47
20	43	10	35	30	46
19	43	9	34	29	45
18	42	8	33	28	45
17	41	7	32	27	44
16	41			26	44
15	40			25	44
14	39			24	43
13	38			23	42
12	37			22	41
11	36			21	40
10	35			20	39
9	34			19	38
8	33			18	38
7	32			17	37
				16	36
				15	35
				14	34
				13	33

SCORE CONVERSION TABLE
A Practice TOEFL, Form 2

SECTION I: LISTENING COMPREHENSION		SECTION II: STRUCTURE AND WRITTEN EXPRESSION		SECTION III: VOCABULARY AND READING COMPREHENSION	
Number Right	Scaled Score	Number Right	Scaled Score	Number Right	Scaled Score
50	68	40	68	60	67
49	68	39	67	59	67
48	67	38	66	58	66
47	66	37	64	57	66
46	65	36	62	56	65
45	64	35	61	55	65
44	64	34	59	54	64
43	62	33	58	53	63
42	61	32	57	52	62
41	61	31	56	51	62
40	60	30	55	50	61
39	59	29	54	49	60
38	59	28	53	48	60
37	58	27	51	47	59
36	58	26	50	46	59
35	56	25	49	45	58
34	55	24	48	44	58
33	54	23	47	43	57
32	54	22	46	42	56
31	53	21	45	41	55
30	51	20	44	40	55
29	50	19	43	39	54
28	50	18	42	38	54
27	49	17	41	37	53
26	48	16	40	36	52
25	47	15	39	35	51
24	47	14	39	34	51
23	46	13	38	33	50
22	45	12	37	32	49
21	45	11	36	31	48
20	44	10	35	30	47
19	44	9	33	29	47
18	43	8	32	28	46
17	42	7	31	27	46
16	42	6	30	26	45
15	41			25	45

SCORE CONVERSION TABLE
A Practice TOEFL, Form 2 (*Cont.*)

SECTION I: LISTENING COMPREHENSION		SECTION II: STRUCTURE AND WRITTEN EXPRESSION		SECTION III: VOCABULARY AND READING COMPREHENSION	
Number Right	Scaled Score	Number Right	Scaled Score	Number Right	Scaled Score
14	40			24	44
13	39			23	43
12	38			22	43
11	37			21	42
10	36			20	41
9	35			19	40
8	34			18	39
7	33			17	38
6	32			16	37
				15	36
				14	35
				13	35
				12	34

SCORE CONVERSION TABLE
A Practice TOEFL, Form 3

SECTION I: LISTENING COMPREHENSION		SECTION II: STRUCTURE AND WRITTEN EXPRESSION		SECTION III: VOCABULARY AND READING COMPREHENSION	
Number Right	Scaled Score	Number Right	Scaled Score	Number Right	Scaled Score
50	68	40	68	60	67
49	67	39	67	59	67
48	67	38	66	58	66
47	66	37	64	57	66
46	66	36	63	56	66
45	65	35	61	55	65
44	64	34	60	54	64
43	63	33	59	53	64
42	62	32	58	52	63
41	61	31	56	51	63
40	61	30	55	50	62
39	60	29	54	49	62
38	59	28	53	48	61
37	58	27	51	47	60
36	57	26	50	46	59
35	56	25	49	45	59
34	55	24	48	44	58
33	54	23	47	43	57
32	53	22	46	42	56
31	52	21	45	41	55
30	52	20	44	40	55
29	51	19	43	39	54
28	50	18	42	38	53
27	49	17	41	37	53
26	48	16	40	36	52
25	47	15	39	35	52
24	47	14	39	34	51
23	46	13	38	33	51
22	45	12	37	32	50
21	44	11	36	31	50
20	43	10	35	30	49
19	43	9	34	29	49
18	42	8	33	28	48
17	42	7	32	27	47
16	40	6	30	26	47
15	40			25	46

SCORE CONVERSION TABLE
A Practice TOEFL, Form 3 (*Cont.*)

SECTION I: LISTENING COMPREHENSION		SECTION II: STRUCTURE AND WRITTEN EXPRESSION		SECTION III: VOCABULARY AND READING COMPREHENSION	
Number Right	Scaled Score	Number Right	Scaled Score	Number Right	Scaled Score
14	39			24	45
13	38			23	44
12	37			22	44
11	36			21	43
10	35			20	42
9	34			19	41
8	33			18	40
7	32			17	39
				16	38
				15	37
				14	36
				13	35
				12	33

Print your full name here _____
(last)   (first)   (middle)

A PRACTICE TOEFL

FORM 1

General Directions

This is a test of your ability to use the English language. It is divided into three sections, some of which have more than one part. Each section or part of the test begins with a set of specific directions that include sample questions. Be sure you understand what you are to do before you begin to work on a section.

The supervisor will tell you when to start each section and when to go on to the next section. You should work quickly but carefully. Do not spend too much time on any one question. If you finish a section early, you may review your answers on that section only. You may not go on to the next section and you may not go back to a section you have already worked on.

You will find that some of the questions are more difficult than others, but you should try to answer every one. Your score will be based on the number of questions you answer correctly—that is, the number for which you choose the best answer from among the choices given. If you are not sure of the answer to a question, make the best guess that you can. It is to your advantage to answer every question, even if you have to guess the answer.

Do not mark your answers in this test book. You must mark all of your answers on the separate answer sheet that is inside this test book. When you mark your answer to a question on your answer sheet, you must:

— Use a medium-soft (#2 or HB) black lead pencil.
— Be careful to mark the space that corresponds to the answer you choose for each question. Also, make sure you mark your answer in the row with the same number as the number of the question you are answering. You will not be permitted to make any corrections after time is called.
— Mark only one answer to each question.
— Carefully and completely fill each intended oval with a dark mark so that you cannot see the letter inside the oval; light or partial marks may not be read properly by the scoring machine.
— Erase all extra marks completely and thoroughly. If you change your mind about an answer after you have marked it on your answer sheet, completely erase your old answer and then mark your new answer.

The examples below show you the correct and wrong ways of marking an answer sheet. Be sure to fill in the ovals on your answer sheet the correct way.

CORRECT	WRONG	WRONG	WRONG	WRONG
Ⓐ Ⓑ ● Ⓓ	Ⓐ Ⓑ ⓒ̸ Ⓓ	Ⓐ Ⓑ ⓧ Ⓓ	Ⓐ Ⓑ Ⓒ Ⓓ	Ⓐ Ⓑ Ⓒ Ⓓ

Some or all of the passages for this test have been adapted from published material to provide the examinee with significant problems for analysis and evaluation. To make the passages suitable for testing purposes, the style, content, or point of view of the original may have been altered in some cases.

Note: On an actual TOEFL examination, the General Directions page appears on the last page of the test booklet. These directions are included here for your convenience. This test is to be used with the listening comprehension test tape found in the *Newbury House TOEFL Preparation Kit* and the multiple-choice answer sheets found at the end of this book.

1 • 1 • 1 • 1 • 1 • 1 • 1

SECTION 1
LISTENING COMPREHENSION

In this section of the test, you will have an opportunity to demonstrate your ability to understand spoken English. There are three parts to this section, with special directions for each part.

Part A

<u>Directions</u>: For each question in Part A, you will hear a short sentence. Each sentence will be spoken just one time. The sentences you hear will not be written out for you. Therefore, you must listen carefully to understand what the speaker says.

After you hear a sentence, read the four choices in your test book, marked (A), (B), (C), and (D), and decide which <u>one</u> is closest in meaning to the sentence you heard. Then, on your sheet, find the number of the question and fill in the space that corresponds to the letter of the answer you have chosen. Fill in the space so that the letter inside the oval cannot be seen.

Example I

You will hear:

You will read: (A) Mary outswam the others.
(B) Mary ought to swim with them.
(C) Mary and her friends swam to the island.
(D) Mary's friends owned the island.

<u>Sample Answer</u>
Ⓐ Ⓑ ● Ⓓ

The speaker said, "Mary swam out to the island with her friends." Sentence (C), "Mary and her friends swam to the island," is closest in meaning to the sentence you heard. Therefore, you should choose answer (C).

GO ON TO THE NEXT PAGE ➤

1 · 1 · 1 · 1 · 1 · 1 · 1

Example II   Sample Answer
                                                        Ⓐ ● Ⓒ Ⓓ
  You will hear:
  You will read: (A) Please remind me to
                      read this book.
                  (B) Could you help me carry
                      these books?
                  (C) I don't mind if you help
                      me.
                  (D) Do you have a heavy
                      course load this term?

The speaker said, "Would you mind helping me with this load of books?" Sentence (B), "Could you help me carry these books?" is closest in meaning to the sentence you heard. Therefore, you should choose answer (B).

1. (A) Bob's sister exercises every day, but he doesn't.
   (B) Bob and his sister exercise every day.
   (C) Bob doesn't like his sister to exercise.
   (D) Bob exercises every day, but his sister doesn't.

2. (A) May I drive the car?
   (B) How do I put gas in the car?
   (C) How much gas does my car use?
   (D) Shall I buy some gas?

3. (A) The bus will be here at 9:25.
   (B) Busses come more frequently before nine o'clock.
   (C) After nine, there are four busses per hour.
   (D) The schedule you looked at was out of date.

4. (A) John needs to study more to be promoted.
   (B) John is a hard worker, so he will pass.
   (C) In the past, John had two jobs.
   (D) John must have a pass where he works.

GO ON TO THE NEXT PAGE ▶

5. (A) Please give the book back to me.
   (B) Remind me to return the book to you.
   (C) Be sure to take the book back to the library.
   (D) Go back to the library and get my book.

6. (A) We spent two days visiting museums.
   (B) A good day to see museums is Monday.
   (C) We didn't expect to go to two museums.
   (D) We are planning to visit two museums.

7. (A) Jane didn't call the electric company today.
   (B) Jane wanted to call Bill, but there was no electricity.
   (C) Jane paid the electric bill by telephone.
   (D) Jane paid only one bill today.

8. (A) We're driving instead of taking a taxi.
   (B) We usually go downtown by taxi.
   (C) We aren't going to drive downtown today.
   (D) Where can you catch a taxi into town?

9. (A) I walked into the apartment.
   (B) The party was at my apartment.
   (C) I rented the apartment.
   (D) I installed a new door in my apartment.

10. (A) Most students won't study their lessons at home.
    (B) If the students don't know the teacher, they won't work at home.
    (C) Students usually write their homework only if they are sure the teacher will look at it.
    (D) Most teachers give students grades for written assignments.

11. (A) That farm was once a shop.
    (B) Stores stand today where once there was a farm.
    (C) A shop is in the center of that farm.
    (D) Farmers no longer shop there.

12. (A) How did Kate get to school?
    (B) Was Kate's house a long way from school?
    (C) How many years of education does Kate have?
    (D) Did Kate attend classes?

A Practice TOEFL

13. (A) The students wish they could leave with the complete test.
    (B) The students wish they could take a break and then finish the test.
    (C) Some students want to finish the examination outside the classroom.
    (D) Students don't have to stay in the room if they have finished the exam.

14. (A) He can't stay in his classes.
    (B) He doesn't like his classes.
    (C) His classes are cancelled this semester.
    (D) He can't stand up in class.

15. (A) Did Betty put two envelopes in here?
    (B) Is the envelope in here, or is it someplace else.
    (C) Are both envelopes inside this desk?
    (D) Did Betty forget this envelope, or that one?

16. (A) The driver heard the weather forecast while he was parking.
    (B) Because he was parking, the driver needed to hear the weather.
    (C) A dog was barking as the driver listened to the radio.
    (D) The weather reporter listened to the driver parking.

17. (A) Movies about drug problems are common.
    (B) Many drug stores develop photographs.
    (C) You can buy film at most drug stores.
    (D) You can rent movies at most drug stores.

18. (A) This room is not only small, but it is also far away.
    (B) Fewer than two hundred guests will come, so we need a smaller room.
    (C) We must reduce our guest list by one hundred.
    (D) Two hundred people won't fit in this room.

19. (A) Don't believe the news you hear.
    (B) The newspaper is too hard to understand.
    (C) You shouldn't let the information bother you.
    (D) The new report isn't so difficult.

20. (A) I'm going to help my three friends move.
    (B) I'm going to need some help when I move.
    (C) Two friends are helping me move Thursday.
    (D) My friends are going to move in two days.

GO ON TO THE NEXT PAGE

1 • 1 • 1 • 1 • 1 • 1 • 1

Part B

Directions: In Part B you will hear short conversations between two speakers. At the end of each conversation, a third person will ask a question about what was said. You will hear each conversation and question about it just one time. Therefore, you must listen carefully to understand what each speaker says. After you hear a conversation and question about it, read the four possible answers in your test book and decide which one is the best answer to the question you heard. Then, on your answer sheet, find the number of the question and fill in the space that corresponds to the letter of the answer you have chosen.

Look at the following example.

Sample Answer
● Ⓑ Ⓒ Ⓓ

You will hear:

You will read: (A) Present Professor Smith with a picture.
(B) Photograph Professor Smith.
(C) Put glass over the photograph.
(D) Replace the broken headlight.

From the conversation you learn that the woman thinks Professor Smith would like a photograph of the class. The best answer to the question "What does the woman think the class should do?" is (A), "Present Professor Smith with a picture." Therefore, you should choose answer (A).

21. (A) How do you pronounce that?
    (B) He seldom sees the program.
    (C) Who can you see on this program?
    (D) It's often hard to look at.

22. (A) At a vending machine.
    (B) In a bus.
    (C) At the bank.
    (D) In a department store.

GO ON TO THE NEXT PAGE

A Practice TOEFL 163

1 · 1 · 1 · 1 · 1 · 1 · 1

23. (A) She knows he missed one day.
    (B) Half the class doesn't come.
    (C) No one else missed the class.
    (D) She isn't surprised.

24. (A) Take care of his back.
    (B) Have a physical examination.
    (C) Have his car fixed.
    (D) Return a musical instrument.

25. (A) Mind the children.
    (B) Take the children to school.
    (C) Park at the university.
    (D) Take the children to the park.

26. (A) She's too busy to help.
    (B) She would not like to help him.
    (C) She owns one, too.
    (D) She helped him once this week.

27. (A) Don't talk about his ideas.
    (B) Jack is never content.
    (C) Don't worry about Jack.
    (D) Jack's ideas are very poor.

28. (A) He doesn't have a job.
    (B) He doesn't make enough money.
    (C) His house isn't for sale.
    (D) His paycheck is already spent.

29. (A) She will make another order.
    (B) She's pleased with the prompt service.
    (C) She won't consider the company again.
    (D) She's had too many visitors.

30. (A) Weighing boxes.
    (B) Marketing.
    (C) Setting the table.
    (D) Moving.

31. (A) An electrician.
    (B) A carpenter.
    (C) An engineer.
    (D) A plumber.

32. (A) It's not fair.
    (B) It's not yet time.
    (C) It's likely.
    (D) It's not important.

33. (A) Mary's mother agrees with me.
    (B) Mary seems agreeable.
    (C) Mary likes being a mother.
    (D) Mary thinks so, too.

34. (A) In a travel agency.
    (B) In a library.
    (C) In a hotel.
    (D) In a night club.

35. (A) Make up a test.
    (B) Take next month off.
    (C) Go to graduate school.
    (D) Take examinations.

GO ON TO THE NEXT PAGE

1·1·1·1·1·1·1

Part C

<u>Directions:</u> In this part of the test, you will hear short talks and conversations. After each of them, you will be asked some questions. You will hear the talks and conversations and the questions about them just one time. They will not be written out for you. Therefore, you must listen carefully to understand what each speaker says.

After you hear a question, read the four possible answers in your test book and decide which <u>one</u> is the best answer to the question you heard. Then, on your answer sheet, find the number of the question and fill in the space that corresponds to the letter of the answer you have chosen.

Answer all questions on the basis of what is <u>stated</u> or <u>implied</u> in the talk or conversation.

Listen to this sample talk.

You will hear:

Now look at the following example.

You will hear:

You will read: (A) They are impossible to guide.
(B) They may go up in flames.
(C) They tend to leak gas.
(D) They are cheaply made.

<u>Sample Answer</u>
Ⓐ ● Ⓒ Ⓓ

The best answer to the question "Why are gas balloons considered dangerous?" is (B), "They may go up in flames." Therefore, you should choose answer (B).

Now look at this example.

You will hear:

You will read: (A) Watch for changes in weather.
(B) Watch their altitude.
(C) Check for weak spots in their balloons.
(D) Test the strength of the ropes.

<u>Sample Answer</u>
● Ⓑ Ⓒ Ⓓ

The best answer to the question "According to the speaker, what must balloon pilots be careful to do?" is (A) "Watch for changes in weather." Therefore, you should choose answer (A).

GO ON TO THE NEXT PAGE

1 · 1 · 1 · 1 · 1 · 1 · 1

36. (A) Its decoration.
    (B) Its heaviness.
    (C) Its design.
    (D) Its price.

37. (A) Between 1800 and 1850.
    (B) From 1850 to 1900.
    (C) Between 1900 and 1950.
    (D) From 1950 to the present.

38. (A) Six.
    (B) Twelve.
    (C) Nineteen.
    (D) Twenty.

39. (A) Shaker museums.
    (B) Shaker craftsmanship.
    (C) Shaker history.
    (D) Shaker worship.

40. (A) They will make new furniture.
    (B) They will leave the United States.
    (C) They will gain many new members.
    (D) They will gradually die out.

41. (A) Industrial development.
    (B) Declining water quality.
    (C) High forms of aquatic life.
    (D) Sewage treatment plants.

42. (A) On a boat.
    (B) In a classroom.
    (C) On a street.
    (D) In a laboratory.

43. (A) Reduce levels of oxygen.
    (B) Increase plant reproduction.
    (C) Reduce levels of nitrogen.
    (D) Increase amounts of algae.

44. (A) There is insufficient oxygen.
    (B) There are not enough small plants.
    (C) There is no nitrogen.
    (D) There are no bacteria.

45. (A) Discharges from industry.
    (B) Agricultural runoff.
    (C) Storm water runoff.
    (D) Hydroelectric dams.

46. (A) Raising garter snakes.
    (B) Observing the habits of snakes.
    (C) Guessing the origin of snake myths.
    (D) Describing the garter snake.

GO ON TO THE NEXT PAGE

47. (A) It doesn't lay eggs.
    (B) It isn't harmful.
    (C) It swallows creatures whole.
    (D) It is quite colorful.

48. (A) It is often found in homes.
    (B) It lives in cultivated areas.
    (C) It is sold in pet stores.
    (D) It is bred commercially.

49. (A) Ten.
    (B) Fifteen.
    (C) Thirty.
    (D) Fifty.

50. (A) Substantive.
    (B) Fanciful.
    (C) Provocative.
    (D) Morbid.

THIS IS THE END OF THE LISTENING COMPREHENSION SECTION OF THE TEST.

THE NEXT PART OF THE TEST IS SECTION 2. TURN TO THE DIRECTIONS FOR SECTION 2 IN YOUR TEST BOOK. READ THEM, AND BEGIN WORK.
DO NOT READ OR WORK ON ANY OTHER SECTION OF THE TEST.

A Practice TOEFL

2 · 2 · 2 · 2 · 2 · 2 · 2

SECTION 2
STRUCTURE AND WRITTEN EXPRESSION

Time—25 minutes

This section is designed to measure your ability to recognize language that is appropriate for standard written English. There are two types of questions in this section, with special directions for each type.

Directions: Questions 1-15 are incomplete sentences. Beneath each sentence you will see four words or phrases, marked (A), (B), (C), and (D). Choose the one word or phrase that best completes the sentence. Then, on your answer sheet, find the number of the question and fill in the space that corresponds to the letter of the answer you have chosen. Fill in the space so that the letter inside the oval cannot be seen.

Example I

Vegetables are an excellent source ------- vitamins.

(A) of
(B) has
(C) where
(D) that

Sample Answer

● Ⓑ Ⓒ Ⓓ

The sentence should read, "Vegetables are an excellent source of vitamins." Therefore, you should choose answer (A).

Example II

------- in history when remarkable progress was made within a relatively short span of time.

(A) Periods
(B) Throughout periods
(C) There have been periods
(D) Periods have been

Sample Answer

Ⓐ Ⓑ ● Ⓓ

The sentence should read, "There have been periods in history when remarkable progress was made within a relatively short span of time." Therefore, you should choose answer (C).

After you read the directions, begin work on the questions.

GO ON TO THE NEXT PAGE

1. The focusing properties of an optical lens depend on the fact ------- the velocity of light is smaller in glass than in air.

   (A) if
   (B) that
   (C) when
   (D) and

2. Most of the early federal labor laws dealt only with railroads and their employees ------- extending into other industries.

   (A) without
   (B) except
   (C) no
   (D) nor

3. The nature of agricultural production on the prairies is distinct from ------- of the rest of Canada.

   (A) what is
   (B) those
   (C) that
   (D) it is

4. ------- Robert Fulton invented the steamship and improved the submarine, his main achievement lay in making steamboats profitable.

   (A) Although
   (B) However
   (C) If
   (D) That

5. The Cherokee Indians were divided ------- seven clans with members in every village.

   (A) at
   (B) of
   (C) into
   (D) in

6. The importance of the laser lies in the great variety of uses it now has, and the still greater number ------- in the future.

   (A) expects
   (B) expecting
   (C) expect
   (D) expected

7. ------- a short time after the Civil War, Atlanta has become the principal center of transportation and commerce and finance in the southeastern United States.

   (A) While rebuilt
   (B) Rebuilt
   (C) It was rebuilt
   (D) When rebuilt

8. The upper and lower surfaces of the segments of a centipede's body ------- by a flexible membrane.

   (A) joining
   (B) joined
   (C) to join
   (D) are joined

GO ON TO THE NEXT PAGE

A Practice TOEFL

9. By far the most famous member of the Harlem Renaissance movement of the 1920s ------- Langston Hughes.

   (A) has been
   (B) was
   (C) was being
   (D) had been

10. ------- Canada has never developed a national press is most likely due to regional differences of outlook and interests.

    (A) Because of
    (B) Although
    (C) It is
    (D) That

11. Throughout the United States, insurance laws follow a general pattern ------- provisions can vary from state to state.

    (A) whether
    (B) wherever
    (C) although
    (D) unless

12. Edgar Allan Poe is certainly one of the ------- American writers.

    (A) read most widely
    (B) read widely most
    (C) most widely read
    (D) most read widely

13. By 1945, electronic equipment had become so complex ------- often too large to be convenient or too heavy to be portable.

    (A) which it was
    (B) that was
    (C) which was
    (D) that it was

14. Antibiotics are chemical substances which are able to inhibit growth of and even ------- bacteria and other microorganisms.

    (A) destroyed
    (B) destroying
    (C) to destroy
    (D) they destroy

15. Most amateur cameras make use of the rotary shutter, ------- has the form of a half circle.

    (A) which
    (B) that
    (C) who
    (D) what

GO ON TO THE NEXT PAGE

2 · 2 · 2 · 2 · 2 · 2 · 2

Directions: In questions 16-40 each sentence has four underlined words or phrases. The four underlined parts of the sentence are marked (A), (B), (C), and (D). Identify the <u>one</u> underlined word or phrase that must be changed in order for the sentence to be correct. Then, on your answer sheet, find the number of the question and fill in the space that corresponds to the letter of the answer you have chosen.

Example I

A ray of light passing <u>through</u> <u>the center</u> of a
                            A   B
thin lens <u>keep</u> its <u>original</u> direction.
         C   D

Sample Answer
Ⓐ Ⓑ Ⓒ ●

The sentence should read, "A ray of light passing through the center of a thin lens keeps its original direction." Therefore, you should choose answer (C).

Example II

The mandolin, a musical <u>instrument</u> <u>that has</u>
                           A   B
strings, was probably copied <u>from</u> the lute, a
                          C
<u>many</u> older instrument.
 D

Sample Answer
Ⓐ Ⓑ Ⓒ ●

The sentence should read, "The mandolin, a musical instrument that has strings, was probably copied from the lute, a much older instrument." Therefore, you should choose answer (D).

After you read the directions, begin work on the questions.

16. <u>With</u> his clear blue eyes and small <u>softly</u> hands, Jesse James
    A   B
impressed people <u>as</u> a <u>kind person</u>.
                  C   D

17. A balance <u>between</u> cheap production and <u>high</u> quality <u>have</u> been a
              A   B   C
<u>major concern</u> in the field of crafts.
     D

GO ON TO THE NEXT PAGE ➤

18. Toronto, the capital <u>of</u> Ontario, <u>has become</u> Canada's commercial
                        A   B
    and <u>manufacturing center</u> and one of the country's <u>modernest</u> cities.
              C   D

19. A <u>complex</u> division of labor <u>has contributed</u> most to increase
        A   B
    production, promote general welfare, and <u>raising</u> the standard of
                                                C
    living in <u>industrial</u> countries.
                 D

20. Hummingbirds are found <u>most often frequently</u> in <u>warm, humid</u>
                                    A   B
    regions <u>where</u> flowers and small insects <u>abound</u>.
              C   D

21. The Santa Fe Opera House is a modern, <u>partly roofed</u>, open-air
                                               A
    theatre <u>build</u> into a <u>mountainside</u> five miles north <u>of</u> the city.
              B   C   D

22. Wheat <u>accounts</u> for almost sixty <u>percent</u> of the <u>totally</u> world grain
              A   B   C
    <u>exports</u>.
       D

23. A whale <u>it</u> bears a superficial resemblance <u>to</u> a fish in external form
              A   B
    and <u>is</u> streamlined <u>for</u> aquatic life.
           C   D

24. <u>Is</u> Katherine Hepburn, <u>with</u> her four Academy Awards, won <u>more</u>
      A   B   C
    than <u>any</u> other actress?
            D

25. The behavior of <u>any</u> gas <u>may be described</u> in <u>terms</u> of <u>their</u> pressure,
                       A   B   C   D
    volume and temperature.

26. The first British settlement in New England was <u>founded</u> in 1607
                                                         A
    <u>from</u> the <u>mouth</u> of the Kennebec River in <u>what is</u> now the state of
       B   C   D
    Maine.

27. Over the past hundred years, scientists have gradually unraveled
    A   B   C
    many of the mystery of genetic inheritance.
                D

28. About ten percent of the Earth's land area, or nearly 5.8 millions
                             A   B   C
    square miles, is covered by glacial ice.
                  D

29. Martin Luther King distinguished himself as an American
                       A   B   C
    clergyman or nonviolent civil rights leader.
              D

30. By its presence, a catalyst affects the speed of a chemical reaction
       A
    but do not appear in the product resulting from the chemical
        B   C   D
    change.

31. Thanksgiving, which began as a daily of religious celebration of the
                  A   B
    harvest among the Pilgrims in Plymouth, is now a secular
            C   D
    observance.

32. While a infinite number of systems of measurement is conceivable,
          A   B
    only a few are in widespread use.
    C   D

33. Honeysuckle vines have been cultivated and grown extensively for
                       A   B   C
    their tubular or bell-shaped flowers.
                     D

34. A relatively completion record of veterinary practice has been
                 A   B
    pieced together from ancient historical records.
           C   D

35. Euclidean geometry is a branch of mathematics designed to
                          A B   C
    represent and studying space.
                 D

36. Many <u>early black</u> <u>musicals</u> learned to play band instruments <u>from</u>
              A   B   C
Claiborne Williams, who went from town to town <u>in response</u> to the
                                                                            D
pleadings of young adults.

37. The Department of Agriculture <u>inspects</u> meat, poultry, and other
                                           A
food products and sets <u>standards of</u> quality <u>from</u> every major
                                 B   C
<u>agricultural</u> commodity.
     D

38. <u>The</u> great majority of <u>action</u> volcanoes <u>are</u> located in just two great
   A   B   C
<u>zones</u>.
 D

39. Sight hounds <u>use</u> their vision <u>to hunt</u>, and their supple <u>narrowly</u>
                 A   B   C
bodies are built <u>for speed</u>.
               D

40. Arbitration is distinguished <u>from</u> mediation as a form of <u>settlement</u>
                                 A   B
disputes <u>since</u> arbitrators have the authority to make
          C
<u>binding decisions</u>.
     D

THIS IS THE END OF SECTION 2

IF YOU FINISH BEFORE TIME IS CALLED, CHECK YOUR WORK ON SECTION 2 ONLY.
DO NOT READ OR WORK ON ANY OTHER SECTION OF THE TEST.
THE SUPERVISOR WILL TELL YOU WHEN TO BEGIN WORK ON SECTION 3.

3 · 3 · 3 · 3 · 3 · 3 · 3

SECTION 3
VOCABULARY AND READING COMPREHENSION

Time—45 minutes

This section is designed to measure your comprehension of standard written English. There are two types of questions in this section, with special directions for each type.

Directions: In questions 1-30 each sentence has an underlined word or phrase. Below each sentence are four other words or phrases, marked (A), (B), (C), and (D). You are to choose the one word or phrase that best keeps the meaning of the original sentence if it is substituted for the underlined word or phrase. Then, on your answer sheet, find the number of the question and fill in the space that corresponds to the letter you have chosen. Fill in the space so that the letter inside the oval cannot be seen.

Example

Passenger ships and aircraft are often equipped with ship-to-shore or air-to-land radio telephones.

(A) highways
(B) railroads
(C) planes
(D) sailboats

Sample Answer

Ⓐ Ⓑ ● Ⓓ

The best answer is (C) because "Passenger ships and planes are often equipped with ship-to-shore or air-to-land radio telephones" is closest in meaning to the original sentence. Therefore, you should choose answer (C).

After you read the directions, begin work on the questions.

GO ON TO THE NEXT PAGE ➤

A Practice TOEFL

1. New York City's numerous skyscrapers give the city its special character.
   (A) large
   (B) pretty
   (C) many
   (D) tall

2. A coat of paint will develop small cracks as it shrinks over time.
   (A) fades
   (B) contracts
   (C) peels
   (D) hardens

3. Rhythm, although associated most often with music, is a component of poetry as well.
   (A) an element
   (B) an attraction
   (C) a virtue
   (D) a material

4. The brittle bones of an elderly person may fracture easily.
   (A) dense
   (B) infirm
   (C) fragile
   (D) slender

5. The entomologist scours the world for new types of insects.
   (A) torments
   (B) scorns
   (C) searches
   (D) resists

6. Cream is the principal by-product of milk.
   (A) best
   (B) last
   (C) only
   (D) main

7. A type of barrier sometimes used by farmers to control predators is a wide furrow plowed around a field.
   (A) floods
   (B) weeds
   (C) pests
   (D) crops

8. Toxic fumes can trigger severe headaches.
   (A) soften
   (B) prevent
   (C) intensify
   (D) cause

9. The physical geography of Canada has a marked influence on its climate.
   (A) finite
   (B) pronounced
   (C) stable
   (D) curious

GO ON TO THE NEXT PAGE

10. The size of one's native language vocabulary reflects one's education, reading and <u>range</u> of interests.

    (A) lack
    (B) pursuit
    (C) extent
    (D) level

11. A camera takes light rays <u>bounced off</u> subjects and focuses them on a sheet of film.

    (A) incorporated by
    (B) defined by
    (C) reflected by
    (D) disguised by

12. The hummingbird is <u>noted</u> for its incredibly small size.

    (A) well-known
    (B) envied
    (C) appreciated
    (D) remarkable

13. Clara Barton will long be remembered for her role in <u>founding</u> the American Red Cross.

    (A) promoting
    (B) assisting
    (C) establishing
    (D) financing

14. The high prairie grass has almost disappeared in Iowa, except for a few <u>patches</u> in state grass preserves.

    (A) orchards
    (B) plots
    (C) blades
    (D) species

15. The Adams House has stood on an impressive <u>thoroughfare</u> on Capitol Hill since the 1890's.

    (A) plot
    (B) foundation
    (C) avenue
    (D) slope

16. Walrus ivory, which the Eskimos used for weapons and carvings, is now very scarce due to the <u>slaughter</u> of the animals.

    (A) migration
    (B) destruction
    (C) dispersal
    (D) inbreeding

17. After the success of her verse, Dorothy Parker became <u>a freelance</u> writer.

    (A) a wealthy
    (B) an academic
    (C) a popular
    (D) an independent

18. The resistance of the human lungs to disease is <u>surprisingly</u> high.

    (A) unmistakably
    (B) undoubtedly
    (C) amazingly
    (D) mysteriously

GO ON TO THE NEXT PAGE

19. Do many people wonder about the relationship of reading speed and reading comprehension?

    (A) speculate on
    (B) recognize
    (C) acknowledge
    (D) lecture

20. Much of the state of Nevada has an arid climate.

    (A) a dry
    (B) a cool
    (C) a healthy
    (D) a changeable

21. When minerals are extracted from land surface mines, grasses and trees must be removed causing erosion of the bare earth.

    (A) exposed
    (B) disturbed
    (C) frail
    (D) destroyed

22. To near-sighted people, faraway things look blurry without glasses.

    (A) unfamiliar
    (B) rigid
    (C) indistinct
    (D) colorless

23. The bridal processions of the wealthy are typically luxurious.

    (A) wedding
    (B) holiday
    (C) extravagant
    (D) casual

24. In the north of Kansas are located the Smoky Hills Uplands, whose eastern slopes contain Dakota sandstone.

    (A) summits
    (B) inclines
    (C) canyons
    (D) plains

25. The eyes of an octopus stick out on stalks so that it can see in all directions.

    (A) develop
    (B) occur
    (C) depend
    (D) protrude

26. The Gulf Stream is a current of warm water flowing in a north-easterly direction on the western margin of the North Atlantic Ocean.

    (A) half
    (B) corner
    (C) area
    (D) edge

GO ON TO THE NEXT PAGE

27. The Amish have long been renowned for making ordinary soil magically productive.

    (A) famous
    (B) distrusted
    (C) envied
    (D) responsible

28. The earliest grave markers of New England were the work of itinerant carvers.

    (A) ministers
    (B) sculptors
    (C) architects
    (D) merchants

29. The National Park system sets aside areas of natural beauty for preservation and public enjoyment.

    (A) recreation
    (B) cultivation
    (C) restoration
    (D) conservation

30. Probably no commodity on Earth is as much in demand, although essentially useless, as a precious gem.

    (A) unavoidably
    (B) extremely
    (C) uniquely
    (D) basically

3 • 3 • 3 • 3 • 3 • 3 • 3

Directions: In the rest of this section you will read several passages. Each one is followed by several questions about it. For questions 31-60, you are to choose the one best answer, (A), (B), (C), or (D), to each question. Then, on your answer sheet, find the number of the question and fill in the space that corresponds to the letter of the answer you have chosen.

Answer all questions following a passage on the basis of what is stated or implied in that passage.

Read the following passage:

The rattles with which a rattlesnake warns of its presence are formed by loosely interlocking hollow rings of hard skin, which make a buzzing sound when its tail is shaken. As a baby, the snake begins to form its rattles from the button at the very tip of its tail. Thereafter, each time it sheds its skin, a new ring is formed. Popular belief holds that a snake's age can be told by counting the rings, but this idea is fallacious. In fact, a snake may lose its old skin as often as four times a year. Also, rattles tend to wear or break off with time.

Example I

A rattlesnake's rattles are made of

(A) skin
(B) bone
(C) wood
(D) muscle

Sample Answer
● Ⓑ Ⓒ Ⓓ

According to the passage, a rattlesnake's rattles are made out of rings of hard skin. Therefore, you should choose answer (A).

Example II

How often does a rattlesnake shed its skin?

(A) Once every four years
(B) Once every four months
(C) Up to four times every year
(D) Four times more often than other snakes

Sample Answer
Ⓐ Ⓑ ● Ⓓ

The passage states that "a snake may lose its old skin as often as four times a year." Therefore, you should choose answer (C).

After you read the directions, begin work on the questions.

GO ON TO THE NEXT PAGE ➤

Questions 31-36

In the great cosmic dark there are countless stars and planets both younger and older than our solar system. Although we cannot yet be certain, the same processes that led on Earth to evolution of life and intelligence should have been operating throughout the Cosmos. There may be a million worlds in the Milky Way Galaxy alone that at this moment are inhabited by beings who are very different from us, and far more advanced. Knowing a great deal is not the same as being smart; intelligence is not information alone but also judgment, the manner in which information is coordinated and used. Still, the amount of information to which we have access is one index of our intelligence. The measuring rod, the unit of information, is something called a bit (for binary digit). It is an answer—either yes or no—to an unambiguous question. To specify whether a lamp is on or off requires a single bit of information. To designate one letter out of the twenty-six in the Latin alphabet takes five bits ($2^5 = 2 \times 2 \times 2 \times 2 \times 2 = 32$, which is more than 26).

The total number of bits that characterizes an hour-long television program is about 10^{12}. The information in all the libraries on the Earth is something like 10^{17} bits. This number demonstrates that all of the books in the world would contain no more information than is broadcast on television in a single large American city in a single year.

Such a number represents crudely what humans know. But elsewhere, in older worlds, where life evolved billions of years earlier than on Earth, perhaps 10^{30} is known—not just more information but significantly different information.

31. What is the best title for this passage?

   (A) The Evolution of Knowledge
   (B) Worlds of the Milky Way Galaxy
   (C) An Index of Intelligence
   (D) A Definition of Human Knowledge

32. According to the passage, which is the number of bits that corresponds to what humans know?

   (A) 2^5
   (B) 10^{12}
   (C) 10^{17}
   (D) 10^{30}

33. The paragraph following the passage most probably discusses
    (A) human exploration of Mars
    (B) how knowledge in outer space is coordinated
    (C) the evolution of intelligence on other worlds
    (D) the dramatic influence of T.V. on society

34. The author characterizes a bit as
    (A) an hour-long TV program
    (B) use of judgment
    (C) a process of understanding
    (D) an answer to a question

35. Which of the following is NOT mentioned as a characteristic of human intelligence?
    (A) Knowledge of information
    (B) Coordination of knowledge
    (C) Capacity to think quickly
    (D) Application of knowledge

36. The author implies that the likelihood that life can be found on other planets is
    (A) remote
    (B) high
    (C) non-existent
    (D) certain

GO ON TO THE NEXT PAGE

Questions 37-42

Successful innovations have driven many older technologies to extinction and have resulted in higher productivity, greater consumption of energy, increased demand for raw materials, accelerated flow of materials through the economy and increased quantities of metals and other substances in use per capita. The history of industrial development abounds with examples.

In 1870, horses and mules were the prime source of power on U.S. farms. One horse or mule was required to support four human beings—a ratio that remained almost constant for many decades. At that time, had a national commission been asked to forecast the horse and mule population for 1970, its answer probably would have depended on whether its consultants were of an economic or technological turn of mind. Had they been "economists," they would probably have projected the 1970 horse and mule population to be more than 50 million. Had they been "technologists," they would have recognized that the power of steam had already been harnessed to industry and to land and ocean transport. They would have recognized further that it would be only a matter of time before steam would be the prime source of power on the farm. It would have been difficult for them to avoid the conclusion that the horse and mule population would decline rapidly.

37. According to the passage, what supplied most of the power on U.S. farms in 1870?

    (A) Animals
    (B) Humans
    (C) Engines
    (D) Water

38. Which of the following is NOT mentioned by the author as a consequence of new technological developments?

    (A) Older technologies die away.
    (B) The quality of life is improved.
    (C) Overall productivity increases.
    (D) More raw materials become necessary.

39. It can be inferred from the passage that by 1870

    (A) technology began to be more economical
    (B) the steam engine had been invented
    (C) the U.S. horse population was about 10 million
    (D) a national commission on agriculture had been established

40. With which of the following statements would the author of the passage be most likely to agree?

    (A) Technological developments influence society's future.
    (B) Technicians are more useful to society than economists.
    (C) The economy is independent of technological transformation.
    (D) Technological innovations are almost always successful.

41. In the second paragraph, the author suggests that "economists" would

    (A) plan the economy through yearly forecasts
    (B) fail to consider the influence of technological innovation
    (C) value the economic contribution of farm animals
    (D) consult for the national commission on the economy

42. What is the author's attitude toward changes brought on by technological innovation?

    (A) He is excited about them.
    (B) He accepts them as natural.
    (C) He is disturbed by them.
    (D) He questions their usefulness.

GO ON TO THE NEXT PAGE

Questions 43-48

 Before the Nobel Prize in literature was awarded to John Steinbeck in 1962, only five Americans had been previously thus honored, the most recent being Ernest Hemingway in 1954 and William Faulkner in 1949. Steinbeck had been considered on those occasions and also in 1945. As the honor is by far the greatest any writer can receive, Steinbeck was elated. The feeling of elation was tempered slightly, however, by the observation expressed by Steinbeck in 1956, that recipients of the Nobel Prize seldom write anything of value afterwards. He cited Hemingway and Faulkner as examples, minimizing the point that by the time of their selection most writers had already written their best work. At the age of sixty, when he received the award himself, Steinbeck wrote to a friend that he would not have accepted the award had he not believed that he would continue to write well, that he "could beat the rap." Like his contemporaries, and others as well, however, he did not.
 There was no expectation or need that the writer do so, for Steinbeck had long since made his mark in modern American literature.

43. According to the passage, Steinbeck observed that authors who receive the Nobel Prize for literature

 (A) had already finished writing popular works
 (B) should follow the examples of Hemingway and Faulkner
 (C) rarely write significant works afterwards
 (D) are among the greatest contemporary writers

44. In what year was Steinbeck sixty years old?

 (A) 1949
 (B) 1954
 (C) 1956
 (D) 1962

45. According to the passage, Steinbeck wrote his best work

 (A) in an expressive style
 (B) before receiving the Nobel Prize
 (C) while he was feeling elated
 (D) guided by his contemporaries

46. Before 1949, how many Americans had received the Nobel prize for literature?

    (A) Two
    (B) Three
    (C) Four
    (D) Five

47. In the second paragraph, the phrase "do so" refers to

    (A) feel elated at receiving the Nobel Prize
    (B) accept the Nobel Prize if nominated
    (C) write well after receiving the Nobel Prize earlier
    (D) honor Nobel Prize winners of the past

48. What is the author's attitude toward John Steinbeck?

    (A) Steinbeck was an exceptionally different author.
    (B) Steinbeck should have received the Nobel Prize earlier.
    (C) Steinbeck wrote equally well throughout his life.
    (D) Steinbeck earned his reputation well before 1962.

Questions 49-54

The University Health Service is an outpatient facility which provides primary health care to the university community. The Health Service personnel includes a family practice physician, two nurse practitioners and a medical secretary. The nurse practitioners have responsibility to provide the health care to the students, and to obtain physician consultation as needed. Services include chronic, acute, and routine medical care, laboratory tests, allergy injections, physical examinations, and counseling and health education. Referrals are made to nearby specialists when necessary. For examination purposes, blood is drawn on premises and sent to a local lab. Laboratory tests such as urinalysis and microscopic examinations may be done on premises at no charge. Referrals are made to a nearby facility for x-rays. Medicines are not dispensed at the University Health Service; however, samples are given as available. Prescriptions can be filled at one of the local pharmacies.

49. Which of the following is not performed at the facilities of the University Health Service?

(A) counseling
(B) x-rays
(C) allergy shots
(D) urinalysis

50. What is the main purpose of the passage?

(A) To describe on-campus medical care
(B) To report the most common health complaints
(C) To describe the qualifications of the staff
(D) To outline routine insurance policies

51. The paragraph immediately following the passage probably discusses
    (A) courses in health education
    (B) how to call an ambulance
    (C) the business hours of the Health Service
    (D) why the Health Service is useful

52. Which of the following best describes the tone of the passage?
    (A) Alarmed
    (B) Superior
    (C) Liberal
    (D) Objective

53. Most of the primary health care is provided by
    (A) a doctor
    (B) nurses
    (C) a medical secretary
    (D) lab technicians

54. In the sixth sentence, "Blood is drawn" means that
    (A) blood data is recorded
    (B) blood is evaluated
    (C) blood test results are confidential
    (D) blood is taken from the body

GO ON TO THE NEXT PAGE

Questions 55-60

Artists use caricature to distort the human face or figure for comic effect, while at the same time capturing an identifiable likeness and suggesting the essence of personality or character beneath the surface. The humor lies in the fact that the caricature is recognizable, and yet exaggerated.

From its origins in Europe as witty sketches, caricature grew through the eighteenth and nineteenth centuries, becoming enormously popular in the United States early in this century. In the 1920s and 1930s especially, this lively form of illustration appeared in newspapers and magazines throughout the country. The caricaturists in this era drew their portraits of important figures primarily to entertain. In spirit their work was closer to the humor of the fast-developing comic strip and gag cartoon than to the sting of political satire. Their subjects were more often amused than offended by their amiable attacks.

55. Which of the following words does NOT describe a typical caricature?

(A) Humorous
(B) Distorted
(C) Topical
(D) Solemn

56. The caricatures discussed in the passage are

(A) photographs
(B) drawings
(C) etchings
(D) paintings

57. Producing a caricature is most like which of the following?

(A) Singing a song
(B) Making a speech
(C) Reciting a poem
(D) Telling a joke

58. According to the passage, the people who were caricatured were often

(A) angered
(B) puzzled
(C) entertained
(D) shocked

GO ON TO THE NEXT PAGE

59. Which of the following does the passage tell us?

   (A) Caricature was popular in early twentieth century America.
   (B) Caricature is common in times of stress.
   (C) Caricature evolved into a serious mode of self expression.
   (D) Caricature is one of the few art forms that originated in America.

60. The paragraph immediately following the passage probably discusses

   (A) the early history of American comedy films
   (B) popular jokes of the twentieth century
   (C) the change in American caricature in the 1940s
   (D) how to develop skills as a caricaturist

THIS IS THE END OF SECTION 3

IF YOU FINISH BEFORE TIME IS CALLED, CHECK YOUR WORK ON SECTION 3 ONLY.
DO NOT READ OR WORK ON ANY OTHER SECTION OF THE TEST.

Print your
full name here _____
(last)　　　　　　　(first)　　　　　　(middle)

A PRACTICE TOEFL

FORM 2

General Directions

This is a test of your ability to use the English language. It is divided into three sections, some of which have more than one part. Each section or part of the test begins with a set of specific directions that include sample questions. Be sure you understand what you are to do before you begin to work on a section.

The supervisor will tell you when to start each section and when to go on to the next section. You should work quickly but carefully. Do not spend too much time on any one question. If you finish a section early, you may review your answers on that section only. You may not go on to the next section and you may not go back to a section you have already worked on.

You will find that some of the questions are more difficult than others, but you should try to answer every one. Your score will be based on the number of questions you answer correctly—that is, the number for which you choose the best answer from among the choices given. If you are not sure of the answer to a question, make the best guess that you can. It is to your advantage to answer every question, even if you have to guess the answer.

Do not mark your answers in this test book. You must mark all of your answers on the separate answer sheet that is inside this test book. When you mark your answer to a question on your answer sheet, you must:

- Use a medium-soft (#2 or HB) black lead pencil.
- Be careful to mark the space that corresponds to the answer you choose for each question. Also, make sure you mark your answer in the row with the same number as the number of the question you are answering. You will not be permitted to make any corrections after time is called.
- Mark only one answer to each question.
- Carefully and completely fill each intended oval with a dark mark so that you cannot see the letter inside the oval; light or partial marks may not be read properly by the scoring machine.
- Erase all extra marks completely and thoroughly. If you change your mind about an answer after you have marked it on your answer sheet, completely erase your old answer and then mark your new answer.

The examples below show you the correct and wrong ways of marking an answer sheet. Be sure to fill in the ovals on your answer sheet the correct way.

CORRECT	WRONG	WRONG	WRONG	WRONG
Ⓐ Ⓑ ● Ⓓ	Ⓐ Ⓑ ✓ Ⓓ	Ⓐ Ⓑ ✗ Ⓓ	Ⓐ Ⓑ Ⓒ Ⓓ	Ⓐ Ⓑ Ⓒ Ⓓ

Some or all of the passages for this test have been adapted from published material to provide the examinee with significant problems for analysis and evaluation. To make the passages suitable for testing purposes, the style, content, or point of view of the original may have been altered in some cases.

Note: On an actual TOEFL examination, the general directions page appears on the last page of the test booklet. These directions are included here for your convenience. This test is to be used with the listening comprehension test tape found in the *Newbury House TOEFL Preparation Kit* and the multiple-choice answer sheets found at the end of this book.

1 • 1 • 1 • 1 • 1 • 1 • 1

SECTION 1
LISTENING COMPREHENSION

In this section of the test, you will have an opportunity to demonstrate your ability to understand spoken English. There are three parts to this section, with special directions for each part.

Part A

<u>Directions</u>: For each question in Part A, you will hear a short sentence. Each sentence will be spoken just one time. The sentences you hear will not be written out for you. Therefore, you must listen carefully to understand what the speaker says.

After you hear a sentence, read the four choices in your test book, marked (A), (B), (C), and (D), and decide which <u>one</u> is closest in meaning to the sentence you heard. Then, on your sheet, find the number of the question and fill in the space that corresponds to the letter of the answer you have chosen. Fill in the space so that the letter inside the oval cannot be seen.

Example I

You will hear:

You will read: (A) Mary outswam the others.
(B) Mary ought to swim with them.
(C) Mary and her friends swam to the island.
(D) Mary's friends owned the island.

<u>Sample Answer</u>
Ⓐ Ⓑ ● Ⓓ

The speaker said, "Mary swam out to the island with her friends." Sentence (C), "Mary and her friends swam to the island," is closest in meaning to the sentence you heard. Therefore, you should choose answer (C).

GO ON TO THE NEXT PAGE ➔

1 • 1 • 1 • 1 • 1 • 1 • 1

Example II

You will hear:

You will read:
(A) Please remind me to read this book.
(B) Could you help me carry these books?
(C) I don't mind if you help me.
(D) Do you have a heavy course load this term?

Sample Answer
Ⓐ ● Ⓒ Ⓓ

The speaker said, "Would you mind helping me with this load of books?" Sentence (B), "Could you help me carry these books?" is closest in meaning to the sentence you heard. Therefore, you should choose answer (B).

1. (A) While driving in snow, one cannot pass.
   (B) Traffic here is slow all the time.
   (C) It's well known that cars break down here.
   (D) Driving in snow here is very difficult.

2. (A) We're using four colors to paint the living room.
   (B) We left the painting on the wall.
   (C) The living room has walls of beautifully painted wood.
   (D) The colors in the painting aren't right for the living room.

3. (A) Greg goes to school, but he doesn't work full time.
   (B) Greg doesn't go to school, but he does have a job.
   (C) Greg walks to school, but not to work.
   (D) Greg works full time and he goes to school.

4. (A) If you'll phone when you're in town, we can meet.
   (B) When you leave town, I'll go with you.
   (C) Call me if you forget my address.
   (D) We can get a gift together downtown.

GO ON TO THE NEXT PAGE

1 • 1 • 1 • 1 • 1 • 1 • 1

5. (A) It's never hot in the suburbs.
   (B) The city gets cold before the suburbs do.
   (C) Compared to the suburbs, city temperatures are higher.
   (D) Suburban schools are open year-round, unlike city schools.

6. (A) Joanna left home without an umbrella.
   (B) Joanna didn't hear the rain.
   (C) Joanna's umbrella didn't work.
   (D) Joanna had the day off due to the weather.

7. (A) People prefer traditional buildings.
   (B) Old styles of architecture are cold.
   (C) The modern style is better than the old.
   (D) Modern buildings are poorly heated.

8. (A) More than fifty persons is too large for one class.
   (B) Miss Moore has failed half of the class.
   (C) People who fail must make up 50% of the classwork.
   (D) Those who are absent more than half the time should fail.

9. (A) I laughed when I locked my book in the library.
   (B) The bookstore is closed, so I can't get a book.
   (C) I don't have my library book with me.
   (D) The school library is closed.

10. (A) The church is around the corner.
    (B) The church is at the next corner.
    (C) The church has a cross on it.
    (D) The church is three blocks away.

11. (A) How much is the fee for this class?
    (B) What do you think of this class?
    (C) How can you understand this class?
    (D) Do you think the room is comfortable?

12. (A) There are a lot of parking spaces for students here.
    (B) Students like to reserve a space before they apply.
    (C) If a student parks illegally, he must pay a fine of $15.
    (D) A student must fill out a form and pay a fee for a parking space.

GO ON TO THE NEXT PAGE ➤

A Practice TOEFL

13. (A) Jack will go to the theater next door.
    (B) Jack arrived too late for the beginning of the movie.
    (C) Jack saw seven people waiting beside the theater.
    (D) Jack arrived at seven o'clock.

14. (A) The figures on these tax forms are difficult to see.
    (B) My income tax figures never come out right.
    (C) I don't know how people can understand these forms.
    (D) I can't look at anyone else's figures.

15. (A) You should write down your daily activities in a journal.
    (B) It's a good idea to read the paper every day.
    (C) You should keep a record of the music you've heard.
    (D) After your trip, you should record what you see.

16. (A) Latin isn't a required course.
    (B) She never married the Latin student.
    (C) Mary is taking a Latin course.
    (D) They will never require Latin.

17. (A) I'm sorry, but there's only one chair here.
    (B) Is this seat taken?
    (C) May I put one seat in here?
    (D) I'm terribly sorry, but someone is sitting here.

18. (A) You can use your own cassette to listen to tapes on Fridays.
    (B) The lab is usually open late, except on Fridays.
    (C) The usual time to record lessons is on Friday.
    (D) You can use the language lab late every Friday.

19. (A) The outline of the course made it sound difficult.
    (B) Everyone watched as the teacher drew on the board.
    (C) It was hard to pay attention to the teacher.
    (D) Few people listened to the teacher's outline of the course.

20. (A) Dick might have mailed a letter without a stamp.
    (B) The stamp Dick put on the letter was pretty.
    (C) Dick received a letter today with no stamp on it.
    (D) Dick wrote a letter today, but I forgot to mail it.

Part B

Directions: In Part B you will hear short conversations between two speakers. At the end of each conversation, a third person will ask a question about what was said. You will hear each conversation and question about it just one time. Therefore, you must listen carefully to understand what each speaker says. After you hear a conversation and question about it, read the four possible answers in your test book and decide which one is the best answer to the question you heard. Then, on your answer sheet, find the number of the question and fill in the space that corresponds to the letter of the answer you have chosen.

Look at the following example.

Sample Answer
● Ⓑ Ⓒ Ⓓ

You will hear:

You will read: (A) Present Professor Smith with a picture.
(B) Photograph Professor Smith.
(C) Put glass over the photograph.
(D) Replace the broken headlight.

From the conversation you learn that the woman thinks Professor Smith would like a photograph of the class. The best answer to the question "What does the woman think the class should do?" is (A), "Present Professor Smith with a picture." Therefore, you should choose answer (A).

GO ON TO THE NEXT PAGE

1 • 1 • 1 • 1 • 1 • 1 • 1

21. (A) Writing a letter.
    (B) Filling out a form.
    (C) Answering an invitation.
    (D) Cashing a check.

22. (A) He's going to the fourth floor.
    (B) He gets off at two o'clock.
    (C) He's going to Room 44.
    (D) He gets off the train.

23. (A) A grade list.
    (B) The notes.
    (C) A news report.
    (D) An announcement.

24. (A) Every Thursday.
    (B) Every two evenings.
    (C) Twice a week.
    (D) Once a week.

25. (A) Keep busy.
    (B) Talk to Marie.
    (C) Remember to call.
    (D) Touch Marie.

26. (A) In a clothing store.
    (B) On a bus.
    (C) In a car.
    (D) At a travel agency.

27. (A) Leave in two minutes.
    (B) Get off the bus.
    (C) Wait for two students.
    (D) Wait for the second bus.

28. (A) I'll see you later.
    (B) I'll be up soon.
    (C) You can leave it with me.
    (D) You can decide that.

29. (A) Going to a movie.
    (B) Writing a schedule.
    (C) Getting change for $25.
    (D) Parking a car.

30. (A) The back yard.
    (B) A map.
    (C) Stolen property.
    (D) A photograph.

31. (A) He might not make the bus.
    (B) She can see the bus stop.
    (C) He lost his watch on the bus.
    (D) She won't let him leave.

32. (A) She's already sent hers in.
    (B) Frank should send it in soon.
    (C) She's going to get one next week.
    (D) Frank can wait two weeks.

33. (A) Return from Montreal early.
    (B) Leave him in Montreal.
    (C) Go to Montreal without Alice.
    (D) Go back to Montreal later.

1 • 1 • 1 • 1 • 1 • 1 • 1

34. (A) A story in last week's newspaper.
    (B) A scientific writing method.
    (C) The way the teacher writes.
    (D) The difficulty of writing papers.

35. (A) She needs to join her friends.
    (B) She has no umbrella.
    (C) Her raincoat doesn't fit.
    (D) Her legs and arms hurt.

Part C

Directions: In this part of the test, you will hear short talks and conversations. After each of them, you will be asked some questions. You will hear the talks and conversations and the questions about them just one time. They will not be written out for you. Therefore, you must listen carefully to understand what each speaker says.

After you hear a question, read the four possible answers in your test book and decide which one is the best answer to the question you heard. Then, on your answer sheet, find the number of the question and fill in the space that corresponds to the letter of the answer you have chosen.

Answer all questions on the basis of what is stated or implied in the talk or conversation.

Listen to this sample talk.

You will hear:

Now look at the following example.   Sample Answer
                                                             Ⓐ ● Ⓒ Ⓓ
You will hear:

You will read: (A) They are impossible to guide.
               (B) They may go up in flames.
               (C) They tend to leak gas.
               (D) They are cheaply made.

The best answer to the question "Why are gas balloons considered dangerous?" is (B), "They may go up in flames." Therefore, you should choose answer (B).

GO ON TO THE NEXT PAGE ▶

A Practice TOEFL   201

1 • 1 • 1 • 1 • 1 • 1 • 1

Now look at this example.   Sample Answer
                              ● Ⓑ Ⓒ Ⓓ

You will hear:

You will read: (A) Watch for changes in the weather.
(B) Watch their altitude.
(C) Check for weak spots in their balloons.
(D) Test the strength of the ropes.

The best answer to the question "According to the speaker, what must balloon pilots be careful to do?" is (A) "Watch for changes in weather." Therefore, you should choose answer (A).

36. (A) In a studio.
    (B) In a gallery.
    (C) In an art supplies shop.
    (D) In a psychologist's clinic.

37. (A) On the floor.
    (B) On the wall.
    (C) In the gallery.
    (D) In an asylum.

38. (A) Logic.
    (B) Size.
    (C) Humor.
    (D) Honesty.

39. (A) Tedious.
    (B) Spontaneous.
    (C) Uninterested.
    (D) Painstaking.

40. (A) Realistic.
    (B) Disproportionate.
    (C) Abstract.
    (D) Unfinished.

41. (A) He hates modern art.
    (B) He wants to understand the art.
    (C) He doesn't trust psychologists.
    (D) He isn't interested in the explanations.

42. (A) The climate.
    (B) Time.
    (C) Light.
    (D) The soil.

43. (A) Its rings get thinner.
    (B) It adds a ring of wood.
    (C) Its value increases.
    (D) It becomes darker in color.

44. (A) They can build more quickly.
    (B) They can use it to measure buildings.
    (C) It provides a dating procedure.
    (D) It explains cultural evolution.

GO ON TO THE NEXT PAGE

1 • 1 • 1 • 1 • 1 • 1 • 1

45. (A) 2000 years ago.
    (B) In the eighteenth century.
    (C) In the early twentieth century.
    (D) Early in this decade.

46. (A) What jellyfish look like.
    (B) How jellyfish move.
    (C) What jellyfish eat.
    (D) Where jellyfish live.

47. (A) On a boat.
    (B) At an aquarium.
    (C) In school.
    (D) At the seashore.

48. (A) Like a bell.
    (B) Like a long stick.
    (C) Like a small locomotive.
    (D) Like a flattened ball.

49. (A) By dangling its tentacles.
    (B) By using tiny jets.
    (C) By waving its tail.
    (D) By expelling water.

50. (A) While contracting its bell.
    (B) When surrounded by fish.
    (C) When near the shore.
    (D) When sinking downward.

THIS IS THE END OF THE LISTENING COMPREHENSION SECTION OF THE TEST.

THE NEXT PART OF THE TEST IS SECTION 2. TURN TO THE DIRECTIONS FOR SECTION 2 IN YOUR TEST BOOK. READ THEM, AND BEGIN WORK.
DO NOT READ OR WORK ON ANY OTHER SECTION OF THE TEST.

STOP STOP STOP STOP STOP STOP STOP

A Practice TOEFL

2 • 2 • 2 • 2 • 2 • 2 • 2

SECTION 2
STRUCTURE AND WRITTEN EXPRESSION

Time—25 minutes

This section is designed to measure your ability to recognize language that is appropriate for standard written English. There are two types of questions in this section, with special directions for each type.

Directions: Questions 1-15 are incomplete sentences. Beneath each sentence you will see four words or phrases, marked (A), (B), (C), and (D). Choose the one word or phrase that best completes the sentence. Then, on your answer sheet, find the number of the question and fill in the space that corresponds to the letter of the answer you have chosen. Fill in the space so that the letter inside the oval cannot be seen.

Example I   Sample Answer
                                                     ● Ⓑ Ⓒ Ⓓ
Vegetables are an
excellent source -------
vitamins.

(A) of
(B) has
(C) where
(D) that

The sentence should read, "Vegetables are an excellent source of vitamins." Therefore, you should choose answer (A).

Example II   Sample Answer
                                                     Ⓐ Ⓑ ● Ⓓ
------- in history when
remarkable progress was
made within a relatively
short span of time.

(A) Periods
(B) Throughout periods
(C) There have been periods
(D) Periods have been

The sentence should read, "There have been periods in history when remarkable progress was made within a relatively short span of time." Therefore, you should choose answer (C).

After you read the directions, begin work on the questions.

GO ON TO THE NEXT PAGE ➤

2 • 2 • 2 • 2 • 2 • 2 • 2

1. Several glaciers have been under study ------- whether their size is declining, increasing or remaining about the same.

   (A) determined
   (B) is determined
   (C) to determine
   (D) determining

2. ------- its ability to use water from body tissues alone, the camel can afford to sweat.

   (A) Although
   (B) Because of
   (C) Even if
   (D) Since

3. At the peak of United States immigration, one million immigrants ------- at Ellis Island each year.

   (A) were processing
   (B) processed
   (C) were processed
   (D) which were processed

4. Not only ------- beautiful silver jewelry, but they also weave high-quality rugs of wool.

   (A) make the Navaho Indians
   (B) do the Navaho Indians make
   (C) the Navaho Indians are making
   (D) do make the Navaho Indians

5. Does the west coast of Canada have ------- than the east?

   (A) a milder a climate
   (B) a climate and milder
   (C) a climate is milder
   (D) a milder climate

6. A chessboard is placed between two players ------- each has a white square on the right side.

   (A) and that
   (B) as a result
   (C) so that
   (D) therefore

7. Virginia Dare was ------- of English descent to be born to the New World.

   (A) the person the first
   (B) the first of persons
   (C) first person
   (D) the first person

8. ------- eight known ways in which genes function.

   (A) There are at least
   (B) At least
   (C) At least the
   (D) For at least are

9. Besides his geodesic domes, Buckminster Fuller is known for his invention of the Dymaxion world map that ------- into a globe.

   (A) it can fold
   (B) is folding
   (C) can be folded
   (D) it is folded

GO ON TO THE NEXT PAGE

10. ------- amphibians have lungs, they breathe partly through their skins.

    (A) Because of
    (B) However
    (C) Despite
    (D) Although

11. Cape Canaveral offers the advantage of weather conditions ------- to take place all year long.

    (A) that operations allow
    (B) that allow operations
    (C) operations that allow
    (D) operations allow that

12. ------- the exception of a few parasitic ants, all ants are colony-making social insects.

    (A) In spite of
    (B) Although
    (C) But
    (D) With

13. The raw material for speech is the air ------- in and out of the sublaryngeal organs.

    (A) directs
    (B) directed
    (C) is directed
    (D) has directed

14. ------- on Lake Michigan, Chicago covers a large area of land.

    (A) It is situated
    (B) Situated
    (C) Situation
    (D) Its situation

15. The way ------- political campaigns are conducted varies widely from country to country.

    (A) in that
    (B) which for
    (C) in which
    (D) when

GO ON TO THE NEXT PAGE

Directions: In questions 16-40 each sentence has four underlined words or phrases. The four underlined parts of the sentence are marked (A), (B), (C), and (D). Identify the <u>one</u> underlined word or phrase that must be changed in order for the sentence to be correct. Then, on your answer sheet, find the number of the question and fill in the space that corresponds to the letter of the answer you have chosen.

Example I   Sample Answer
                                                                          Ⓐ Ⓑ ● Ⓓ
A ray of light passing <u>through</u> <u>the center</u> of a
                         A   B
thin lens <u>keep</u> its <u>original</u> direction.
           C   D

The sentence should read, "A ray of light passing through the center of a thin lens keeps its original direction." Therefore, you should choose answer (C).

Example II   Sample Answer
                                                                          Ⓐ Ⓑ Ⓒ ●
The mandolin, a musical <u>instrument</u> <u>that has</u>
                              A   B
strings, was probably copied <u>from</u> the lute, a
                                 C
<u>many</u> older instrument.
   D

The sentence should read, "The mandolin, a musical instrument that has strings, was probably copied from the lute, a much older instrument." Therefore, you should choose answer (D).

After you read the directions, begin work on the questions.

16. <u>Most</u> Canadians <u>live</u> <u>along</u> the boundary between Canada <u>or</u> the
       A   B   C   D
    United States.

17. The human brain <u>is protected</u> by the bones <u>of</u> the cranium
                         A   B
    somewhat <u>as a</u> walnut kernel is protected by <u>their shells</u>.
                C   D

18. How it is possible to discuss postwar American art without
        A   B
    making mention of David Smith's achievements in sculpture?
        C   D

19. When a gas, liquids, or a solid changes to another state, it is said
              A   B
    to undergo a change of form.
        C   D

20. By the middle of the last century, the greenhouse
        A
    had been transformed from a mere refuge from a hostile climate
           B
    into a controlled environment adapted to the diverse need of
                                                          C
    particular plants.
        D

21. Many of today's business institutions already exist in the ancient
                       A   B
    world, although obviously on a much smaller scale and in a much
                       C   D
    cruder form.

22. Pocahontas, the Virginia Indian princess, gave birth of a son,
                 A   B
    Thomas, in 1615, a year before she went to Europe.
                        C   D

23. The katydid, a long-horned grasshopper, make noise by rubbing the
                    A   B   C
    edges of the front wings together.
                          D

24. The impact of Eli Whitney's invention of the cotton gin it was felt
                                                            A
    in American agriculture as well as in the textile industry.
              B   C   D

25. It is predicted that the enjoyment of hobbies will to continue to
            A   B
    increase as the required working hours in industry decrease.
                        C   D

GO ON TO THE NEXT PAGE

26. Most Americans <u>best know</u> George Washington Carver for his
          A
    scientific research <u>on</u> the peanut, <u>from which</u> he derived over 300
                        B   C
    <u>differents</u> products.
        D

27. Imagination is always based <u>upon</u> <u>what</u> is <u>known</u> of the <u>reality</u>
                                 A   B   C   D
    world.

28. <u>Though</u> <u>born</u> in England, the comedian Bob Hope has lived <u>most</u> of
        A   B   C
    <u>the</u> life in the United States.
        D

29. Glacial <u>streams appear</u> green <u>rather than</u> blue <u>because suspended</u>
                    A   B   C
    calcium carbonate in <u>the water</u>.
                              D

30. The <u>gold</u> depository at Fort Knox, a military reservation <u>whose</u> not
            A   B
    far from Louisville, Kentucky, <u>houses</u> U.S. <u>government</u> gold
                                       C   D
    reserves.

31. Some U.S. investigators <u>predict that</u> significant alterations
                                  A
    <u>in climate</u> patterns <u>will come apparent</u> <u>by the turn</u> of the century.
          B   C   D

32. The practice of <u>refraining from</u> <u>work</u> on holidays <u>seem</u> to be <u>almost</u>
                           A   B   C   D
    universal.

33. <u>Next to</u> Maine, New Hampshire <u>is the</u> <u>most dense</u> wooded state <u>in</u>
          A   B   C   D
    the Union.

34. Edith Wharton <u>is known for</u> <u>the penetrating wit</u> she
                         A   B
    <u>displayed and showed</u> <u>in her writings</u>.
              C   D

35. The electronic analog computer was introduced less than fifty years,
                                                    A   B
    and has since become a fixture in the modern office.
            C   D

36. Santa Fe, New Mexico, derives much of its incomes from tourism
                                              A
    and the sale of Indian arts and crafts.
        B   C   D

37. Rembrandt Peale was a member of a large and long-lived dynasty of
                                   A   B
    painters in Philadelphia in the nineteen century.
               C   D

38. When the ice began to withdraw from the terminal moraine about
    A   B
    10,000 B.C., the tundra and fringing spruce woodlands followed it
                                                C
    of the north.
    D

39. Polar explorer Richard Byrd demonstrated when his air expeditions
                                              A   B
    in Antarctica that the airplane is an important tool in exploration.
                  C   D

40. Houston, Texas, is a city of more than 1200 churches that reveal a
                                 A   B
    rich mixture and blend of conventional and modern architecture.
         C   D

THIS IS THE END OF SECTION 2

IF YOU FINISH BEFORE TIME IS CALLED, CHECK YOUR WORK
ON SECTION 2 ONLY.
DO NOT READ OR WORK ON ANY OTHER SECTION OF THE
TEST. THE SUPERVISOR WILL TELL YOU WHEN TO BEGIN
WORK ON SECTION 3.

3 • 3 • 3 • 3 • 3 • 3 • 3

SECTION 3
VOCABULARY AND READING COMPREHENSION

Time—45 minutes

This section is designed to measure your comprehension of standard written English. There are two types of questions in this section, with special directions for each type.

<u>Directions:</u> In questions 1-30 each sentence has an underlined word or phrase. Below each sentence are four other words or phrases, marked (A), (B), (C), and (D). You are to choose the <u>one</u> word or phrase that <u>best keeps the meaning</u> of the original sentence if it is substituted for the underlined word or phrase. Then, on your answer sheet, find the number of the question and fill in the space that corresponds to the letter you have chosen. Fill in the space so that the letter inside the oval cannot be seen.

Example

Passenger ships and <u>aircraft</u> are often equipped with ship-to-shore or air-to-land radio telephones.

(A) highways
(B) railroads
(C) planes
(D) sailboats

Sample Answer
Ⓐ Ⓑ ● Ⓓ

The best answer is (C) because "Passenger ships and planes are often equipped with ship-to-shore or air-to-land radio telephones" is closest in meaning to the original sentence. Therefore, you should choose answer (C).

After you read the directions, begin work on the questions.

1. Of all the species of nightshade, the potato is the most <u>prominent</u>.

   (A) cultivated
   (B) significant
   (C) digestible
   (D) profitable

2. Notwithstanding the strength of the Canadian mineral industry, it must <u>face</u> some serious challenges.

   (A) avoid
   (B) seek
   (C) define
   (D) meet

GO ON TO THE NEXT PAGE

A Practice TOEFL   211

3. A marine propeller is mounted on the end of a shaft near the stern of a ship.

   (A) bottom
   (B) controls
   (C) engine
   (D) rear

4. At the time of the Louisiana Purchase, it was obvious to the Americans that France needed funds to finance its war with England.

   (A) evident
   (B) advantageous
   (C) surprising
   (D) disappointing

5. Although the hazards of space travel are many, the rewards make it a worthwhile endeavor.

   (A) expenses
   (B) difficulties
   (C) pressures
   (D) risks

6. Interest rates generally fluctuate in a cyclical manner depending upon the strength and weakness of the economic system.

   (A) vary
   (B) inflate
   (C) decrease
   (D) behave

7. The Indians in California fashion baskets from a variety of plant materials.

   (A) clothes
   (B) weapons
   (C) containers
   (D) utensils

8. Most scholars agree that American composer George Gershwin's talent was largely self-developed.

   (A) wealth
   (B) fame
   (C) character
   (D) ability

9. Are typewriters fast becoming obsolete with the advent of computers?

   (A) complicated
   (B) neglected
   (C) outmoded
   (D) disdained

10. Steel stretches in hot weather, so suspension bridges can sag a foot or more on a hot day.

    (A) shrink
    (B) droop
    (C) bounce
    (D) rise

GO ON TO THE NEXT PAGE

11. Many species of catfish are <u>gregarious,</u> but move only short distances from their birthplaces.

    (A) unsightly
    (B) sociable
    (C) inactive
    (D) huge

12. Susan B. Anthony, the American champion of woman's suffrage, was also <u>a participant in</u> the movement to end slavery.

    (A) a partaker in
    (B) an observer in
    (C) a leader in
    (D) a supporter of

13. The history of public education in the United States dates from the society of the early <u>pioneers</u>.

    (A) settlers
    (B) Indian reservations
    (C) business leaders
    (D) missionaries

14. Biologists define a species as a group of organisms that interbreed naturally, producing <u>offspring</u>.

    (A) eggs
    (B) progeny
    (C) genes
    (D) nutrients

15. Thomas Jefferson was a <u>staunch</u> protector of the sovereign rights of citizens.

    (A) devoted
    (B) competent
    (C) celebrated
    (D) successful

16. Rocky Mountain National Park covers a region of <u>vast</u> natural splendor.

    (A) extensive
    (B) attractive
    (C) exploited
    (D) renowned

17. Americans were immediately attracted to the <u>vibrant</u> images made possible by neon technology.

    (A) symbolic
    (B) graphic
    (C) elegant
    (D) lively

18. The <u>townspeople</u> of Williamsburg are proud of their historic houses.

    (A) architects
    (B) patriots
    (C) citizens
    (D) leaders

GO ON TO THE NEXT PAGE

19. The stock market crash in 1929 touched off the Great Depression.

    (A) extended
    (B) hastened
    (C) initiated
    (D) justified

20. In North Carolina, textile manufacturing ranks as the most important industry.

    (A) cloth
    (B) furniture
    (C) plastic
    (D) apparel

21. Emily Dickinson, the writer, was so shy that she rarely left her room.

    (A) retiring
    (B) indigent
    (C) wayward
    (D) egregious

22. The United States has instituted a set of auto emission standards to reduce pollution.

    (A) suggested
    (B) established
    (C) published
    (D) accepted

23. Gypsum is a widespread mineral, occurring both in sedimentary beds and in veins.

    (A) valuable
    (B) common
    (C) hard
    (D) expensive

24. Baldness, the abnormal or premature loss of hair, is an inherited trait transmitted by a sex-influenced gene.

    (A) characteristic
    (B) disease
    (C) quality
    (D) mark

25. Robert Todd Lincoln, the son of Abraham Lincoln, jealously guarded his privacy.

    (A) cruelly
    (B) voluntarily
    (C) appropriately
    (D) protectively

26. Today many Texans feel their heritage is threatened by newcomers from the North.

    (A) enhanced
    (B) ridiculed
    (C) endangered
    (D) appreciated

27. During most of the history of humankind, meteorites have been an intriguing mystery.

    (A) a fascinating
    (B) an incomprehensible
    (C) a secretive
    (D) an unsolvable

28. At the onset of dry rot, leather develops a peculiar hue.

    (A) layer
    (B) shape
    (C) edge
    (D) color

29. An atom smasher speeds up the movement of atoms, allowing scientists to study them better.

    (A) reflects
    (B) directs
    (C) accelerates
    (D) prolongs

30. At the time of the American Revolution, the population of the United States was almost entirely rural.

    (A) hostile
    (B) coastal
    (C) agricultural
    (D) illiterate

Directions: In the rest of this section you will read several passages. Each one is followed by several questions about it. For questions 31-60, you are to choose the one best answer, (A), (B), (C), or (D), to each question. Then, on your answer sheet, find the number of the question and fill in the space that corresponds to the letter of the answer you have chosen.

Answer all questions following a passage on the basis of what is stated or implied in that passage.

Read the following passage:

   The rattles with which a rattlesnake warns of its presence are formed by loosely interlocking hollow rings of hard skin, which make a buzzing sound when its tail is shaken. As a baby, the snake begins to form its rattles from the button at the very tip of its tail. Thereafter, each time it sheds its skin, a new ring is formed. Popular belief holds that a snake's age can be told by counting the rings, but this idea is fallacious. In fact, a snake may lose its old skin as often as four times a year. Also, rattles tend to wear or break off with time.

3 • 3 • 3 • 3 • 3 • 3 • 3

Example I

A rattlesnake's rattles are made of

(A) skin
(B) bone
(C) wood
(D) muscle

Sample Answer
● Ⓑ Ⓒ Ⓓ

According to the passage, a rattlesnake's rattles are made out of rings of hard skin. Therefore, you should choose answer (A).

Example II

How often does a rattlesnake shed its skin?

(A) Once every four years
(B) Once every four months
(C) Up to four times every year
(D) Four times more often than other snakes

Sample Answer
Ⓐ Ⓑ ● Ⓓ

The passage states that "a snake may lose its old skin as often as four times a year." Therefore, you should choose answer (C).

After you read the directions, begin work on the questions.

GO ON TO THE NEXT PAGE

Questions 31-36

The common experience of having a name or word on the tip of the tongue seems related to specific perceptual attributes. In particular, people who report the tip-of-the-tongue feeling tend to identify the word's first letter and number of syllables with an accuracy that far exceeds mere guessing. There is evidence that the mind may encode data about when information was learned and about how often it has been experienced. Some memories seem to embrace spatial information; e.g., one remembers a particular news item to be on the lower right-hand side of the front page of a newspaper. Research indicates that the rate of forgetting varies for different attributes. For example, memories in which auditory attributes seem dominant tend to be more rapidly forgotten than those with minimal acoustic characteristics.

If a designated (target) memory consists of a collection of attributes, its recall or retrieval should be enhanced by any cue that indicates one of the attributes. For example, on failing to recall the term horse (included in a list they have just seen), people may be asked if an associated term (say, barn or zebra) helps them recall the word. While some additional recall has been observed with this kind of help, failures are common even with ostensibly relevant cues. Though it is possible that the cues frequently are inappropriate, nevertheless, if words were not learned (encoded or stored) with accompanying attributes, cuing of any kind should be ineffective.

31. With which of the following statements would the author be MOST likely to agree?

    (A) Words that are only heard are easily forgotten.
    (B) The brain always remembers the moment words are first learned.
    (C) Auditory cues are more helpful than spatial cues.
    (D) Uncommon words are normally remembered with visual cues.

32. It can be concluded from the passage that all encoded words are

    (A) remembered without help
    (B) learned without cues
    (C) stored with attributes
    (D) forgotten if not used

33. What does the passage mainly discuss?

    (A) How a person remembers words
    (B) The origin of the expression "tip-of-the-tongue"
    (C) How a person uses new words
    (D) How cues are used to pronounce words

34. According to the passage, words learned with few attributes will be

    (A) easily spelled
    (B) retrieved with fewer cues
    (C) well encoded
    (D) recalled with difficulty

35. Which of the following does the author mention as a cause for forgettng?

    (A) The need for more precise spatial information
    (B) The creation of ostensibly relevant cues
    (C) The learning of words without corresponding attributes
    (D) The use of inappropriate auditory cues

36. Which is NOT mentioned as a tendency among people who encounter the tip-of-the-tongue experience?

    (A) Knowing the number of syllables in a word
    (B) Remembering where words were seen
    (C) Knowing the first letter of the word
    (D) Recognizing the word when heard

Questions 37-42

There is perhaps no other event in the natural world that is as characteristic of a season as a full chorus of spring peepers. It is not only that the voices of living things are calling once more after the long silence of winter, there is something about the atmosphere in which the chorus takes place that epitomizes the season. There is a certain moist smell in the air on rainy spring nights, slow mists rise from rafts of ice floating in dark marshes, everywhere on roads through wet areas the small white forms of migrating spring peepers, wood frogs, green frogs, and pickerel frogs appear, and all around you the air will be filled with a high bell-like ringing, a little like a distant horse-drawn sleigh. That distant chorus is the voice of the spring peeper, a small tree frog no larger than the end of a little finger. Throughout history naturalists have referred to it as the voice of spring.

In actuality you may be a long way from the pond or marsh that the peepers are calling from. The voice of spring peepers can carry as much as a mile on still spring nights, and once you learn to recognize the song, there will be nights when it is difficult to escape their incessant calling. The sound will accompany you through spring, a sort of background music to the events that will be taking place around you during the season.

37. What is the best title for this passage?

(A) Spring Comes to the Country
(B) The Voice of Spring
(C) Migration of Frogs
(D) A Rainy Spring Night

38. What kind of animal is a spring peeper?

(A) A wood frog
(B) A pickerel frog
(C) A tree frog
(D) A green frog

39. Which of the following is NOT mentioned by the author as a characteristic of the spring season?

    (A) Animal sounds
    (B) New odors
    (C) Rising mists
    (D) Tree blossoms

40. Which of the following best describes the spring climate of the area of the country the author is describing?

    (A) Cold and dry
    (B) Warm and humid
    (C) Cool and wet
    (D) Dry and warm

41. Which of the following generalizations is supported by the passage?

    (A) Each time of year has its own special features.
    (B) As seasons change, so do people.
    (C) Tiny sounds can be of great importance.
    (D) Spring is the most beloved season of all.

42. The paragraph following the passage most likely discusses

    (A) natural signs of fall
    (B) springtime changes in nature
    (C) other kinds of frogs
    (D) summertime weather

GO ON TO THE NEXT PAGE

Questions 43-48

Pie doughs and similar products are usually unleavened, but most bakery products are leavened, or aerated, by gas bubbles developed naturally or folded in from the atmosphere. Leavening may result from yeast or bacterial fermentation, from chemical reactions, or from the distribution in the batter of atmospheric or injected gases.

Bakers' yeast performs its leavening function by fermenting such sugars as glucose, fructose, maltose, and sucrose. It cannot use lactose, the predominant sugar of milk or certain other carbohydrates. The principal products of fermentation are carbon dioxide, the leavening agent, and ethanol, an important component of the aroma of freshly baked bread. Other yeast activity products also flavor the baked product and change the physical properties of the dough.

The rate at which gas is evolved by yeast during the various stages of dough preparation is important to the success of bread manufacture. Gas production is partially governed by the rate at which fermentable carbohydrates become available to the yeast. The sugars naturally present in the flour and the initial stock of added sugar are rapidly exhausted. A relatively quiescent period follows, during which the yeast cells become adapted to the use of maltose, a sugar consantly being produced in the dough by the action of diastatic enzymes on starch. The rate of yeast activity is also governed not only by temperature but also by a phenomena known as osmotic pressure.

43. What is the best title for this passage?

   (A) The Process of Bacterial Fermentation
   (B) The Role of Yeast in the Baking Process
   (C) How Bread is Made
   (D) Types of Chemical Reactions

44. According to the passage, which sugar is fermented in the final states of the baking process?

   (A) Fructose
   (B) Sucrose
   (C) Maltose
   (D) Glucose

45. Which of the following generalizations is supported by the passage?

    (A) Sugars must be present for fermentation to occur.
    (B) Very few sugars are naturally present in flour.
    (C) Yeast prevents changes in the texture of dough.
    (D) Leavening can take place only when yeast is present.

46. The paragraph immediately following the passage most likely discusses

    (A) osmotic pressure
    (B) even temperature
    (C) uses of sugar in baking
    (D) atmospheric gases

47. Which of the following products would least likely contain yeast?

    (A) White bread
    (B) Dinner rolls
    (C) Doughnuts
    (D) Apple pie

48. What material accounts for the pleasing smell of recently baked bread?

    (A) Lactose
    (B) Carbon dioxide
    (C) Ethanol
    (D) Salt

GO ON TO THE NEXT PAGE

Questions 49-54

A major in modern languages and literatures provides its graduates with both a specific area of skills and a sense of their relationship between their particular discipline and the larger body of knowledge that is the patrimony of liberally educated persons. Majors learn to express themselves clearly and correctly through required advanced language courses (301, 302, 401, 402). They acquire a general knowledge of the literature as a whole in survey courses and a deeper knowledge of special areas in the courses that follow, including a number of 500 and 600 electives. The final course taken by the major, the senior seminar, coordinates all knowledge and skills acquired. A joint B.A./M.A. program is available to qualified students.

Students may choose to develop a concentration in French, German, or Spanish. Consult the individual language programs below for further details.

For students not majoring in languages, distribution requirements in literature as well as in humanities may be fulfilled by a number of courses offered by the department.

49. What is the purpose of the passage?

(A) To persuade students to study modern languages
(B) To describe a university language program
(C) To argue for language requirements for all students
(D) To encourage enrollment in advanced language programs

50. According to the passage, in which of the following languages is it NOT possible to major?

(A) Russian
(B) French
(C) German
(D) Spanish

51. The last course required for a modern languages student is identified in the passage as

   (A) a survey course
   (B) a senior seminar
   (C) a concentration
   (D) an M.A. program

52. Survey courses in literature probably emphasize

   (A) accurate grammar usage
   (B) a wide range of reading
   (C) a specific writer's work
   (D) advanced reading skills

53. According to the passage, which courses are the most specialized?

   (A) Those dealing with literature
   (B) Those numbered 301, 302, 401, and 402
   (C) Those required for a B.A.
   (D) Those numbered in the 500s and 600s.

54. In the first sentence, the word "their" refers to

   (A) language
   (B) literature
   (C) graduates
   (D) skills

GO ON TO THE NEXT PAGE

Questions 55-60

In its short history, the art of motion pictures has frequently undergone changes that seemed fundamental, such as that resulting from the introduction of sound. It exists today in styles that differ significantly from country to country and in forms as diverse as the documentary created by one man with a hand-held camera and the multimillion-dollar "epic," involving hundreds of performers and technicians. Despite its diversity, however, an essential unchanging nature can be discerned in most of its manifestations.

A number of factors immediately come to mind in connection with the motion picture experience. For one thing, there is something mildly hypnotic about the illusion of movement that holds the attention and may even lower critical resistance. Also, the accuracy of the motion picture image is compelling because it is made by a nonhuman, scientific process. And, the motion picture gives what has been called a strong sense of being present: the film image always appears to be in the present tense. There is also the concrete nature of film; it appears to show the actual people and things.

No less important than any of the above are the conditions under which the motion picture ideally is seen, where everything helps to dominate the spectator. He or she is taken from the everyday environment, partially isolated from others, and comfortably seated in an air-conditioned auditorium. There, the darkness concentrates attention and prevents comparison of the image on the screen with the objects or people around the viewer. For a while, the motion picture unfolds the world in which the spectator lives.

55. Which of the following statements best expresses the main idea of the passage?

   (A) Motion pictures vary greatly from country to country.
   (B) The fundamental characteristics of motion pictures remain unchanged.
   (C) Motion pictures have been modified over the years.
   (D) The styles of motion pictures have become significantly different.

56. According to the passage, which can be the most simply made type of motion picture?

   (A) A documentary
   (B) An accurate one
   (C) An epic
   (D) A hypnotic one

57. Which of the following statements does the author NOT include as part of the motion picture experience?

    (A) The viewing environment controls the spectator.
    (B) The spectator is somewhat apart from other viewers.
    (C) The viewer becomes fascinated by the action on the screen.
    (D) The spectator realizes that events on the screen are false.

58. The nature of movies is most comparable to which one of the following activities?

    (A) Dancing at a party
    (B) Drawing a picture
    (C) Describing a painting
    (D) Reading a book

59. The author most probably believes that the main purpose of movies is to allow the audience to

    (A) see actual places, people and things
    (B) be entertained in a comfortable setting
    (C) escape from the real world
    (D) enjoy the results of a scientific process

60. The passage supports which of the following conclusions?

    (A) Motion projected on the screen captivates viewers.
    (B) Viewers feel detached from the action on the screen.
    (C) The viewing environment is of minor importance.
    (D) Documentaries and epics have universal appeal.

THIS IS THE END OF SECTION 3

IF YOU FINISH BEFORE TIME IS CALLED, CHECK YOUR WORK ON SECTION 3 ONLY.
DO NOT READ OR WORK ON ANY OTHER SECTION OF THE TEST.

Print your full name here _____
(last)   (first)   (middle)

A PRACTICE TOEFL

FORM 3

General Directions

This is a test of your ability to use the English language. It is divided into three sections, some of which have more than one part. Each section or part of the test begins with a set of specific directions that include sample questions. Be sure you understand what you are to do before you begin to work on a section.

The supervisor will tell you when to start each section and when to go on to the next section. You should work quickly but carefully. Do not spend too much time on any one question. If you finish a section early, you may review your answers on that section only. You may not go on to the next section and you may not go back to a section you have already worked on.

You will find that some of the questions are more difficult than others, but you should try to answer every one. Your score will be based on the number of questions you answer correctly—that is, the number for which you choose the best answer from among the choices given. If you are not sure of the answer to a question, make the best guess that you can. It is to your advantage to answer every question, even if you have to guess the answer.

Do not mark your answers in this test book. You must mark all of your answers on the separate answer sheet that is inside this test book. When you mark your answer to a question on your answer sheet, you must:

— Use a medium-soft (#2 or HB) black lead pencil.
— Be careful to mark the space that corresponds to the answer you choose for each question. Also, make sure you mark your answer in the row with the same number as the number of the question you are answering. You will not be permitted to make any corrections after time is called.
— Mark only one answer to each question.
— Carefully and completely fill each intended oval with a dark mark so that you cannot see the letter inside the oval; light or partial marks may not be read properly by the scoring machine.
— Erase all extra marks completely and thoroughly. If you change your mind about an answer after you have marked it on your answer sheet, completely erase your old answer and then mark your new answer.

The examples below show you the correct and wrong ways of marking an answer sheet. Be sure to fill in the ovals on your answer sheet the correct way.

CORRECT	WRONG	WRONG	WRONG	WRONG
Ⓐ Ⓑ ● Ⓓ	Ⓐ Ⓑ ✓Ⓒ Ⓓ	Ⓐ Ⓑ ✗Ⓒ Ⓓ	Ⓐ Ⓑ Ⓒ Ⓓ	Ⓐ Ⓑ Ⓒ Ⓓ

Some or all of the passages for this test have been adapted from published material to provide the examinee with significant problems for analysis and evaluation. To make the passages suitable for testing purposes, the style, content, or point of view of the original may have been altered in some cases.

Note: On an actual TOEFL examination, the general directions page appears on the last page of the test booklet. This test is to be used with the listening comprehension test tape found in the *Newbury House TOEFL Preparation Kit* and the multiple-choice answer sheets found at the end of this book.

1 • 1 • 1 • 1 • 1 • 1 • 1

SECTION 1
LISTENING COMPREHENSION

In this section of the test, you will have an opportunity to demonstrate your ability to understand spoken English. There are three parts to this section, with special directions for each part.

Part A

Directions: For each question in Part A, you will hear a short sentence. Each sentence will be spoken just one time. The sentences you hear will not be written out for you. Therefore, you must listen carefully to understand what the speaker says.

After you hear a sentence, read the four choices in your test book, marked (A), (B), (C), and (D), and decide which one is closest in meaning to the sentence you heard. Then, on your sheet, find the number of the question and fill in the space that corresponds to the letter of the answer you have chosen. Fill in the space so that the letter inside the oval cannot be seen.

Example I   Sample Answer
                                               Ⓐ Ⓑ ● Ⓓ
You will hear:

You will read: (A) Mary outswam the others.
(B) Mary ought to swim with them.
(C) Mary and her friends swam to the island.
(D) Mary's friends owned the island.

The speaker said, "Mary swam out to the island with her friends." Sentence (C), "Mary and her friends swam to the island," is closest in meaning to the sentence you heard. Therefore, you should choose answer (C).

GO ON TO THE NEXT PAGE

A Practice TOEFL   231

1 • 1 • 1 • 1 • 1 • 1 • 1

Example II

You will hear:

You will read: (A) Please remind me to read this book.
(B) Could you help me carry these books?
(C) I don't mind if you help me.
(D) Do you have a heavy course load this term?

Sample Answer
Ⓐ ● Ⓒ Ⓓ

The speaker said, "Would you mind helping me with this load of books?" Sentence (B), "Could you help me carry these books?" is closest in meaning to the sentence you heard. Therefore, you should choose answer (B).

1. (A) I can't get many postcards on that side.
   (B) I can't decide on any postcards to send.
   (C) Where can I go to get more postcards?
   (D) How many postcards should I buy?

2. (A) We should pick those stamps up off the floor.
   (B) Should we ask for a print at that door?
   (C) Let's buy some stamps now for Dorothy.
   (D) Can we put prints up in the dormitory?

3. (A) Are classes already in session?
   (B) Are the classrooms ready?
   (C) Have they read it in class yet?
   (D) Have half the classes started yet?

4. (A) You have paint from the door on your coat.
   (B) You should paint the door again.
   (C) You should wear another coat when you go.
   (D) You have to leave by another door.

5. (A) They sold the papers outside today.
   (B) Two daily papers are sold there.
   (C) They don't have any more newspapers.
   (D) Their paper is two days old.

GO ON TO THE NEXT PAGE

1 • 1 • 1 • 1 • 1 • 1 • 1

6. (A) Did the letter for Jimmy come yet?
   (B) What was the first letter Jimmy received?
   (C) Did Jimmy expect the letter he received?
   (D) Was Jimmy's letter sent on time?

7. (A) Is it too late for you to hand me that?
   (B) Will you help me with my Latin assignment?
   (C) Please let me in so you can give me this.
   (D) I wonder if you can pass Latin without my help.

8. (A) Because of this project, Bess won't have a vacation.
   (B) She is finishing her project on her vacation.
   (C) After the project is completed, Bess will go on vacation.
   (D) The best time for vacation will be in the summer.

9. (A) Students use this lot on campus.
   (B) There used to be a lot of students here.
   (C) On this campus you can rent used bikes.
   (D) Many students here ride bicycles.

10. (A) Julia wants to change classes.
    (B) Julia's new glasses change her looks.
    (C) Julia's point of view makes her different.
    (D) Julia sees things differently.

11. (A) Sarah and George didn't go to the botany lecture.
    (B) Did George attend the botany lecture with Sarah?
    (C) Didn't Sarah see George at the end of the lecture?
    (D) Neither Sarah nor George bought any last year.

12. (A) The history museum is as pretty as the train station.
    (B) You'll see pretty clothes in the history museum.
    (C) The museum and the station are near each other.
    (D) The museum next to the train station is closed.

13. (A) Janet changed her parking space.
    (B) Janet needs some coins for the meter.
    (C) Janet parked so we could meet her.
    (D) Janet wants to park, for a change.

GO ON TO THE NEXT PAGE

14. (A) Minutes go by quickly.
    (B) That clock is too slow.
    (C) You should wind the clock.
    (D) The clock needs to be reset.

15. (A) Have many students enrolled for Professor Smith's course?
    (B) Four more students are too many for that course.
    (C) A lot of students are registered for one class.
    (D) Do many students ever show up for Professor's Smith class?

16. (A) We never go shopping for coffee on Eighth Street.
    (B) At eight o'clock, let's meet right outside the coffee shop.
    (C) The front of the shop is eight feet wide.
    (D) Let's meet behind the coffee shop at eight.

17. (A) Hurry and walk right off the campus.
    (B) Here he's working late so he can take off later.
    (C) The hair stylist works at night off campus.
    (D) Harry has a night job near school now.

18. (A) You have to present identification to the guard.
    (B) You must identify the guard when you come in.
    (C) The guard will give you a form to fill out quickly.
    (D) You should get an idea of the building when you enter.

19. (A) I don't pay much attention to the weather in summer.
    (B) I don't like the humid weather in summer here.
    (C) Summertime isn't very hot here.
    (D) In summer, it gets hot in no time here.

20. (A) Remember, their group is on the right side.
    (B) Henry's group forgot to talk about the lecture.
    (C) People will discuss the lecture afterwards.
    (D) Don't forget to turn right after you talk to Henry.

Part B

Directions: In Part B you will hear short conversations between two speakers. At the end of each conversation, a third person will ask a question about what was said. You will hear each conversation and question about it just one time. Therefore, you must listen carefully to understand what each speaker says. After you hear a conversation and question about it, read the four possible answers in your test book and decide which one is the best answer to the question you heard. Then, on your answer sheet, find the number of the question and fill in the space that corresponds to the letter of the answer you have chosen.

Look at the following example.

Sample Answer
● Ⓑ Ⓒ Ⓓ

You will hear:

You will read: (A) Present Professor Smith with a picture.
(B) Photograph Professor Smith.
(C) Put glass over the photograph.
(D) Replace the broken headlight.

From the conversation you learn that the woman thinks Professor Smith would like a photograph of the class. The best answer to the question "What does the woman think the class should do?" is (A), "Present Professor Smith with a picture." Therefore, you should choose answer (A).

21. (A) She recently arrived from abroad.
    (B) She was in the country.
    (C) She came back to earn more money.
    (D) She's just come from the bank.

22. (A) The Nelsons are wealthy.
    (B) Mr. Nelson doesn't know how to drive.
    (C) The Nelsons must not spend much money.
    (D) Mr. Nelson doesn't make that much money.

23. (A) It's very difficult to enroll.
    (B) No one has seen the sign.
    (C) Few people show interest in it.
    (D) It costs too much money.

24. (A) In a taxi.
    (B) In an elevator.
    (C) On the subway.
    (D) At a post office.

GO ON TO THE NEXT PAGE

25. (A) She shouldn't have been late.
    (B) Her timing was very poor.
    (C) She probably wasn't having fun.
    (D) Before long, she was enjoying it.

26. (A) At a department store.
    (B) At an airport.
    (C) In a supermarket.
    (D) In a bank.

27. (A) May will be a bad month.
    (B) They can be optimistic.
    (C) Will prices keep rising?
    (D) Did they look them up?

28. (A) Jack will probably not pass the class.
    (B) Jack will not make the project in class.
    (C) Jack's class is very difficult.
    (D) Jack's accounting project is incomplete.

29. (A) It's not polite to ask.
    (B) The question is naive.
    (C) He did hear the question.
    (D) He was born in the city.

30. (A) At a florist shop.
    (B) At a sporting goods store.
    (C) At a grocery store.
    (D) At a service station.

31. (A) Only six people are here.
    (B) They could be sick.
    (C) It's not late at all.
    (D) Four more people will come.

32. (A) A professor.
    (B) A businessman.
    (C) A secretary.
    (D) A doctor.

33. (A) The books are on the right shelf.
    (B) Sixteen copies of the book remain.
    (C) The books are to his right.
    (D) The text is not available.

34. (A) His check was lost.
    (B) He's unable to find his watch.
    (C) He can't set his watch.
    (D) His check didn't arrive.

35. (A) At a restaurant.
    (B) At the dry cleaners.
    (C) At a barber shop.
    (D) At a tailor shop.

GO ON TO THE NEXT PAGE

1 · 1 · 1 · 1 · 1 · 1 · 1

Part C

Directions: In this part of the test, you will hear short talks and conversations. After each of them, you will be asked some questions. You will hear the talks and conversations and the questions about them just one time. They will not be written out for you. Therefore, you must listen carefully to understand what each speaker says.

After you hear a question, read the four possible answers in your test book and decide which one is the best answer to the question you heard. Then, on your answer sheet, find the number of the question and fill in the space that corresponds to the letter of the answer you have chosen.

Answer all questions on the basis of what is stated or implied in the talk or conversation.

Listen to this sample talk.

You will hear:

Now look at the following example.   Sample Answer
                                                                         Ⓐ ● Ⓒ Ⓓ
You will hear:
You will read: (A) They are impossible to guide.
                (B) They may go up in flames.
                (C) They tend to leak gas.
                (D) They are cheaply made.

The best answer to the question "Why are gas balloons considered dangerous?" is (B), "They may go up in flames." Therefore, you should choose answer (B).

Now look at this example.   Sample Answer
                                                                         ● Ⓑ Ⓒ Ⓓ
You will hear:
You will read: (A) Watch for changes in the
                    weather.
                (B) Watch their altitude.
                (C) Check for weak spots in
                    their balloons.
                (D) Test the strength of the ropes.

The best answer to the question "According to the speaker, what must balloon pilots be careful to do?" is (A) "Watch for changes in weather." Therefore, you should choose answer (A).

GO ON TO THE NEXT PAGE ➤

36. (A) How water animals mature.
    (B) How crabs develop cracks.
    (C) How joints and sections are made.
    (D) How crabs grow.

37. (A) When its shell is soft.
    (B) When it cannot move.
    (C) When it develops a crack.
    (D) When it is weak.

38. (A) 1/3 larger.
    (B) 1/2 larger.
    (C) 3/4 larger.
    (D) Double its previous size.

39. (A) The joints and sections.
    (B) The front.
    (C) The back.
    (D) The bottom half.

40. (A) About two years.
    (B) Four hours.
    (C) Six hours.
    (D) Eight hours.

41. (A) After six months.
    (B) After twelve months.
    (C) After thirty-six months.
    (D) After sixty-eight months.

42. (A) At a drug store.
    (B) At a university.
    (C) On the street.
    (D) On a train.

43. (A) Meet someone from Alaska.
    (B) Go to a wedding in Los Angeles.
    (C) Give the woman a telephone call.
    (D) Ask the woman to his house.

44. (A) Alaska.
    (B) Los Angeles.
    (C) San Francisco.
    (D) New York.

45. (A) She can't leave right after work.
    (B) She doesn't know the man's brother yet.
    (C) She didn't give the man a call.
    (D) She can't accept the man's invitation.

46. (A) Chemistry lab grades.
    (B) Test make-ups.
    (C) Class assignments.
    (D) Class attendance policy.

47. (A) They may fail the course.
    (B) They may not make up the work.
    (C) They may read additional assignments.
    (D) They may not understand the class.

GO ON TO THE NEXT PAGE

1 • 1 • 1 • 1 • 1 • 1 • 1

48. (A) None.
    (B) One.
    (C) Three.
    (D) Five.

49. (A) Bring a note.
    (B) Notify the professor.
    (C) Make up the work.
    (D) Explain it to the dean.

50. (A) From noon to four o'clock.
    (B) For two hours on Thursday.
    (C) Three days a week.
    (D) On a daily basis.

THIS IS THE END OF THE LISTENING COMPREHENSION SECTION OF THE TEST

THE NEXT PART OF THE TEST IS SECTION 2. TURN TO THE
DIRECTIONS FOR SECTION 2 IN YOUR TEST BOOK,
READ THEM, AND BEGIN WORK.
DO NOT READ OR WORK ON ANY OTHER SECTION OF THE
TEST.

A Practice TOEFL   **239**

SECTION 2
STRUCTURE AND WRITTEN EXPRESSION

Time—25 minutes

This section is designed to measure your ability to recognize language that is appropriate for standard written English. There are two types of questions in this section, with special directions for each type.

<u>Directions:</u> Questions 1–15 are incomplete sentences. Beneath each sentence you will see four words or phrases, marked (A), (B), (C), and (D). Choose the <u>one</u> word or phrase that best completes the sentence. Then, on your answer sheet, find the number of the question and fill in the space that corresponds to the letter of the answer you have chosen. Fill in the space so that the letter inside the oval cannot be seen.

Example I

Vegetables are an excellent source ------- of vitamins.

(A) of
(B) has
(C) where
(D) that

<u>Sample Answer</u>
● Ⓑ Ⓒ Ⓓ

The sentence should read, "Vegetables are an excellent source of vitamins." Therefore, you should choose answer (A).

Example II

------- in history when remarkable progress was made within a relatively short span of time.

(A) Periods
(B) Throughout periods
(C) There have been periods
(D) Periods have been

<u>Sample Answer</u>
Ⓐ Ⓑ ● Ⓓ

The sentence should read, "There have been periods in history when remarkable progress was made within a relatively short span of time." Therefore, you should choose answer (C).

After you read the directions, begin work on the questions.

GO ON TO THE NEXT PAGE

1. When Columbus ------- America in 1492, the continents may have been peopled by as many as twenty-five to fifty million Indians.

   (A) who discovered
   (B) discovering
   (C) discovered
   (D) to discover

2. The sport of jogging needs no special equipment ------- good shoes.

   (A) and
   (B) only
   (C) also
   (D) except

3. There are nearly four hundred Girl Scout Councils throughout the United States, making it possible for a girl to become a scout no matter ------- .

   (A) is where she lives
   (B) where she lives
   (C) where does she live
   (D) she lives where

4. Chlorine is a gaseous chemical element ------- in a large number of chlorine-containing compounds.

   (A) which
   (B) which exists
   (C) which it exists
   (D) in which it exists

5. The Art Institute of Chicago is one of the four ------- art museums in America.

   (A) largest
   (B) of larger
   (C) the largest
   (D) of large

6. The loss of memory ------- as amnesia may be produced by any severe emotional shock.

   (A) to know
   (B) knowing
   (C) known
   (D) know

7. Since the earliest frogs were aquatic, the question has arisen as to how ------- .

   (A) did the jumping adaptation of the frog originate
   (B) was the jumping adaptation of the frog originated
   (C) the jumping adaptation of the frog originated
   (D) the jumping adaptation of the frog to originate.

8. ------- agriculture, mining and forestry are all important to the Canadian economy, Canada is also a major industrial power.

   (A) Although
   (B) That
   (C) However
   (D) In spite of

9. Marian Anderson made her debut at the Metropolitan Opera in New York in 1955, ------- the first black singer ever to sing with the company.

    (A) became
    (B) to becoming
    (C) she became
    (D) becoming

10. The shipment and storage of canned goods presents ------- .

    (A) few relatively problems
    (B) relatively few problems
    (C) problems relatively few
    (D) few problems relatively

11. The subject of comparative anatomy as taught in colleges ------- universities usually deals only with animals.

    (A) and
    (B) some
    (C) but
    (D) nor

12. The Gypsy Moth, ------- into the United States for the silk industry, was responsible for a major caterpillar plague that caused immense destruction to forests.

    (A) introduced
    (B) was introduced
    (C) it was introduced
    (D) when it was introduced

13. Jimmy Carter was the first president elected from the Deep South since before ------- .

    (A) the Civil War
    (B) the Civil War was
    (C) it was the Civil War
    (D) the time the Civil War was

14. Although the mechanics of faulting are not clearly understood, it is known that ------- .

    (A) commonly subjected to great stress are deeply buried rocks
    (B) deeply buried rocks to great stress are commonly subjected
    (C) deeply buried rocks are commonly subjected to great stress
    (D) commonly subjected to great stress deeply buried rocks are.

15. Anemia is a condition of the body ------- the normal number of red blood cells is reduced.

    (A) which
    (B) in which
    (C) in which is
    (D) in which it is

GO ON TO THE NEXT PAGE

Directions: In questions 16–40 each sentence has four underlined words or phrases. The four underlined parts of the sentence are marked (A), (B), (C), and (D). Identify the one underlined word or phrase that must be changed in order for the sentence to be correct. Then, on your answer sheet, find the number of the question and fill in the space that corresponds to the letter of the answer you have chosen.

Example I

A ray of light passing <u>through</u> <u>the center</u> of a
                                 A   B

thin lens <u>keep</u> its <u>original</u> direction.
         C   D

Sample Answer
Ⓐ Ⓑ ● Ⓓ

The sentence should read, "A ray of light passing through the center of a thin lens keeps its original direction." Therefore, you should choose answer (C).

Example II

The mandolin, a musical <u>instrument</u> <u>that has</u>
                              A   B

strings, was probably copied <u>from</u> the lute, a
                              C

<u>many</u> older instrument.
 D

Sample Answer
Ⓐ Ⓑ Ⓒ ●

The sentence should read, "The mandolin, a musical instrument that has strings, was probably copied from the lute, a much older instrument." Therefore, you should choose answer (D).

After you read the directions, begin work on the questions.

16. Lion-fish are <u>noted</u> for <u>its</u> venomous fin spines, which <u>are</u> capable of
                    A   B   C
producing painful, <u>though</u> rarely fatal, puncture wounds.
                        D

17. As would <u>to be</u> expected in <u>a mild</u> climate, <u>outdoor sports</u>
              A   B   C
<u>flourish in</u> Hawaii.
    D

GO ON TO THE NEXT PAGE

18. The opening of rich farmlands to settlement provided the main
        A
    impetus for immigration to Canada during the early years of it's
                    B   C D
    history.

19. Most of the shortwave and visible radiation from the Sun that is not
     A   B
    scattered back to the atmosphere was transmitted to the surface
                                        C
    of the Earth.
      D

20. After the Civil War, Union troops they occupied Texas, marking the
         A   B
    beginning of the Reconstruction period that lasted until 1874.
                                            C   D

21. How many people there are who can recall the role of Carrie
                    A   B   C
    Chapman Catt in the women's movement?
                        D

22. Alligators hunt at night, the young feeding on insects and
                    A   B
    crustaceans and the adults eating a variety of animal, including
                        C   D
    snakes and turtles.

23. The oldest and most widespread celebrations are them connected
                         A   B
    with the harvesting of the first fruits.
             C   D

24. At the American Indian view of nature, land could not be the
    A   B   C
    personal property of any individual.
                            D

25. Materials for making plastics can be classified in terms of whether it
             A   B   C
    can be softened or formed only once, or as often as desired.
                                         D

GO ON TO THE NEXT PAGE

26. The wide variety of forms and the regional diversity <u>represented at</u> the historical village of Deerfield offer <u>both</u> the novice and the connoisseur the <u>opportunity appreciate</u> the <u>broad</u> spectrum of American art.

A   B   C   D

27. Helen Keller, <u>the</u> famous blind and deaf American author and educator, <u>is regarded</u> <u>by many</u> as one of the most remarkable <u>woman</u> in history.

A   B   C   D

28. <u>Much</u> species of cowbirds do not build nests of their <u>own</u>, but <u>lay</u> their eggs in the nests of other species <u>whose nests</u> are similar in size.

A   B   C   D

29. <u>The</u> most <u>successfully</u> advertisements are <u>based</u> on appeals <u>to</u> universal human likes and dislikes.

A   B   C   D

30. Most <u>sedimentary</u> rocks are layered, and, <u>as is implied</u> by the name, <u>has originated</u> <u>by the sedimentation</u> of particles.

A   B   C   D

31. On the <u>ground floor</u> of the Kennedy Center in Washington is a <u>mirrored</u> grand <u>foyer</u> illuminated <u>of eighteen</u> crystal chandeliers.

A   B   C   D

32. Tree <u>ducks</u>, or <u>whistling</u> ducks, <u>are</u> small, timid, <u>color</u> birds.

A   B   C   D

33. The Pennsylvania Dutch, <u>whose</u> culture is <u>unique</u> American, have <u>developed</u> a <u>distinctive</u> tradition in folk art.

A   B   C   D

GO ON TO THE NEXT PAGE

34. Greenheart wood, both strong and dense, <u>are used</u>, chiefly in
    A
    Europe, for <u>underwater</u> <u>applications</u>, <u>such as</u> pilings for wharves
              B   C   D
    and bridges.

35. Buster Keaton is <u>recognized by</u> many as the <u>most gifted</u> and
                    A   B
    influential silent screen <u>comedy</u> <u>after</u> Charlie Chaplin.
                               C   D

36. <u>In</u> the technique <u>knowing</u> as Kirlian photography, the object to be
    A   B
    photographed is placed <u>directly</u> on the film emulsion <u>itself</u>.
                            C   D

37. Weeds have <u>marked</u> capacities to spread and <u>success</u> <u>under</u> great
                A   B   C
    variety of <u>conditions</u>.
                D

38. What is <u>most striking</u> about New York City is <u>the fact that</u> so many
            A   B
    people visit it <u>without seeing</u> the real inner beauty of that
                     C
    <u>enormous, huge city</u>.
     D

39. <u>Speed</u> records <u>for</u> pacer horses are slightly <u>fast</u> than for <u>trotters</u>.
     A   B   C   D

40. The <u>majority theme</u> of Robert Penn Warren's <u>novels is</u> <u>the paradox</u>
         A   B   C
    <u>of human</u> action.
     D

THIS IS THE END OF SECTION 2

IF YOU FINISH BEFORE TIME IS CALLED, CHECK YOUR WORK
ON SECTION 2 ONLY.
DO NOT READ OR WORK ON ANY OTHER SECTION OF THE
TEST. THE SUPERVISOR WILL TELL YOU WHEN TO BEGIN
WORK ON SECTION 3.

SECTION 3
VOCABULARY AND READING COMPREHENSION

Time—45 minutes

This section is designed to measure your comprehension of standard written English. There are two types of questions in this section, with special directions for each type.

<u>Directions</u>: In questions 1–30 each sentence has an underlined word or phrase. Below each sentence are four other words or phrases, marked (A), (B), (C), and (D). You are to choose the <u>one</u> word or phrase that <u>best keeps the meaning</u> of the original sentence if it is substituted for the underlined word or phrase. Then, on your answer sheet, find the number of the question and fill in the space that corresponds to the letter you have chosen. Fill in the space so that the letter inside the oval cannot be seen.

Example

Passenger ships and <u>aircraft</u> are often equipped with ship-to-shore or air-to-land radio telephones.

(A) highways
(B) railroads
(C) planes
(D) sailboats

Sample Answer
Ⓐ Ⓑ ● Ⓓ

The best answer is (C) because "Passenger ships and planes are often equipped with ship-to-shore or air-to-land radio telephones" is closest in meaning to the original sentence. Therefore, you should choose answer (C).

After you read the directions, begin work on the questions.

1. Rosin is brittle solid which varies in color from <u>pale</u> yellow to near black.

    (A) dazzling
    (B) luminous
    (C) faint
    (D) opaque

2. During the Great Depression, social and economic pressures in the United States were <u>deep-rooted</u>.

    (A) superficial
    (B) extremely complex
    (C) unfavorable
    (D) indescribable

3. The camel is a very <u>lethargic</u> animal and has a reputation for stupidity.

    (A) irrational
    (B) boring
    (C) messy
    (D) sluggish

4. American author Nathaniel Hawthorne was never <u>at ease</u> with other writers unless he could talk to them privately.

    (A) honest
    (B) talkative
    (C) argumentative
    (D) relaxed

5. The soles of your feet are <u>thick-skinned</u> compared to the rest of your body.

    (A) tough
    (B) flexible
    (C) fragrant
    (D) harsh

6. The Hawaiian Islands were <u>previously</u> called the Sandwich Islands.

    (A) formerly
    (B) mistakenly
    (C) commonly
    (D) occasionally

7. In general, sea bass <u>attain</u> a weight of slightly over eight pounds.

    (A) maintain
    (B) reach
    (C) exceed
    (D) favor

8. Consideration of the bill was delayed by <u>a bloc</u> of the senators determined to defeat the legislation.

    (A) a veto
    (B) an appeal
    (C) a barricade
    (D) a group

GO ON TO THE NEXT PAGE

9. A psychotherapist must maintain an impartial attitude toward a patient's conflicts.

   (A) attentive
   (B) inquisitive
   (C) objective
   (D) affirmative

10. Helen Hayes's voice may be quiet and refined, but her audience sits up and takes notice.

    (A) mannerly
    (B) natural
    (C) inferior
    (D) immodest

11. Because of the rugged terrain found in some western states, much of the land is uninhabited.

    (A) desolate
    (B) rough
    (C) arid
    (D) remote

12. Adult butterflies often form large aggregations while sipping water at wet places.

    (A) stomachs
    (B) gatherings
    (C) eggs
    (D) displays

13. During his life, millionaire, Howard Hughes often kept his whereabouts secret.

    (A) location
    (B) thoughts
    (C) wealth
    (D) accomplishments

14. The fundamental element of a word is known as its root.

    (A) final
    (B) important
    (C) simple
    (D) basic

15. In colonial times, merchants peddled their goods from door to door.

    (A) moved
    (B) received
    (C) provided
    (D) sold

16. The appeal of jade lies in its compact structure, which permits very delicate carving.

    (A) density
    (B) value
    (C) attraction
    (D) essence

17. The changes in food demands as our population burgeons are offset by the technical revolution in farming.

    (A) relocates
    (B) intermarries
    (C) matures
    (D) expands

GO ON TO THE NEXT PAGE

18. The Peace Corps was set up by President Kennedy to promote peace and friendship between the United States and developing countries.

    (A) established
    (B) proposed
    (C) supported
    (D) proclaimed

19. Some surgeons believe that there is no place for levity in the operating room.

    (A) unhappiness
    (B) humor
    (C) haste
    (D) kindness

20. In astronomy, any cloud-like structure observed outside the solar system is called a nebula.

    (A) found
    (B) seen
    (C) recorded
    (D) photographed

21. When the painting was reported missing, the whole community was distraught.

    (A) annoyed
    (B) upset
    (C) misinformed
    (D) unaffected

22. Few other waterfalls exceed the volume of water that passes over Niagara Falls.

    (A) surpass
    (B) generate
    (C) sustain
    (D) endure

23. The parrot fish will gnaw hard barnacles off rocks in the sea.

    (A) chew
    (B) slice
    (C) push
    (D) lick

24. Lorraine Hansbury received the acclaim she deserved for her Broadway play *A Raisin in the Sun*.

    (A) assistance
    (B) acceptance
    (C) praise
    (D) stipend

25. When a supernova collapses, the resulting blast creates light equal to hundreds of millions of stars.

    (A) motion
    (B) agitation
    (C) reaction
    (D) explosion

26. Spring inevitably brings scorching winds into the desert regions of the American Southwest.

    (A) sweltering
    (B) intermittent
    (C) vehement
    (D) disquieting

GO ON TO THE NEXT PAGE

27. In the quest to find a cure for cancer, scientists must draw on a collective information base.

    (A) diagnosis
    (B) remedy
    (C) cause
    (D) symptom

28. During a respite of three years from public duties, Jefferson began to remodel his house at Monticello.

    (A) laws
    (B) speeches
    (C) responsibilities
    (D) concerts

29. Scientists found the prints of several extinct species in the cave.

    (A) fragile
    (B) vanished
    (C) related
    (D) active

30. The queen honeybee exudes a smell that inhibits worker bees from laying eggs.

    (A) substance
    (B) sound
    (C) liquid
    (D) scent

GO ON TO THE NEXT PAGE

3 • 3 • 3 • 3 • 3 • 3 • 3

Directions: In the rest of this section you will read several passages. Each one is followed by several questions about it. For questions 31-60, you are to choose the one best answer, (A), (B), (C), or (D), to each question. Then, on your answer sheet, find the number of the question and fill in the space that corresponds to the letter of the answer you have chosen.

Answer all questions following a passage on the basis of what is stated or implied in that passage.

Read the following passage:

The rattles with which a rattlesnake warns of its presence are formed by loosely interlocking hollow rings of hard skin, which make a buzzing sound when its tail is shaken. As a baby, the snake begins to form its rattles from the button at the very tip of its tail. Thereafter, each time it sheds its skin, a new ring is formed. Popular belief holds that a snake's age can be told by counting the rings, but this idea is fallacious. In fact, a snake may lose its old skin as often as four times a year. Also, rattles tend to wear or break off with time.

Example I

A rattlesnake's rattles are made of

(A) skin
(B) bone
(C) wood
(D) muscle

Sample Answer
● Ⓑ Ⓒ Ⓓ

According to the passage, a rattlesnake's rattles are made out of rings of hard skin. Therefore, you should choose answer (A).

Example II

How often does a rattlesnake shed its skin?

(A) Once every four years
(B) Once every four months
(C) Up to four times every year
(D) Four times more often than other snakes

Sample Answer
Ⓐ Ⓑ ● Ⓓ

The passage states that "a snake may lose its old skin as often as four times a year." Therefore, you should choose answer (C).

After you read the directions, begin work on the questions.

GO ON TO THE NEXT PAGE

Questions 31–36

Up to about 1830, both American English and British English shared an identical development; both owe their present accepted national forms to the effects of authoritarianism working on bourgeois credulity; both succumbed, in the period of the Industrial Revolution, to a process of refinement at the hands of grammarian and lexicographer. But there the resemblance begins to break down. The American English which emerged from the crucible, chiefly a literary language smelted down from good New England ore, was immediately forged by John Adams, Noah Webster, and their like into an instrument to promote the national unity and emerging national aspiration of the country. On the other hand, the British English, which was both a literary and a spoken language, was molded to the purposes of a powerful ruling class.

31. The author suggests that American English differs from British English because

(A) the Industrial Revolution came later to America
(B) American English developed in an evolving society
(C) there was no early American literary tradition
(D) the American bourgeoisie was antiauthoritarian

32. What is the main purpose of the passage?

(A) To demonstrate the superiority of American English
(B) To examine the contributions of John Adams and Noah Webster
(C) To compare and contrast American and British English
(D) To denounce the influence of the Industrial Revolution on the English Language

33. The author compares the evolution of American English to

   (A) a musical composition
   (B) gardening
   (C) a new art form
   (D) metalworking

34. What is the "instrument" that is mentioned in the sixth line?

   (A) Refinement
   (B) A national literature
   (C) American English
   (D) The Industrial Revolution

35. According to the passage, American English served to foster

   (A) nationalism
   (B) conversation
   (C) industry
   (D) authoritarianism

36. The author uses the word "forged" in the fifth line to mean

   (A) debased
   (B) separated
   (C) diverted
   (D) shaped

GO ON TO THE NEXT PAGE

Questions 37–43

It must be acknowledged that the psychoanalytical biographer works at a disadvantage in comparison with the psychoanalyst. The psychographer must content himself with records that are necessarily incomplete; the psychoanalyst has before him a living patient. Critics hostile to psychography never tire of pointing out this discrepancy. Yet the psychographer may have certain advantages over the psychoanalyst which are less well recognized.

The average person in psychoanalysis is young, generally not past his thirties. This means that he has yet to encounter some of those stages of life which are so revelatory of personality. For example, he may not yet have married, have children, achieved the peak of his career, and so on. Neither the analyst nor the patient knows how the patient will react to these events. Thus, certain aspects of the patient's personality may remain inaccessible for purposes of examination and understanding. But the subject of the psychographer has lived his entire life. Not only the development and mid-stages of his life are available for inspection but also its ultimate unfolding and final resolution. Thus, one advantage is that in discovering the dominant psychological themes of his subject's emotional evolution, the psychoanalytic biographer has at his disposal a broader spectrum of behavior through more decades of life than has the analyst with a living patient.

37. What two groups of people does the author compare in this passage?

   (A) Psychologists and psychiatrists
   (B) Psychotherapists and psychoanalysts
   (C) Psychographers and psychologists
   (D) Psychoanalysts and psychographers

38. According to its critics, what is the main disadvantage of psychography?

   (A) It relies on a necessarily limited amount of information.
   (B) It only uses recorded speech to analyze the subject.
   (C) It fails to help people solve their most serious problems.
   (D) It has no means to analyze the emotions of the subject.

39. According to the author, what compensates for the shortcomings of psychography?

   (A) Accessible personality traits are more easily uncovered.
   (B) A wider range of information on the subject can be used.
   (C) It includes the examination of the subject's ancestors.
   (D) Evolutionary theory more strongly supports psychography.

40. The author implies that personality characteristics can often be most completely revealed by

   (A) the patient's behavior as a young person
   (B) interviewing the patient's spouse, children and parents
   (C) how a patient handles life's common stages
   (D) exploring the patient's intellectual life

41. With which of the following statements would the author be most likely to agree?

   (A) Psychography may reveal a more complete picture of a subject's personality than psychoanalysis.
   (B) In the long run, psychoanalysis has more disadvantages than advantages.
   (C) Psychoanalysis can only be adequately done by a person trained in psychography.
   (D) A patient under 30 years of age may not be adequately helped by psychoanalysis.

42. The paragraph following this passage most probably discusses

   (A) the importance of psychoanalysis in maintaining mental health
   (B) further advantages of the method of psychography
   (C) the history and development of psychography in this century
   (D) criticism of psychoanalysis in the modern world

43. The author's main purpose in writing this passage most probably is

   (A) to interest the reader in studying psychology
   (B) to promote the status of behavioral scientists
   (C) to describe the disadvantages of psychoanalysis
   (D) to defend the work of the psychoanalytic biographer

Questions 44–48

Over a period of time, many habitats change with respect to the types of plants and animals that live there. This change is known as succession.

Succession occurs because plants and animals cause a change in the environment in which they live. The first weed and grasses that appear on a bare field, for example, change the environment by shielding the soil from direct sunlight. As these plants spread, the ground surface becomes cooler and more moist than it was originally. Thus, the environment at the ground surface has been changed. The new surface conditions favor the sprouting of shrubs. As shrubs grow, they kill the grasses by preventing light from reaching them and also build up the soil in the area. In addition, they attract animals that also enhance the soil. Pine seedlings soon take hold and as they grow, they in turn shade out the shrubs. They are not able to shade out oak and hickory seedlings, however, that have found the forest floor suitable. These seedlings grow into large trees that eventually shade out the pines.

44. What is the best title of this passage?

(A) The Importance of Weeds and Grasses
(B) How Environmental Habitats Change
(C) The Success of Oak and Hickory
(D) Animal and Plant Habitats

45. Which is the correct order of plant succession in the example in the passage?

(A) Weeds, pines, shrubs, oak
(B) Oak, pines, shrubs, weeds
(C) Weeds, shrubs, pines, oak
(D) Shrubs, weeds, pines, oak

46. According to the passage, how do weeds and grasses affect the soil?

    (A) They make it cooler and wetter.
    (B) They attract animals to it.
    (C) They spread seeds on it.
    (D) They add nutrients to it.

47. It can be inferred from the passage that

    (A) oak and hickory trees grow taller than pines
    (B) weeds and grasses prefer cold climates
    (C) pines and grasses can exist together
    (D) birds discourage the growth of shrubs

48. Which of the following is a stage of succession as described in the passage?

    (A) A forest cut down to build an airport
    (B) A flood washing away a crop of wheat
    (C) Wildflowers growing in an unused parking lot
    (D) Animals being tamed by children

Questions 49–54

Resources can be said to be scarce in both an absolute and in a relative sense: the surface of the Earth is finite, imposing absolute scarcity; but the scarcity that concerns economists is the relative scarcity of resources in different uses. Materials used for one purpose cannot at the same time be used for other purposes; if the quantity of an input is limited, the increased use of it in one manufacturing process must cause it to become less available for other uses.

The cost of a product in terms of money may not measure its true cost to society. The true cost of, say, the construction of a supersonic jet is the value of the schools and refrigerators that will never be built as a result. Every act of production uses up some of society's available resources; it means the foregoing of an opportunity to produce something else. In deciding how to use resources most effectively to satisfy the wants of the community, this opportunity cost must ultimately be taken into account.

In a market economy the price of a good and the quantity supplied depends on the cost of making it, and that cost, ultimately, is the cost of not making other goods. The market mechanism enforces this relationship. The cost of, say, a pair of shoes is the price of the leather, the labor, the fuel, and other elements used up in producing them. But the price of these inputs, in turn, depends on what they can produce elsewhere—if the leather can be used to produce handbags that are valued highly by consumers, the price of leather will be bid up correspondingly.

49. What does this passage mainly discuss?

   (A) The scarcity of manufactured goods
   (B) The value of scarce materials
   (C) The manufacturing of scarce goods
   (D) The cost of producing shoes

50. According to the passage, what are the opportunity costs of an item?

   (A) The amount of time and money spent in producing it.
   (B) The opportunities a person has to buy it.
   (C) The value of what could have been produced instead.
   (D) The value of the resources used in its production.

51. According to the passage, what is the relationship between production and resources?

    (A) Available resources stimulate production.
    (B) Resources are totally independent of production.
    (C) Production increases as resources increase.
    (D) Production lessens the amount of available resources.

52. What determines the price of a good in a market economy?

    (A) The cost of all elements of production
    (B) The cost of making other goods
    (C) The efficiency of the manufacturing process
    (D) The quantity of materials supplied

53. Which of the following examples best reflects a cost to society as defined in the passage?

    (A) A family buying a dog
    (B) Eating in a restaurant instead of at home
    (C) Using land for a house instead of a park
    (D) Staying at home instead of going to school

54. With which of the following statements would the author of the passage be most likely to agree?

    (A) The price of a good reflects its usefulness to society.
    (B) Opportunity costs are reflected in the price of a good.
    (C) Opportunity costs increase with availability.
    (D) The cost of a good depends on its quality.

GO ON TO THE NEXT PAGE

Questions 55–60

From about 1900 to 1950, most organs in America used an electrical, pneumatic, or electro-pneumatic system to open the valves under the pipes which admit air to them, causing them to sound. Before that time, organs were constructed with a system of levers and pulling connections (called trackers) to connect the keyboards to the valves under the pipes. Today, the tracker system is again becoming popular. In this system, the only power used for the key action comes from the player's fingers or feet. While this might seem to be disadvantageous for the player, in reality, with careful design and engineering, the touch of a good tracker organ is very light and it is easy to play.

The inherent simplicity of this purely mechanical action makes it durable and free from malfunction. There are organs in Europe dating from as far back as 1380 that use this system and are still performing faithfully!

In order to understand the artistic superiority of tracker action we might apply a bit of information theory. With most typical electrical or pneumatic actions, only two "bits" of information are transmitted from the player to the pipe, namely, "off" or "on". Furthermore, the transmission of information flows in only one direction, from the player to the pipe.

With mechanical action, the link between the player and pipe is literally an extension of the player's finger. Thus, the player can control the speed of the opening valve, as well as the closing, and hence the way the pipe starts and stops its sound.

The differences are subtle, of course (not nearly so dramatic as touch control on a piano, for example), but very important in truly artistic performance. Moreover, the "information" sent by the player is reciprocated. The player can "feel" what he or she is doing, which gives a marvelous sense of security to the player, and this security further adds to the artistic effect of the performance.

55. What is the main subject of the passage?

    (A) The advantages of tracker organs
    (B) The development of the electric organ
    (C) The superiority of the organ over the piano
    (D) The manufacture of organs in the early twentieth century

56. The tracker organ differs from the electric organ in that

    (A) the foot pedals are not necessary for full sound
    (B) its valves always open quickly
    (C) the player supplies all the power for its keys
    (D) its levers are not connected to the valves

57. The author of the passage implies that

    (A) most organists prefer not to use their feet
    (B) tracker organs require frequent maintenance
    (C) most organists would prefer to play a tracker organ
    (D) listeners prefer the sound of electropneumatic organs

58. The tone of the passage is best described as

    (A) neutral
    (B) positive
    (C) curious
    (D) impassioned

59. According to the first paragraph, how many types of organ systems have been in use since 1900?

    (A) Two
    (B) Four
    (C) Seven
    (D) Eight

60. Ultimately, the best reasons for playing a tracker organ are probably

    (A) financial
    (B) academic
    (C) logistical
    (D) artistic

THIS IS THE END OF SECTION 3

IF YOU FINISH BEFORE TIME IS CALLED, CHECK YOUR WORK ON SECTION 3 ONLY.
DO NOT READ OR WORK ON ANY OTHER SECTION OF THE TEST.

Newbury House TOEFL Preparation Kit — Answer Sheet

Name _____

Newbury House TOEFL Preparation Kit — Answer Sheet

Name _____

Newbury House TOEFL Preparation Kit – Answer Sheet

Name _____

Section 1

1. Ⓐ Ⓑ Ⓒ Ⓓ
2. Ⓐ Ⓑ Ⓒ Ⓓ
3. Ⓐ Ⓑ Ⓒ Ⓓ
4. Ⓐ Ⓑ Ⓒ Ⓓ
5. Ⓐ Ⓑ Ⓒ Ⓓ
6. Ⓐ Ⓑ Ⓒ Ⓓ
7. Ⓐ Ⓑ Ⓒ Ⓓ
8. Ⓐ Ⓑ Ⓒ Ⓓ
9. Ⓐ Ⓑ Ⓒ Ⓓ
10. Ⓐ Ⓑ Ⓒ Ⓓ
11. Ⓐ Ⓑ Ⓒ Ⓓ
12. Ⓐ Ⓑ Ⓒ Ⓓ
13. Ⓐ Ⓑ Ⓒ Ⓓ
14. Ⓐ Ⓑ Ⓒ Ⓓ
15. Ⓐ Ⓑ Ⓒ Ⓓ
16. Ⓐ Ⓑ Ⓒ Ⓓ
17. Ⓐ Ⓑ Ⓒ Ⓓ
18. Ⓐ Ⓑ Ⓒ Ⓓ
19. Ⓐ Ⓑ Ⓒ Ⓓ
20. Ⓐ Ⓑ Ⓒ Ⓓ
21. Ⓐ Ⓑ Ⓒ Ⓓ
22. Ⓐ Ⓑ Ⓒ Ⓓ
23. Ⓐ Ⓑ Ⓒ Ⓓ
24. Ⓐ Ⓑ Ⓒ Ⓓ
25. Ⓐ Ⓑ Ⓒ Ⓓ
26. Ⓐ Ⓑ Ⓒ Ⓓ
27. Ⓐ Ⓑ Ⓒ Ⓓ
28. Ⓐ Ⓑ Ⓒ Ⓓ
29. Ⓐ Ⓑ Ⓒ Ⓓ
30. Ⓐ Ⓑ Ⓒ Ⓓ
31. Ⓐ Ⓑ Ⓒ Ⓓ
32. Ⓐ Ⓑ Ⓒ Ⓓ
33. Ⓐ Ⓑ Ⓒ Ⓓ
34. Ⓐ Ⓑ Ⓒ Ⓓ
35. Ⓐ Ⓑ Ⓒ Ⓓ
36. Ⓐ Ⓑ Ⓒ Ⓓ
37. Ⓐ Ⓑ Ⓒ Ⓓ
38. Ⓐ Ⓑ Ⓒ Ⓓ
39. Ⓐ Ⓑ Ⓒ Ⓓ
40. Ⓐ Ⓑ Ⓒ Ⓓ
41. Ⓐ Ⓑ Ⓒ Ⓓ
42. Ⓐ Ⓑ Ⓒ Ⓓ
43. Ⓐ Ⓑ Ⓒ Ⓓ
44. Ⓐ Ⓑ Ⓒ Ⓓ
45. Ⓐ Ⓑ Ⓒ Ⓓ
46. Ⓐ Ⓑ Ⓒ Ⓓ
47. Ⓐ Ⓑ Ⓒ Ⓓ
48. Ⓐ Ⓑ Ⓒ Ⓓ
49. Ⓐ Ⓑ Ⓒ Ⓓ
50. Ⓐ Ⓑ Ⓒ Ⓓ

Section 2

1. Ⓐ Ⓑ Ⓒ Ⓓ
2. Ⓐ Ⓑ Ⓒ Ⓓ
3. Ⓐ Ⓑ Ⓒ Ⓓ
4. Ⓐ Ⓑ Ⓒ Ⓓ
5. Ⓐ Ⓑ Ⓒ Ⓓ
6. Ⓐ Ⓑ Ⓒ Ⓓ
7. Ⓐ Ⓑ Ⓒ Ⓓ
8. Ⓐ Ⓑ Ⓒ Ⓓ
9. Ⓐ Ⓑ Ⓒ Ⓓ
10. Ⓐ Ⓑ Ⓒ Ⓓ
11. Ⓐ Ⓑ Ⓒ Ⓓ
12. Ⓐ Ⓑ Ⓒ Ⓓ
13. Ⓐ Ⓑ Ⓒ Ⓓ
14. Ⓐ Ⓑ Ⓒ Ⓓ
15. Ⓐ Ⓑ Ⓒ Ⓓ
16. Ⓐ Ⓑ Ⓒ Ⓓ
17. Ⓐ Ⓑ Ⓒ Ⓓ
18. Ⓐ Ⓑ Ⓒ Ⓓ
19. Ⓐ Ⓑ Ⓒ Ⓓ
20. Ⓐ Ⓑ Ⓒ Ⓓ
21. Ⓐ Ⓑ Ⓒ Ⓓ
22. Ⓐ Ⓑ Ⓒ Ⓓ
23. Ⓐ Ⓑ Ⓒ Ⓓ
24. Ⓐ Ⓑ Ⓒ Ⓓ
25. Ⓐ Ⓑ Ⓒ Ⓓ
26. Ⓐ Ⓑ Ⓒ Ⓓ
27. Ⓐ Ⓑ Ⓒ Ⓓ
28. Ⓐ Ⓑ Ⓒ Ⓓ
29. Ⓐ Ⓑ Ⓒ Ⓓ
30. Ⓐ Ⓑ Ⓒ Ⓓ
31. Ⓐ Ⓑ Ⓒ Ⓓ
32. Ⓐ Ⓑ Ⓒ Ⓓ
33. Ⓐ Ⓑ Ⓒ Ⓓ
34. Ⓐ Ⓑ Ⓒ Ⓓ
35. Ⓐ Ⓑ Ⓒ Ⓓ
36. Ⓐ Ⓑ Ⓒ Ⓓ
37. Ⓐ Ⓑ Ⓒ Ⓓ
38. Ⓐ Ⓑ Ⓒ Ⓓ
39. Ⓐ Ⓑ Ⓒ Ⓓ
40. Ⓐ Ⓑ Ⓒ Ⓓ

Section 3

1. Ⓐ Ⓑ Ⓒ Ⓓ
2. Ⓐ Ⓑ Ⓒ Ⓓ
3. Ⓐ Ⓑ Ⓒ Ⓓ
4. Ⓐ Ⓑ Ⓒ Ⓓ
5. Ⓐ Ⓑ Ⓒ Ⓓ
6. Ⓐ Ⓑ Ⓒ Ⓓ
7. Ⓐ Ⓑ Ⓒ Ⓓ
8. Ⓐ Ⓑ Ⓒ Ⓓ
9. Ⓐ Ⓑ Ⓒ Ⓓ
10. Ⓐ Ⓑ Ⓒ Ⓓ
11. Ⓐ Ⓑ Ⓒ Ⓓ
12. Ⓐ Ⓑ Ⓒ Ⓓ
13. Ⓐ Ⓑ Ⓒ Ⓓ
14. Ⓐ Ⓑ Ⓒ Ⓓ
15. Ⓐ Ⓑ Ⓒ Ⓓ
16. Ⓐ Ⓑ Ⓒ Ⓓ
17. Ⓐ Ⓑ Ⓒ Ⓓ
18. Ⓐ Ⓑ Ⓒ Ⓓ
19. Ⓐ Ⓑ Ⓒ Ⓓ
20. Ⓐ Ⓑ Ⓒ Ⓓ
21. Ⓐ Ⓑ Ⓒ Ⓓ
22. Ⓐ Ⓑ Ⓒ Ⓓ
23. Ⓐ Ⓑ Ⓒ Ⓓ
24. Ⓐ Ⓑ Ⓒ Ⓓ
25. Ⓐ Ⓑ Ⓒ Ⓓ
26. Ⓐ Ⓑ Ⓒ Ⓓ
27. Ⓐ Ⓑ Ⓒ Ⓓ
28. Ⓐ Ⓑ Ⓒ Ⓓ
29. Ⓐ Ⓑ Ⓒ Ⓓ
30. Ⓐ Ⓑ Ⓒ Ⓓ
31. Ⓐ Ⓑ Ⓒ Ⓓ
32. Ⓐ Ⓑ Ⓒ Ⓓ
33. Ⓐ Ⓑ Ⓒ Ⓓ
34. Ⓐ Ⓑ Ⓒ Ⓓ
35. Ⓐ Ⓑ Ⓒ Ⓓ
36. Ⓐ Ⓑ Ⓒ Ⓓ
37. Ⓐ Ⓑ Ⓒ Ⓓ
38. Ⓐ Ⓑ Ⓒ Ⓓ
39. Ⓐ Ⓑ Ⓒ Ⓓ
40. Ⓐ Ⓑ Ⓒ Ⓓ
41. Ⓐ Ⓑ Ⓒ Ⓓ
42. Ⓐ Ⓑ Ⓒ Ⓓ
43. Ⓐ Ⓑ Ⓒ Ⓓ
44. Ⓐ Ⓑ Ⓒ Ⓓ
45. Ⓐ Ⓑ Ⓒ Ⓓ
46. Ⓐ Ⓑ Ⓒ Ⓓ
47. Ⓐ Ⓑ Ⓒ Ⓓ
48. Ⓐ Ⓑ Ⓒ Ⓓ
49. Ⓐ Ⓑ Ⓒ Ⓓ
50. Ⓐ Ⓑ Ⓒ Ⓓ
51. Ⓐ Ⓑ Ⓒ Ⓓ
52. Ⓐ Ⓑ Ⓒ Ⓓ
53. Ⓐ Ⓑ Ⓒ Ⓓ
54. Ⓐ Ⓑ Ⓒ Ⓓ
55. Ⓐ Ⓑ Ⓒ Ⓓ
56. Ⓐ Ⓑ Ⓒ Ⓓ
57. Ⓐ Ⓑ Ⓒ Ⓓ
58. Ⓐ Ⓑ Ⓒ Ⓓ
59. Ⓐ Ⓑ Ⓒ Ⓓ
60. Ⓐ Ⓑ Ⓒ Ⓓ

Newbury House TOEFL Preparation Kit — Answer Sheet

Name _____

Newbury House TOEFL Preparation Kit – Answer Sheet

Name _____

Section 1 / Section 2 / Section 3

Newbury House TOEFL Preparation Kit — Answer Sheet

Name _____

Newbury House TOEFL Preparation Kit – Answer Sheet

Name _____

Section 1

Section 2

Section 3